Microsoft®
Training &
Certification

2071B: Querying Microsoft® SQL Server™ 2000 with Transact-SQL

Microsoft®

Course Number: 2071B
Part Number: X09-89608
Released: 09/2001

END-USER LICENSE AGREEMENT FOR MICROSOFT OFFICIAL CURRICULUM COURSEWARE –STUDENT EDITION

PLEASE READ THIS END-USER LICENSE AGREEMENT ("EULA") CAREFULLY. BY USING THE MATERIALS AND/OR USING OR INSTALLING THE SOFTWARE THAT ACCOMPANIES THIS EULA (COLLECTIVELY, THE "LICENSED CONTENT"), YOU AGREE TO THE TERMS OF THIS EULA. IF YOU DO NOT AGREE, DO NOT USE THE LICENSED CONTENT.

1. **GENERAL.** This EULA is a legal agreement between you (either an individual or a single entity) and Microsoft Corporation ("Microsoft"). This EULA governs the Licensed Content, which includes computer software (including online and electronic documentation), training materials, and any other associated media and printed materials. This EULA applies to updates, supplements, add-on components, and Internet-based services components of the Licensed Content that Microsoft may provide or make available to you unless Microsoft provides other terms with the update, supplement, add-on component, or Internet-based services component. Microsoft reserves the right to discontinue any Internet-based services provided to you or made available to you through the use of the Licensed Content. This EULA also governs any product support services relating to the Licensed Content except as may be included in another agreement between you and Microsoft. An amendment or addendum to this EULA may accompany the Licensed Content.

2. **GENERAL GRANT OF LICENSE.** Microsoft grants you the following rights, conditioned on your compliance with all the terms and conditions of this EULA. Microsoft grants you a limited, non-exclusive, royalty-free license to install and use the Licensed Content solely in conjunction with your participation as a student in an Authorized Training Session (as defined below). You may install and use one copy of the software on a single computer, device, workstation, terminal, or other digital electronic or analog device ("Device"). You may make a second copy of the software and install it on a portable Device for the exclusive use of the person who is the primary user of the first copy of the software. A license for the software may not be shared for use by multiple end users. An "Authorized Training Session" means a training session conducted at a Microsoft Certified Technical Education Center, an IT Academy, via a Microsoft Certified Partner, or such other entity as Microsoft may designate from time to time in writing, by a Microsoft Certified Trainer (for more information on these entities, please visit www.microsoft.com). WITHOUT LIMITING THE FOREGOING, COPYING OR REPRODUCTION OF THE LICENSED CONTENT TO ANY SERVER OR LOCATION FOR FURTHER REPRODUCTION OR REDISTRIBUTION IS EXPRESSLY PROHIBITED.

3. **DESCRIPTION OF OTHER RIGHTS AND LICENSE LIMITATIONS**

    3.1   *Use of Documentation and Printed Training Materials.*

    3.1.1   The documents and related graphics included in the Licensed Content may include technical inaccuracies or typographical errors. Changes are periodically made to the content. Microsoft may make improvements and/ or changes in any of the components of the Licensed Content at any time without notice. The names of companies, products, people, characters and/or data mentioned in the Licensed Content may be fictitious and are in no way intended to represent any real individual, company, product or event, unless otherwise noted.

    3.1.2   Microsoft grants you the right to reproduce portions of documents (such as student workbooks, white papers, press releases, datasheets and FAQs) (the "Documents") provided with the Licensed Content. You may not print any book (either electronic or print version) in its entirety. If you choose to reproduce Documents, you agree that: (a) use of such printed Documents will be solely in conjunction with your personal training use; (b) the Documents will not republished or posted on any network computer or broadcast in any media; (c) any reproduction will include either the Document's original copyright notice or a copyright notice to Microsoft's benefit substantially in the format provided below; and (d) to comply with all terms and conditions of this EULA. In addition, no modifications may made to any Document.

    Form of Notice:

    © 2001. Reprinted with permission by Microsoft Corporation. All rights reserved.

    Microsoft and Windows are either registered trademarks or trademarks of Microsoft Corporation in the US and/or other countries. Other product and company names mentioned herein may be the trademarks of their respective owners.

    3.2   *Use of Media Elements.* The Licensed Content may include certain photographs, clip art, animations, sounds, music, and video clips (together "Media Elements"). You may not modify these Media Elements.

    3.3   *Use of Sample Code.* In the event that the Licensed Content includes sample code in source or object format ("Sample Code"), Microsoft grants you a limited, non-exclusive, royalty-free license to use, copy and modify the Sample Code; if you elect to exercise the foregoing rights, you agree to comply with all other terms and conditions of this EULA, including without limitation Sections 3.4, 3.5, and 6.

    3.4   *Permitted Modifications.* In the event that you exercise any rights provided under this EULA to create modifications of the Licensed Content, you agree that any such modifications: (a) will not be used for providing training where a fee is charged in public or private classes; (b) indemnify, hold harmless, and defend Microsoft from and against any claims or lawsuits, including attorneys' fees, which arise from or result from your use of any modified version of the Licensed Content; and (c) not to transfer or assign any rights to any modified version of the Licensed Content to any third party without the express written permission of Microsoft.

3.5   *Reproduction/Redistribution Licensed Content.* Except as expressly provided in this EULA, you may not reproduce or distribute the Licensed Content or any portion thereof (including any permitted modifications) to any third parties without the express written permission of Microsoft.

4.   **RESERVATION OF RIGHTS AND OWNERSHIP.** Microsoft reserves all rights not expressly granted to you in this EULA. The Licensed Content is protected by copyright and other intellectual property laws and treaties. Microsoft or its suppliers own the title, copyright, and other intellectual property rights in the Licensed Content. You may not remove or obscure any copyright, trademark or patent notices that appear on the Licensed Content, or any components thereof, as delivered to you. **The Licensed Content is licensed, not sold.**

5.   **LIMITATIONS ON REVERSE ENGINEERING, DECOMPILATION, AND DISASSEMBLY.** You may not reverse engineer, decompile, or disassemble the Software or Media Elements, except and only to the extent that such activity is expressly permitted by applicable law notwithstanding this limitation.

6.   **LIMITATIONS ON SALE, RENTAL, ETC. AND CERTAIN ASSIGNMENTS.** You may not provide commercial hosting services with, sell, rent, lease, lend, sublicense, or assign copies of the Licensed Content, or any portion thereof (including any permitted modifications thereof) on a stand-alone basis or as part of any collection, product or service.

7.   **CONSENT TO USE OF DATA.** You agree that Microsoft and its affiliates may collect and use technical information gathered as part of the product support services provided to you, if any, related to the Licensed Content. Microsoft may use this information solely to improve our products or to provide customized services or technologies to you and will not disclose this information in a form that personally identifies you.

8.   **LINKS TO THIRD PARTY SITES.** You may link to third party sites through the use of the Licensed Content. The third party sites are not under the control of Microsoft, and Microsoft is not responsible for the contents of any third party sites, any links contained in third party sites, or any changes or updates to third party sites. Microsoft is not responsible for webcasting or any other form of transmission received from any third party sites. Microsoft is providing these links to third party sites to you only as a convenience, and the inclusion of any link does not imply an endorsement by Microsoft of the third party site.

9.   **ADDITIONAL LICENSED CONTENT/SERVICES.** This EULA applies to updates, supplements, add-on components, or Internet-based services components, of the Licensed Content that Microsoft may provide to you or make available to you after the date you obtain your initial copy of the Licensed Content, unless we provide other terms along with the update, supplement, add-on component, or Internet-based services component. Microsoft reserves the right to discontinue any Internet-based services provided to you or made available to you through the use of the Licensed Content.

10.   **U.S. GOVERNMENT LICENSE RIGHTS**. All software provided to the U.S. Government pursuant to solicitations issued on or after December 1, 1995 is provided with the commercial license rights and restrictions described elsewhere herein. All software provided to the U.S. Government pursuant to solicitations issued prior to December 1, 1995 is provided with "Restricted Rights" as provided for in FAR, 48 CFR 52.227-14 (JUNE 1987) or DFAR, 48 CFR 252.227-7013 (OCT 1988), as applicable.

11.   **EXPORT RESTRICTIONS.** You acknowledge that the Licensed Content is subject to U.S. export jurisdiction. You agree to comply with all applicable international and national laws that apply to the Licensed Content, including the U.S. Export Administration Regulations, as well as end-user, end-use, and destination restrictions issued by U.S. and other governments. For additional information see <http://www.microsoft.com/exporting/>.

12.   **TRANSFER.** The initial user of the Licensed Content may make a one-time permanent transfer of this EULA and Licensed Content to another end user, provided the initial user retains no copies of the Licensed Content. The transfer may not be an indirect transfer, such as a consignment. Prior to the transfer, the end user receiving the Licensed Content must agree to all the EULA terms.

13.   **"NOT FOR RESALE" LICENSED CONTENT.** Licensed Content identified as "Not For Resale" or "NFR," may not be sold or otherwise transferred for value, or used for any purpose other than demonstration, test or evaluation.

14.   **TERMINATION.** Without prejudice to any other rights, Microsoft may terminate this EULA if you fail to comply with the terms and conditions of this EULA. In such event, you must destroy all copies of the Licensed Content and all of its component parts.

15.   <u>DISCLAIMER OF WARRANTIES.</u> **TO THE MAXIMUM EXTENT PERMITTED BY APPLICABLE LAW, MICROSOFT AND ITS SUPPLIERS PROVIDE THE LICENSED CONTENT AND SUPPORT SERVICES (IF ANY) *AS IS AND WITH ALL FAULTS,* AND MICROSOFT AND ITS SUPPLIERS HEREBY DISCLAIM ALL OTHER WARRANTIES AND CONDITIONS, WHETHER EXPRESS, IMPLIED OR STATUTORY, INCLUDING, BUT NOT LIMITED TO, ANY (IF ANY) IMPLIED WARRANTIES, DUTIES OR CONDITIONS OF MERCHANTABILITY, OF FITNESS FOR A PARTICULAR PURPOSE, OF RELIABILITY OR AVAILABILITY, OF ACCURACY OR COMPLETENESS OF RESPONSES, OF RESULTS, OF WORKMANLIKE EFFORT, OF LACK OF VIRUSES, AND OF LACK OF NEGLIGENCE, ALL WITH REGARD TO THE LICENSED CONTENT, AND THE PROVISION OF OR FAILURE TO PROVIDE SUPPORT OR OTHER SERVICES, INFORMATION, SOFTWARE, AND RELATED CONTENT THROUGH THE LICENSED CONTENT, OR OTHERWISE ARISING OUT OF THE USE OF THE LICENSED CONTENT. ALSO, THERE IS NO WARRANTY OR CONDITION OF TITLE, QUIET ENJOYMENT, QUIET POSSESSION, CORRESPONDENCE TO DESCRIPTION OR NON-INFRINGEMENT WITH REGARD TO THE LICENSED CONTENT. THE ENTIRE RISK AS TO THE QUALITY, OR ARISING OUT OF THE USE OR PERFORMANCE OF THE LICENSED CONTENT, AND ANY SUPPORT SERVICES, REMAINS WITH YOU.**

16.   <u>EXCLUSION OF INCIDENTAL, CONSEQUENTIAL AND CERTAIN OTHER DAMAGES.</u> **TO THE MAXIMUM EXTENT PERMITTED BY APPLICABLE LAW, IN NO EVENT SHALL MICROSOFT OR ITS SUPPLIERS BE LIABLE FOR ANY SPECIAL, INCIDENTAL, PUNITIVE, INDIRECT, OR CONSEQUENTIAL DAMAGES WHATSOEVER (INCLUDING, BUT NOT**

LIMITED TO, DAMAGES FOR LOSS OF PROFITS OR CONFIDENTIAL OR OTHER INFORMATION, FOR BUSINESS INTERRUPTION, FOR PERSONAL INJURY, FOR LOSS OF PRIVACY, FOR FAILURE TO MEET ANY DUTY INCLUDING OF GOOD FAITH OR OF REASONABLE CARE, FOR NEGLIGENCE, AND FOR ANY OTHER PECUNIARY OR OTHER LOSS WHATSOEVER) ARISING OUT OF OR IN ANY WAY RELATED TO THE USE OF OR INABILITY TO USE THE LICENSED CONTENT, THE PROVISION OF OR FAILURE TO PROVIDE SUPPORT OR OTHER SERVICES, INFORMATION, SOFTWARE, AND RELATED CONTENT THROUGH THE LICENSED CONTENT, OR OTHERWISE ARISING OUT OF THE USE OF THE LICENSED CONTENT, OR OTHERWISE UNDER OR IN CONNECTION WITH ANY PROVISION OF THIS EULA, EVEN IN THE EVENT OF THE FAULT, TORT (INCLUDING NEGLIGENCE), MISREPRESENTATION, STRICT LIABILITY, BREACH OF CONTRACT OR BREACH OF WARRANTY OF MICROSOFT OR ANY SUPPLIER, AND EVEN IF MICROSOFT OR ANY SUPPLIER HAS BEEN ADVISED OF THE POSSIBILITY OF SUCH DAMAGES. BECAUSE SOME STATES/JURISDICTIONS DO NOT ALLOW THE EXCLUSION OR LIMITATION OF LIABILITY FOR CONSEQUENTIAL OR INCIDENTAL DAMAGES, THE ABOVE LIMITATION MAY NOT APPLY TO YOU.

17. __LIMITATION OF LIABILITY AND REMEDIES.__ NOTWITHSTANDING ANY DAMAGES THAT YOU MIGHT INCUR FOR ANY REASON WHATSOEVER (INCLUDING, WITHOUT LIMITATION, ALL DAMAGES REFERENCED HEREIN AND ALL DIRECT OR GENERAL DAMAGES IN CONTRACT OR ANYTHING ELSE), THE ENTIRE LIABILITY OF MICROSOFT AND ANY OF ITS SUPPLIERS UNDER ANY PROVISION OF THIS EULA AND YOUR EXCLUSIVE REMEDY HEREUNDER SHALL BE LIMITED TO THE GREATER OF THE ACTUAL DAMAGES YOU INCUR IN REASONABLE RELIANCE ON THE LICENSED CONTENT UP TO THE AMOUNT ACTUALLY PAID BY YOU FOR THE LICENSED CONTENT OR US$5.00. THE FOREGOING LIMITATIONS, EXCLUSIONS AND DISCLAIMERS SHALL APPLY TO THE MAXIMUM EXTENT PERMITTED BY APPLICABLE LAW, EVEN IF ANY REMEDY FAILS ITS ESSENTIAL PURPOSE.

18. __APPLICABLE LAW.__ If you acquired this Licensed Content in the United States, this EULA is governed by the laws of the State of Washington. If you acquired this Licensed Content in Canada, unless expressly prohibited by local law, this EULA is governed by the laws in force in the Province of Ontario, Canada; and, in respect of any dispute which may arise hereunder, you consent to the jurisdiction of the federal and provincial courts sitting in Toronto, Ontario. If you acquired this Licensed Content in the European Union, Iceland, Norway, or Switzerland, then local law applies. If you acquired this Licensed Content in any other country, then local law may apply.

19. __ENTIRE AGREEMENT; SEVERABILITY.__ This EULA (including any addendum or amendment to this EULA which is included with the Licensed Content) are the entire agreement between you and Microsoft relating to the Licensed Content and the support services (if any) and they supersede all prior or contemporaneous oral or written communications, proposals and representations with respect to the Licensed Content or any other subject matter covered by this EULA. To the extent the terms of any Microsoft policies or programs for support services conflict with the terms of this EULA, the terms of this EULA shall control. If any provision of this EULA is held to be void, invalid, unenforceable or illegal, the other provisions shall continue in full force and effect.

Should you have any questions concerning this EULA, or if you desire to contact Microsoft for any reason, please use the address information enclosed in this Licensed Content to contact the Microsoft subsidiary serving your country or visit Microsoft on the World Wide Web at http://www.microsoft.com.

__Si vous avez acquis votre Contenu Sous Licence Microsoft au CANADA :__

DÉNI DE GARANTIES. Dans la mesure maximale permise par les lois applicables, le Contenu Sous Licence et les services de soutien technique (le cas échéant) sont fournis _TELS QUELS ET AVEC TOUS LES DÉFAUTS_ par Microsoft et ses fournisseurs, lesquels par les présentes dénient toutes autres garanties et conditions expresses, implicites ou en vertu de la loi, notamment, mais sans limitation, (le cas échéant) les garanties, devoirs ou conditions implicites de qualité marchande, d'adaptation à une fin usage particulière, de fiabilité ou de disponibilité, d'exactitude ou d'exhaustivité des réponses, des résultats, des efforts déployés selon les règles de l'art, d'absence de virus et d'absence de négligence, le tout à l'égard du Contenu Sous Licence et de la prestation des services de soutien technique ou de l'omission de la 'une telle prestation des services de soutien technique ou à l'égard de la fourniture ou de l'omission de la fourniture de tous autres services, renseignements, Contenus Sous Licence, et contenu qui s'y rapporte grâce au Contenu Sous Licence ou provenant autrement de l'utilisation du Contenu Sous Licence. PAR AILLEURS, IL N'Y A AUCUNE GARANTIE OU CONDITION QUANT AU TITRE DE PROPRIÉTÉ, À LA JOUISSANCE OU LA POSSESSION PAISIBLE, À LA CONCORDANCE À UNE DESCRIPTION NI QUANT À UNE ABSENCE DE CONTREFAÇON CONCERNANT LE CONTENU SOUS LICENCE.

EXCLUSION DES DOMMAGES ACCESSOIRES, INDIRECTS ET DE CERTAINS AUTRES DOMMAGES. DANS LA MESURE MAXIMALE PERMISE PAR LES LOIS APPLICABLES, EN AUCUN CAS MICROSOFT OU SES FOURNISSEURS NE SERONT RESPONSABLES DES DOMMAGES SPÉCIAUX, CONSÉCUTIFS, ACCESSOIRES OU INDIRECTS DE QUELQUE NATURE QUE CE SOIT (NOTAMMENT, LES DOMMAGES À L'ÉGARD DU MANQUE À GAGNER OU DE LA DIVULGATION DE RENSEIGNEMENTS CONFIDENTIELS OU AUTRES, DE LA PERTE D'EXPLOITATION, DE BLESSURES CORPORELLES, DE LA VIOLATION DE LA VIE PRIVÉE, DE L'OMISSION DE REMPLIR TOUT DEVOIR, Y COMPRIS D'AGIR DE BONNE FOI OU D'EXERCER UN SOIN RAISONNABLE, DE LA NÉGLIGENCE ET DE TOUTE AUTRE PERTE PÉCUNIAIRE OU AUTRE PERTE

DE QUELQUE NATURE QUE CE SOIT) SE RAPPORTANT DE QUELQUE MANIÈRE QUE CE SOIT À L'UTILISATION DU CONTENU SOUS LICENCE OU À L'INCAPACITÉ DE S'EN SERVIR, À LA PRESTATION OU À L'OMISSION DE LA 'UNE TELLE PRESTATION DE SERVICES DE SOUTIEN TECHNIQUE OU À LA FOURNITURE OU À L'OMISSION DE LA FOURNITURE DE TOUS AUTRES SERVICES, RENSEIGNEMENTS, CONTENUS SOUS LICENCE, ET CONTENU QUI S'Y RAPPORTE GRÂCE AU CONTENU SOUS LICENCE OU PROVENANT AUTREMENT DE L'UTILISATION DU CONTENU SOUS LICENCE OU AUTREMENT AUX TERMES DE TOUTE DISPOSITION DE LA U PRÉSENTE CONVENTION EULA OU RELATIVEMENT À UNE TELLE DISPOSITION, MÊME EN CAS DE FAUTE, DE DÉLIT CIVIL (Y COMPRIS LA NÉGLIGENCE), DE RESPONSABILITÉ STRICTE, DE VIOLATION DE CONTRAT OU DE VIOLATION DE GARANTIE DE MICROSOFT OU DE TOUT FOURNISSEUR ET MÊME SI MICROSOFT OU TOUT FOURNISSEUR A ÉTÉ AVISÉ DE LA POSSIBILITÉ DE TELS DOMMAGES.

LIMITATION DE RESPONSABILITÉ ET RECOURS.   MALGRÉ LES DOMMAGES QUE VOUS PUISSIEZ SUBIR POUR QUELQUE MOTIF QUE CE SOIT (NOTAMMENT, MAIS SANS LIMITATION, TOUS LES DOMMAGES SUSMENTIONNÉS ET TOUS LES DOMMAGES DIRECTS OU GÉNÉRAUX OU AUTRES), LA SEULE RESPONSABILITÉ 'OBLIGATION INTÉGRALE DE MICROSOFT ET DE L'UN OU L'AUTRE DE SES FOURNISSEURS AUX TERMES DE TOUTE DISPOSITION DEU LA PRÉSENTE CONVENTION EULA ET VOTRE RECOURS EXCLUSIF À L'ÉGARD DE TOUT CE QUI PRÉCÈDE SE LIMITE AU PLUS ÉLEVÉ ENTRE LES MONTANTS SUIVANTS : LE MONTANT QUE VOUS AVEZ RÉELLEMENT PAYÉ POUR LE CONTENU SOUS LICENCE OU 5,00 $US. LES LIMITES, EXCLUSIONS ET DÉNIS QUI PRÉCÈDENT (Y COMPRIS LES CLAUSES CI-DESSUS), S'APPLIQUENT DANS LA MESURE MAXIMALE PERMISE PAR LES LOIS APPLICABLES, MÊME SI TOUT RECOURS N'ATTEINT PAS SON BUT ESSENTIEL.

À moins que cela ne soit prohibé par le droit local applicable, la présente Convention est régie par les lois de la province d'Ontario, Canada. Vous consentez Chacune des parties à la présente reconnaît irrévocablement à la compétence des tribunaux fédéraux et provinciaux siégeant à Toronto, dans de la province d'Ontario et consent à instituer tout litige qui pourrait découler de la présente auprès des tribunaux situés dans le district judiciaire de York, province d'Ontario.

Au cas où vous auriez des questions concernant cette licence ou que vous désiriez vous mettre en rapport avec Microsoft pour quelque raison que ce soit, veuillez utiliser l'information contenue dans le Contenu Sous Licence pour contacter la filiale de succursale Microsoft desservant votre pays, dont l'adresse est fournie dans ce produit, ou visitez écrivez à : Microsoft sur le World Wide Web à http://www.microsoft.com

Contents

Module 9: Introduction to Programming Objects

Appendix A: Library Database Case Study

Appendix B: Database Schemas

About This Course

This section provides you with a brief description of the course, audience, suggested prerequisites, and course objectives.

Description

This course provides students with the technical skills required to write basic Transact-SQL queries for Microsoft® SQL Server™ 2000.

This is a revised two-day course. The course content reflects the need to focus on querying with Transact-SQL. The material comes primarily from course 2071A, Querying Microsoft SQL Server 2000 with Transact SQL.

This revised course is a prerequisite for course 2073A, *Programming a Microsoft SQL Server 2000 Database* and course 2072A, *Administering a Microsoft SQL Server 2000 Database*.

Audience

This course is designed for SQL Server database administrators, implementers, system engineers, and developers who are responsible for writing queries.

Student Prerequisites

This course requires that students meet the following prerequisites:

- Experience using the Microsoft Windows® operating system.
- An understanding of basic relational database concepts, including:
  - Logical and physical database design.
  - Data integrity concepts.
  - Relationships between tables and columns (primary key and foreign key, one-to-one, one-to-many, many-to-many).
  - How data is stored in tables (rows and columns).

  For students who do not meet these prerequisites, the following course provides students with the necessary knowledge and skills:

  - Course 1609, *Designing Data Services and Data Models*
- Familiarity with the role of the database administrator.

Course Objectives

At the end of this course, the student will be able to:

- Describe the uses of and ways to execute the Transact-SQL language.
- Use querying tools.
- Write SELECT queries to retrieve data.
- Group and summarize data using Transact-SQL.
- Join data from multiple tables.
- Write queries that retrieve and modify data by using subqueries.
- Modify data in tables.
- Query text fields with full-text search.
- Describe how to create programming objects.

Student Materials Compact Disc Contents

The Student Materials compact disc contains the following files and folders:

- *Default.htm*. This file opens the Student Materials Web page. It provides students with resources pertaining to this course, including additional reading, review and lab answers, lab files, multimedia presentations, and course-related Web sites.

- *Readme.txt*. This file contains a description of the compact disc contents and setup instructions in ASCII format (non-Microsoft Word document).

- *AddRead*. This folder contains additional reading pertaining to this course. If there are no additional reading files, this folder does not appear.

- *Answers*. This folder contains answers to the module review questions and hands-on labs.

- *Appendix*. This folder contains appendix files for this course. If there are no appendix files, this folder does not appear.

- *Batches*. This folder contains batch files and scripts for modules and lab setup.

- *Demo*. This folder contains scripts that are used in the modules.

- *Fonts*. This folder contains fonts that are required to view the PowerPoint presentation and Web-based materials.

- *Labfiles*. This folder contains files that are used in the hands-on labs. These files may be used to prepare the student computers for the hands-on labs.

- *Pptview*. This folder contains the PowerPoint Viewer, which is used to display the PowerPoint slides.

- *Webfiles*. This folder contains the files that are required to view the course Web page. To open the Web page, open Windows Explorer, and in the root directory of the compact disc, double-click **Default.htm**.

- *Wordview*. This folder contains the Word Viewer that is used to view any Word document (.doc) files that are included on the compact disc. If no Word documents are included, this folder does not appear.

Document Conventions

The following conventions are used in course materials to distinguish elements of the text.

Convention	Use
◆	Indicates an introductory page. This symbol appears next to a slide title when additional information on the topic is covered on the page or pages that follow it.
bold	Represents commands, command options, and portions of syntax that must be typed exactly as shown. It also indicates commands on menus and buttons, icons, dialog box titles and options, and icon and menu names.
italic	In syntax statements, indicates placeholders for variable information. Italic is also used for introducing new terms, for book titles, and for emphasis in the text.
Title Capitals	Indicate domain names, user names, computer names, directory names, folders, and file names, except when specifically referring to case-sensitive names. Unless otherwise indicated, you can use lowercase letters when you type a directory name or file name in a dialog box or at a command prompt.
ALL CAPITALS	Indicate the names of keys, key sequences, and key combinations—for example, ALT+SPACEBAR.
`monospace`	Represents code samples, examples of screen text, or entries that you type at a command prompt or in initialization files.
[ ]	In syntax statements, enclose optional items. For example, [*filename*] in command syntax indicates that you can choose to type a file name with the command. Type only the information within the brackets, not the brackets themselves.
{ }	In syntax statements, enclose required items. Type only the information within the braces, not the braces themselves.
|	In syntax statements, separates an either/or choice.
▶	Indicates a procedure with sequential steps.
...	In syntax statements, specifies that the preceding item may be repeated.
. . .	Represents an omitted portion of a code sample.

Microsoft®
Training &
Certification

Introduction

Contents

Microsoft®

Introduction

- Name
- Company Affiliation
- Title/Function
- Job Responsibility
- Database Experience
- SQL Server Experience
- Expectations for the Course

Course Materials

- ■ **Name Card**
- ■ **Student Workbook**
- ■ **Student Materials Compact Disc**
- ■ **Course Evaluation**

The following materials are included with your kit:

- *Name card.* Write your name on both sides of the name card.

- *Student workbook.* The student workbook contains the material covered in class, in addition to the hands-on lab exercises.

- *Student Materials compact disc.* The Student Materials compact disc contains the Web page that provides students with links to resources pertaining to this course, including additional readings, review and lab answers, lab files, multimedia presentations, and course-related Web sites.

Note To open the Web page, insert the Student Materials compact disc into the CD-ROM drive, and then in the root directory of the compact disc, double-click **Default.htm**.

- *Course evaluation.* At the conclusion of this course, please complete the course evaluation to provide feedback on the instructor, course, and software product. Your comments will help us improve future courses.

To provide additional comments on course materials, send e-mail to mstrain@microsoft.com. Be sure to type **Course 2071B** in the subject line.

To provide additional comments or inquire about the Microsoft Certified Professional program, send e-mail to mcp@msprograms.com.

Prerequisites

- **Experience Using a Microsoft Windows Operating System**
- **Understanding of Basic Relational Database Concepts**
- **Familiarity with the Role of the Database Administrator**

This course requires that you meet the following prerequisites:

- Experience using a Microsoft® Windows® operating system.
- Understanding of basic relational database concepts, including:
  - Logical and physical database design.
  - Data integrity concepts.
  - Relationships between tables and columns (primary key and foreign key, one-to-one, one-to-many, many-to-many).
  - How data is stored in tables (rows and columns).

  For students who do not meet these prerequisites, the following course provides students with the necessary knowledge and skills:
  - Course 1609, *Designing Data Services and Data Models*
- Familiarity with the role of the database administrator.

Course Outline

- **Module 1: Introduction to Transact-SQL**
- **Module 2: Using Transact-SQL Querying Tools**
- **Module 3: Retrieving Data**
- **Module 4: Grouping and Summarizing Data**
- **Module 5: Joining Multiple Tables**

Module 1, "Introduction to Transact-SQL," provides a brief overview of Transact-SQL as a programming language and describes different ways to execute Transact-SQL. Students are assumed to be familiar with ANSI-SQL and basic programming concepts, such as functions, operators, variables, and control-of-flow statements. At the end of this module, you will be able to describe the elements of Transact-SQL.

Module 2, "Using Transact-SQL Querying Tools," describes several querying tools available in Microsoft SQL Server™ and how to use them to execute Transact-SQL scripts. At the end of this module, you will be able to describe the primary Transact-SQL querying tools in SQL Server and execute Transact-SQL scripts in various ways.

Module 3, "Retrieving Data," covers the SELECT statement in detail, using many examples to demonstrate how to sort data, eliminate duplicates, and change the format of a result set. At the end of this module, you will be able to use the SELECT statement to retrieve data.

Module 4, "Grouping and Summarizing Data," discusses using aggregate functions to group data, and explains how to generate summary reports and list values in a result set. At the end of this module, you will be able to generate and group summary data for a table.

Module 5, "Joining Multiple Tables," provides information on querying multiple tables by using different types of joins, combining result sets by using the UNION operator, and creating tables by using the SELECT INTO statement. At the end of this module, you will be able to combine data and multiple result sets.

Course Outline *(continued)*

- Module 6: Working with Subqueries
- Module 7: Modifying Data
- Module 8: Querying Full-Text Indexes
- Module 9: Introduction to Programming Objects

Module 6, "Working with Subqueries," presents advanced query techniques, including nested and correlated subqueries, and explains when and how to use them to break down and perform complex queries. At the end of this module, you will be able to write queries that use single-value, multiple-value, and correlated subqueries to restrict result sets and combine multiple processing steps into one SELECT statement.

Module 7, "Modifying Data," explains how transactions work and discusses how to write INSERT, DELETE, and UPDATE statements to modify data in tables. At the end of this module, you will be able to modify data in tables in various ways.

Module 8, "Querying Full-Text Indexes," describes the Microsoft Search service, how to access information about indexes on text fields, and how to query those full-text indexes. At the end of this module, you will be able to describe the functions and components of Microsoft Search, get information about full-text indexes, and write full-text queries.

Module 9, "Introduction to Programming Objects," discusses how to create programming objects that enable the user to look at and manipulate data while hiding the complexity of the underlying database structure. At the end of this module, you will be able to display the text of a programming object and describe the concept and advantage of using views, stored procedures, triggers, and user-defined functions.

Appendices

- **Appendix A: Library Database Case Study**
- **Appendix B: Database Schemas**

Appendix A: Library Database Case Study

This appendix contains a description of the **library** sample database that is used in this course.

Appendix B: Database Schemas

This appendix contains schematic diagrams of the databases that are used in this course.

Microsoft Official Curriculum

- **Microsoft Windows Operating Systems**
- **Microsoft Office**
- **Microsoft BackOffice Small Business Server**
- **Microsoft SQL Server**
- **Microsoft Exchange**
- **Microsoft BackOffice Server Infrastructure and Solutions**
- **Microsoft FrontPage**
- **Microsoft Systems Management Server**
- **Knowledge Management Solutions**

Microsoft® Official Curriculum (MOC) is hands-on facilitated classroom and Web-based training. Microsoft develops skills-based training courses to educate computer professionals who develop, support, and implement solutions by using Microsoft products, solutions, and technologies. MOC courses are available for the following products and solutions:

- Microsoft Windows® operating systems
- Microsoft Office
- Microsoft BackOffice® Small Business Server
- Microsoft SQL Server™
- Microsoft Exchange
- Microsoft BackOffice Server Infrastructure and Solutions
- Microsoft FrontPage®
- Microsoft Systems Management Server
- Knowledge Management Solutions

MOC provides a curriculum path for each product and solution. For more information about the curriculum paths, see the Microsoft Official Curriculum Web page at http://www.microsoft.com/trainingandservices/.

The Microsoft Official Curriculum Web page provides information about MOC courses. In addition, you can find recommended curriculum paths for individuals who are entering the Information Technology (IT) industry, who are continuing their training on Microsoft products and solutions, or who currently support non-Microsoft products.

Microsoft Certified Professional Program

- **Microsoft Certified Systems Engineer (MCSE)**

- **Microsoft Certified Database Administrator (MCDBA)**

- **Microsoft Certified Solution Developer (MCSD)**

- **Microsoft Certified Professional + Site Building (MCP + Site Building)**

- **Microsoft Certified Professional (MCP)**

- **Microsoft Certified Trainer (MCT)**

The Microsoft Certified Professional program provides the best method to prove your command of current Microsoft products and technologies. The following table describes each certification in more detail.

Certification	Description
Microsoft Certified Systems Engineer (MCSE)	MCSEs are qualified to effectively plan, implement, maintain, and support information systems in a wide range of computing environments with Microsoft Windows 2000 and Microsoft BackOffice.
Microsoft Certified Database Administrator (MCDBA)	MCDBAs are qualified to derive physical database designs, develop logical data models, create physical databases, create data services by using Transact-SQL, manage and maintain databases, configure and manage security, monitor and optimize databases, and install and configure Microsoft SQL Server.
Microsoft Certified Solution Developer (MCSD)	MCSDs are qualified to build Web-based, distributed, and commerce applications by using Microsoft products, such as Microsoft SQL Server, Microsoft Visual Studio®, and Component Services.
Microsoft Certified Professional + Site Building (MCP + Site Building)	MCPs with a specialty in site building are qualified to plan, build, maintain, and manage Web sites by using Microsoft technologies and products.
Microsoft Certified Professional (MCP)	MCPs demonstrate in-depth knowledge of at least one product by passing any one exam (except Networking Essentials).
Microsoft Certified Trainer (MCT)	MCTs demonstrate the instructional and technical skills that qualify them to deliver Microsoft Official Curriculum through Microsoft Certified Technical Education Centers (Microsoft CTEC).

Certification Requirements

The certification requirements differ for each certification category and are specific to the products and job functions addressed by the certification. To become a Microsoft Certified Professional, you must pass rigorous certification exams that provide a valid and reliable measure of technical proficiency and expertise.

For More Information See the Microsoft Training and Certification Web site at http://www.microsoft.com/trainingandservices/.

You can also send e-mail to mcp@msprograms.com if you have specific certification questions.

Preparing for an MCP Exam

Microsoft Official Curriculum (MOC) helps you prepare for Microsoft Certified Professional (MCP) exams. However, no one-to-one correlation exists between MOC courses and MCP exams. Microsoft does not expect or intend for MOC to be the sole preparation tool for passing an MCP exam. Practical product knowledge and experience is also necessary to pass an MCP exam.

To help prepare for the MCP exams, you can use the preparation guides that are available for each exam. Each Exam Preparation Guide contains exam-specific information, such as a list of the topics on which you will be tested. These guides are available on the Microsoft Certified Professional Web site at http://www.microsoft.com/trainingandservices/.

Facilities

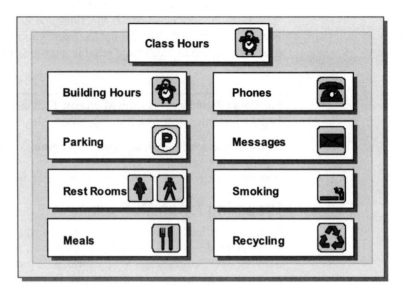

Microsoft®
Training &
Certification

Module 1: Introduction to Transact-SQL

Contents

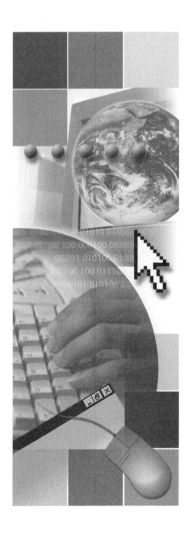

Microsoft®

Overview

- **The Transact-SQL Programming Language**
- **Types of Transact-SQL Statements**
- **Transact-SQL Syntax Elements**

Transact-SQL is a data definition, manipulation, and control language. This module provides a brief overview of Transact-SQL as a programming language. It also describes the types of Transact-SQL statements and syntax elements.

At the end of this module, you will be able to:

- Describe the Transact-SQL programming language.

- Describe the types of Transact-SQL statements.

- Describe Transact-SQL syntax elements.

The Transact-SQL Programming Language

- ■ **Implements Entry-Level ANSI SQL-92 ISO Standard**
- ■ **Can Be Run on Any Entry-Level Compliant Product**
- ■ **Contains Additional Unique Functionality**

The American National Standards Institute (ANSI) and the International Standards Organization (ISO) defined standards for SQL. Using Transact-SQL, Microsoft® SQL Server™ 2000 supports the entry level implementation of SQL-92, the SQL standard published by ANSI and ISO in 1992. The ANSI-SQL compliant language elements of Transact-SQL can be executed from any entry-level ANSI-SQL compliant product. Transact-SQL also contains several extensions to provide increased functionality.

◆ Types of Transact-SQL Statements

- Data Definition Language Statements
- Data Control Language Statements
- Data Manipulation Language Statements

A *query* is a request for data stored in SQL Server. All queries present the result set of a SELECT statement to the user. A *result set* is a tabular arrangement of the data from the SELECT statement, comprising columns and rows.

Writing and executing Transact-SQL statements is one way to issue a query to SQL Server. As you write and execute Transact-SQL statements, you will use:

- Data Definition Language (DDL) statements, which allow you to create objects in the database.

- Data Control Language (DCL) statements, which allow you to determine who can see or modify the data.

- Data Manipulation Language (DML) statements, which allow you to query and modify the data.

Note   This course focuses on using DML statements to query data in SQL Server.

Data Definition Language Statements

- **Define the Database Objects**
  - CREATE *object_name*
  - ALTER *object_name*
  - DROP *object_name*
- **Must Have the Appropriate Permissions**

```
USE northwind
CREATE TABLE customer
(cust_id int, company varchar(40),
contact varchar(30), phone char(12) )
GO
```

Data Definition Language (DDL) statements define the database by creating databases, tables, and user-defined data types. You also use DDL statements to manage your database objects. Some DDL statements include:

- CREATE *object_name*
- ALTER *object_name*
- DROP *object_name*

By default, only members of the **sysadmin**, **dbcreator**, **db_owner**, or **db_ddladmin** role can execute DDL statements. In general, it is recommended that no other accounts be used to create database objects. If different users create their own objects in a database, then each object owner is required to grant the proper permissions to each user of those objects. This causes an administrative burden and should be avoided. Restricting statement permissions to these roles also avoids problems with object ownership that can occur when an object owner has been dropped from a database or when the owner of a stored procedure or view does not own the underlying tables.

Example

The following script creates a table called **customer** in the **Northwind** database. It includes **cust_id**, **company**, **contact**, and **phone** columns.

```
USE northwind
CREATE TABLE customer
(cust_id int, company varchar(40),contact varchar(30),
phone char(12) )
GO
```

Data Control Language Statements

■ **Set or Change Permissions**

    • GRANT

    • DENY

    • REVOKE

■ **Must Have the Appropriate Permissions**

```
USE northwind
GRANT SELECT ON products TO public
GO
```

Data Control Language (DCL) statements are used to change the permissions associated with a database user or role. The following table describes the DCL statements.

Statement	Description
GRANT	Creates an entry in the security system that allows a user to work with data or execute certain Transact-SQL statements.
DENY	Creates an entry in the security system denying a permission from a security account and prevents the user, group, or role from inheriting the permission through its group and role memberships.
REVOKE	Removes a previously granted or denied permission.

By default, only members of the **sysadmin**, **dbcreator**, **db_owner**, or **db_securityadmin** role can execute DCL statements.

Example

This example grants the **public** role permission to query the **products** table.

```
USE northwind
GRANT SELECT ON products TO public
GO
```

Data Manipulation Language Statements

- **USE DML Statements to Change Data or Retrieve Information**
  - SELECT
  - INSERT
  - UPDATE
  - DELETE
- **Must Have the Appropriate Permissions**

```
USE northwind
SELECT categoryid, productname, productid, unitprice
FROM products
GO
```

Data Manipulation Language (DML) statements work with the data in the database. By using DML statements, you can change data or retrieve information. DML statements include:

- SELECT.

- INSERT.

- UPDATE.

- DELETE.

Example

This example retrieves the category ID, product name, product ID, and unit price of the products in the **Northwind** database.

```
USE northwind
SELECT categoryid, productname, productid, unitprice
FROM products
GO
```

◆ Transact-SQL Syntax Elements

- ■ **Batch Directives**
- ■ **Comments**
- ■ **Identifiers**
- ■ **Types of Data**
- ■ **Variables**

- ■ **System Functions**
- ■ **Operators**
- ■ **Expressions**
- ■ **Control-of-Flow Language Elements**
- ■ **Reserved Keywords**

DML statements are constructed by using a number of Transact-SQL syntax elements. These include:

- ■ Batch directives
- ■ Comments
- ■ Identifiers
- ■ Types of data
- ■ Variables
- ■ System functions
- ■ Operators
- ■ Expressions
- ■ Control-of-flow language elements
- ■ Reserved keywords

Batch Directives

- **GO**
  - Delineates batches of Transact-SQL statements to tools and utilities
  - Is not an actual Transact-SQL statement
- **EXEC**
  - Executes a user-defined function, system procedure, user-defined stored procedure, or an extended stored procedure
  - Controls the execution of a character string within a Transact-SQL batch

SQL Server processes single or multiple Transact-SQL statements in batches. A batch directive instructs SQL Server to parse and execute all of the instructions within the batch. There are two basic methods for handing off batches to SQL Server.

GO

SQL Server utilities interpret GO as a signal to send the current batch of Transact-SQL statements to SQL Server. A GO command delineates batches of Transact-SQL statements to tools and utilities and ends the batch. A GO command is not an actual Transact-SQL statement.

When using GO, consider these facts:

- The current batch of statements is composed of all statements entered since the last GO, or since the start of the ad hoc session (or script, if this is the first GO).

- A Transact-SQL statement cannot occupy the same line as a GO command, although the line can contain comments.

- Users must follow the rules for batches.

  For example, some Data Definition Language statements must be executed separately from other Transact-SQL statements by separating the statements with a GO command.

  The scope of local (user-defined) variables is limited to a batch, and cannot be referenced after a GO command.

Note   GO is not an actual Transact-SQL statement; GO is used to delineate batches to tools and utilities.

EXEC

The EXEC directive is used to execute a user-defined function, system procedure, user-defined stored procedure, or an extended stored procedure; it can also control the execution of a character string within a Transact-SQL batch. Parameters can be passed as arguments, and a return status can be assigned.

Comments

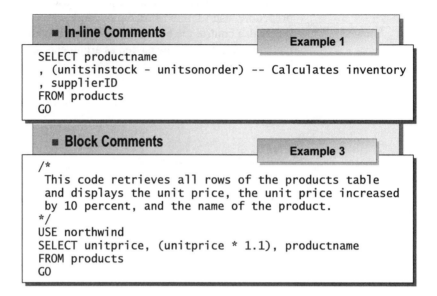

Comments are non-executing strings of text placed in statements to describe the action that the statement is performing or to disable one or more lines of the statement. Comments can be used in one of two ways—in line with a statement or as a block.

In-line Comments

You can create in-line comments using two hyphens (--) to set a comment apart from a statement. Transact-SQL ignores text to the right of the comment characters. This commenting character can also be used to disable lines of a statement.

Example 1

This example uses an in-line comment to explain what a calculation is doing.

```
USE northwind
SELECT productname
  , (unitsinstock - unitsonorder) -- Calculates inventory
  , supplierid
FROM products
GO
```

Example 2

This example uses an in-line comment to prevent the execution of a section of a statement.

```
USE northwind
SELECT productname
  , (unitsinstock - unitsonorder) -- Calculates inventory
-- , supplierid
FROM products
GO
```

Block Comments

You can create multiple line blocks of comments by placing one comment character (/*) at the start of the comment text, typing your comments, and then concluding the comment with a closing comment character (*/).

Use this character designator to create one or more lines of comments or comment headers—descriptive text that documents the statements that follow it. Comment headers often include the author's name, creation and last modification dates of the script, version information, and a description of the action that the statement performs.

Example 3

This example shows a comment header that spans several lines.

```
/*
 This code retrieves all rows of the products table
 and displays the unit price, the unit price increased
 by 10 percent, and the name of the product.
*/
USE northwind
SELECT unitprice, (unitprice * 1.1), productname
 FROM  products
GO
```

Note You should place comments throughout a script to describe the actions that the statements are performing. This is especially important if others must review or implement the script.

Example 4

This section of a script is commented to prevent it from executing. This can be helpful when debugging or troubleshooting a script file.

```
/*
DECLARE @v1 int
SET @v1 = 0
WHILE @v1 < 100
   BEGIN
    SELECT @v1 = (@v1 + 1)
    SELECT @v1
   END
*/
```

◆ Identifiers

- **Standard Identifiers**
  - First character must be alphabetic
  - Other characters can include letters, numerals, or symbols
  - Identifiers starting with symbols have special uses
- **Delimited Identifiers**
  - Use when names contain embedded spaces
  - Use when reserved words are portions of names
  - Enclose in brackets ([ ]) or quotation marks (" ")

SQL Server provides a series of standard naming rules for object identifiers and a method of using delimiters for identifiers that are not standard. It is recommended that you name objects using the standard identifier characters if possible.

Standard Identifiers

Standard identifiers can contain from one to 128 characters, including letters, symbols (_, @, or #), and numbers. No embedded spaces are allowed in standard identifiers. Rules for using identifiers include:

- The first character must be an alphabetic character of a-z or A-Z.

- After the first character, identifiers can include letters, numerals, or the @, $, #, or _ symbol.

- Identifier names starting with a symbol have special uses:

  - An identifier beginning with the @ symbol denotes a local variable or parameter.

  - An identifier beginning with a number sign (#) denotes a temporary table or procedure.

  - An identifier beginning with a double number sign (##) denotes a global temporary object.

Note Names for temporary objects should not exceed 116 characters, including the number (#) or double number (##) sign, because SQL Server gives temporary objects an internal numeric suffix.

Delimited Identifiers

If an identifier complies with all of the rules for the format of identifiers, it can be used with or without delimiters. If an identifier does not comply with one or more of the rules for the format of identifiers, it must always be delimited.

Delimited identifiers can be used in the following situations:

- When names contain embedded spaces

- When reserved words are used for object names or portions of object names

Delimited identifiers must be enclosed in brackets or double quotation marks when they are used in Transact-SQL statements.

- Bracketed identifiers are delimited by square brackets ([ ]):

```
SELECT * FROM [Blanks In Table Name]
```

Note Bracketed delimiters can always be used, regardless of the status of the SET QUOTED_IDENTIFIER option.

- Quoted identifiers are delimited by double quotation marks (""):

```
SELECT * FROM "Blanks in Table Name"
```

Quoted identifiers can only be used if the SET QUOTED_IDENTIFIER option is on.

Naming Guidelines for Identifiers

- **Keep Names Short**
- **Use Meaningful Names Where Possible**
- **Use Clear and Simple Naming Conventions**
- **Use an Identifier That Distinguishes Types of Object**
  - Views
  - Stored procedures
- **Keep Object Names and User Names Unique**
  - **Sales** table and **sales** role

When naming database objects, you should:

- Keep names short.

- Use meaningful names where possible.

- Use a clear and simple naming convention. Decide what works best for your situation and be consistent. Try not to make naming conventions too complex, because they can become difficult to track or understand. For example, you can remove vowels if an object name must resemble a keyword (such as a backup stored procedure named **bckup**).

- Use an identifier that distinguishes the type of object, especially for views and stored procedures. System administrators often mistake views for tables, an oversight that can cause unexpected problems.

- Keep object names and user names unique. For example, avoid creating a **sales** table and a **sales** role within the same database.

Types of Data

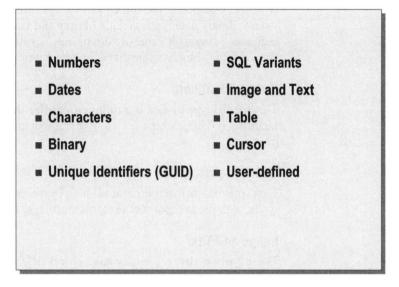

Data types constrain the type of values that you can store in a database. Data types are attributes that specify what type of information can be stored in a column, parameter, or variable. Most Transact-SQL statements do not explicitly reference data types, but the results of most statements are influenced by the interactions between the data types of the objects referenced in the statement.

SQL Server provides system-supplied (base) data types, but you also can create data types. Examples of base data types include:

Numbers

This type of data represents numeric values and includes integers such as **int**, **tinyint**, **smallint**, and **bigint**. It also includes precise decimal values such as **numeric**, **decimal**, **money**, and **smallmoney**. It includes floating point values such as **float** and **real**.

Dates

This type of data represents dates or spans of time. The two date data types are **datetime**, which has a precision of 3.33 milliseconds, and **smalldatetime**, which has a precision of 1-minute intervals.

Characters

This type of data is used to represent character data or strings and includes fixed-width character string data types such as **char** and **nchar**, as well as variable-length string data types such as **varchar** and **nvarchar**.

Binary

This type of data is very similar to character data types in terms of storage and structure, except that the contents of the data are treated as a series of byte values. Binary data types include **binary** and **varbinary**. A data type of **bit** indicates a single bit value of zero or one. A **rowversion** data type indicates a special 8-byte binary value that is unique within a database.

Unique Identifiers

This special type of data is a **uniqueidentifier** that represents a globally unique identifier (GUID), which is a 16-byte hexadecimal value that should always be unique.

SQL Variants

This type of data can represent values of various SQL Server supported data types, with the exception of **text**, **ntext**, **image**, **timestamp** and **rowversion**.

Image and Text

These types of data are binary large object (BLOB) structures that represent fixed- and variable-length data types for storing large non-Unicode and Unicode character and binary data, such as **image**, **text**, and **ntext**.

Tables

The table data type can be used only to define local variables of type table or the return value of a user-defined function.

Cursors

This type of data is used for programming within stored procedures and with low-level client interfaces. The cursor data type is never used as part of a DDL statement.

User-defined Data Types

This data type is created by the database administrator and is based on system data types. Use user-defined data types when several tables must store the same type of data in a column and you must ensure that the columns have exactly the same data type, length, and nullability.

Variables

- **User-defined with DECLARE @ Statement**

- **Assigned Values with SET or SELECT @ Statement**

- **Variables Have Local Scope**

```
USE northwind
DECLARE  @EmpID  varchar(11)
         ,@vlName char(20)
SET @vlname = 'Dodsworth'
SELECT @EmpID = employeeid
 FROM  employees
 WHERE LastName = @vlname
SELECT @EmpID AS EmployeeID
GO
```

Variables are language elements with assigned values. You can use local variables in Transact-SQL.

A local variable is user-defined in a DECLARE statement, assigned an initial value in a SET or SELECT statement, and then used within the statement, batch, or procedure in which it was declared. The scope of a local variable lasts for the duration of the batch in which it is defined. A local variable is shown with one @ symbol preceding its name.

Note   Variables with two @ signs preceding them are a type of function. See *Transact SQL Reference*, *Functions* on the **Contents** tab in SQL Server Books Online for more information.

Syntax

DECLARE {@local_variable data_type} [,...*n*]

SET @*local_variable_name* = *expression*

Example

This example creates the **@EmpID** and **@vlname** local variables, assigns a value to **@vlname**, and then assigns a value to **@EmpID** by querying the **Northwind** database to select the record containing the value of the **@vlname** local variable.

```
USE northwind
DECLARE  @EmpID  varchar(11)
        ,@vlName char(20)
SET @vlname = 'Dodsworth'
SELECT @EmpID = employeeid
 FROM  employees
 WHERE LastName = @vlname
SELECT @EmpID AS EmployeeID
GO
```

Result

EmployeeID
9

```
(1 row(s) affected)
```

◆ System Functions

■ **Aggregate Functions**

```
USE northwind
SELECT AVG (unitprice) AS AvgPrice FROM products
GO
```

■ **Scalar Functions**

```
USE northwind
SELECT DB_NAME() AS 'database'
GO
```

■ **Rowset Functions**

```
SELECT *
 FROM OPENQUERY
   (OracleSvr, 'SELECT name, id FROM owner.titles')
```

You can use functions, including System Functions, anywhere that an expression is allowed in a Transact-SQL query statement. Transact-SQL provides many functions that return information.

Some functions take input parameters and return values that can be used in expressions. Others simply return values without requiring input. The Transact-SQL programming language provides many types of functions. Here are three types of functions that you should be familiar with:

Note See *Transact SQL Reference*, *Functions* on the **Contents** tab in SQL Server Books Online for more information.

Aggregate Functions Operate on the collection of values of a selected column in a resultset but return a single summarizing value.

Example 1

This example determines the average of the **unitprice** column for all products in the **products** table.

```
USE northwind
SELECT AVG(unitprice) AS AvgPrice
 FROM products
GO
```

Result

```
AvgPrice
28.8663

(1 row(s) affected)
```

Scalar Functions   Return a single value operating from none or many single scalar values. These functions can be used wherever an expression is valid. Scalar functions can be grouped into the following categories.

Function category	Description
Configuration	Returns information about the current configuration
Cursor	Returns information about cursors
Date and Time	Performs an operation on a date and time input value and returns a string, numeric, or date and time value
Mathematical	Performs a calculation based on input values provided as parameters to the function and returns a numeric value
Metadata	Returns information about the database and database objects
Security	Returns information about users and roles
String	Performs an operation on a string (**char** or **varchar**) input value and returns a string or numeric value
System	Performs operations and returns information about values, objects, and settings in SQL Server
System Statistical	Returns statistical information about the system
Text and Image	Performs an operation on a text or image input value or column, and returns information about the value

Example 2

This metadata function example returns the name of the database currently in use.

```
USE northwind
SELECT DB_NAME() AS 'database'
GO
```

Result

database

```
Northwind

(1 row(s) affected)
```

Rowset Functions   Can be used like table references in a Transact-SQL statement.

Example 3

This example performs a distributed query to retrieve information from the **titles** table. Note that this example will not execute properly without access to an Oracle database. SQL Server will generate a message to that effect.

```
SELECT *
FROM OPENQUERY(OracleSvr, 'SELECT name, id FROM owner.titles')
GO
```

System Function Examples

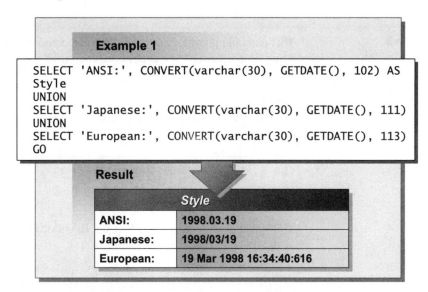

Example 1

```
SELECT 'ANSI:', CONVERT(varchar(30), GETDATE(), 102) AS
Style
UNION
SELECT 'Japanese:', CONVERT(varchar(30), GETDATE(), 111)
UNION
SELECT 'European:', CONVERT(varchar(30), GETDATE(), 113)
GO
```

Result

	Style
ANSI:	1998.03.19
Japanese:	1998/03/19
European:	19 Mar 1998 16:34:40:616

System functions are commonly used when converting date data from the format of one country to that of another.

Note To change date formats, you should use the CONVERT function with the style option to determine the date format that will be returned.

Example 1

This example demonstrates how you can convert dates to different styles.

```
SELECT 'ANSI:', CONVERT (varchar(30), GETDATE(), 102) AS Style
UNION
SELECT 'Japanese:', CONVERT(varchar(30), GETDATE(), 111)
UNION
SELECT 'European:', CONVERT(varchar(30), GETDATE(), 113)
GO
```

Result

```
                    Style
European:    20 Nov 1998 16:44:12:857
Japanese:    11/20/98
ANSI:        1998.11.20
```

Example 2

This example uses the DATEFORMAT option of the SET statement to format dates for the duration of a connection. This setting is used only in the interpretation of character strings as they are converted to date values. It has no effect on the display of date values.

```
SET DATEFORMAT dmy
GO
DECLARE @vdate datetime
SET @vdate = '29/11/98'
SELECT @vdate
GO
```

Result

```
1998-11-29 00:00:00.000

(1 row(s) affected)
```

Example 3

This example returns the current user name and the application that the user is using for the current session or connection. The user in this example is a member of the **sysadmin** role.

```
USE library
SELECT user_name(), app_name()
GO
```

Result

```
dbo              MS SQL Query Analyzer

(1 row(s) affected)
```

Example 4

This example determines whether the **firstname** column in the **member** table of the **library** database allows null values.

A result of zero (false) means that null values are not allowed, and a result of one (true) means that null values are allowed. Notice that the OBJECT_ID function is embedded in the COLUMNPROPERTY function. This allows you to get the **object id** of the **member** table.

```
USE library
SELECT COLUMNPROPERTY(OBJECT_ID('member'), 'firstname',
'AllowsNull')
GO
```

Result

```
0

(1 row(s) affected)
```

Operators

- **Types of Operators**
  - Arithmetic
  - Comparison
  - String concatenation
  - Logical
- **Operator Precedence Levels**

Operators are symbols that perform mathematical computations, string concatenations, and comparisons between columns, constants, and variables. They can be combined and used in search conditions. When you combine them, the order in which the operators are processed is based on a predefined precedence.

Partial Syntax

{*constant* | *column_name* | *function* | (*subquery*)}
  [{*arithmetic_operator* | *string_operator* |
    AND | OR | NOT}
    {*constant* | *column_name* | *function* | (*subquery*)}...]

Types of Operators

SQL Server supports four types of operators: arithmetic, comparison, string concatenation, and logical.

Arithmetic

Arithmetic operators perform computations with numeric columns or constants. Transact-SQL supports multiplicative operators, including multiplication (*), division (/), and modulo (%)—the integer remainder after integer division—and the addition (+) and subtraction (-) additive operators.

Comparison

Comparison operators compare two expressions. Comparisons can be made between variables, columns, and expressions of similar type. Comparison operators include those in the following table.

Operator	Meaning
=	Equal to
>	Greater than
<	Less than
>=	Greater than or equal to
<=	Less than or equal to
<>	Not equal to

String Concatenation

The string concatenation operator (+) concatenates string values. All other string manipulation is handled through string functions. The empty string is never evaluated as a null value.

Logical

The logical operators AND, OR, and NOT connect search conditions in WHERE clauses.

Operator Precedence Levels

If you use multiple operators (logical or arithmetic) to combine expressions, SQL Server processes the operators in order of their precedence, which may affect the resulting value. Operators have the following precedence levels (from highest to lowest).

Type	Operator	Symbol
Grouping	Primary grouping	( )
Arithmetic	Multiplicative	* / %
Arithmetic	Additive	- +
Other	String concatenation	+
Logical	NOT	NOT
Logical	AND	AND
Logical	OR	OR

SQL Server handles the most deeply nested expression first. In addition, if all arithmetic operators in an expression share the same level of precedence, the order is from left to right.

Note The precedence levels of logical operators in SQL Server are different from other programming languages.

Expressions

- **Combination of Symbols and Operators**

- **Evaluation to Single Scalar Value**

- **Result Data Type Dependent on the Elements Within the Expression**

```
USE     northwind
SELECT  OrderID, ProductID
        ,(UnitPrice * Quantity) as ExtendedAmount
 FROM   [Order Details]
 WHERE  (UnitPrice * Quantity) > 10000
 GO
```

Expressions are a combination of symbols and operators that evaluate to a single data value. They can be simple—such as a constant, variable, column or scalar value—or complex expressions created by connecting one or more simple expressions with operators.

The data type of the result depends on the elements within the expression. Implicit data type conversions are frequently done on elements within the expression during evaluation.

Example

The following example calculates the extended amount of a product on an order by multiplying the unit price by the quantity ordered, and then filters the results so that the only rows returned are those orders with products that have an extended amount greater than $10,000.

```
USE     northwind
SELECT  OrderID, ProductID
        ,(UnitPrice * Quantity) as ExtendedAmount
 FROM   [Order Details]
 WHERE  (UnitPrice * Quantity) > 10000
 GO
```

Result

OrderID	ProductID	ExtendedAmount
10353	38	10540.0000
10417	38	10540.0000
10424	38	10329.2000
10865	38	15810.0000
10889	38	10540.0000
10981	38	15810.0000

```
(6 row(s) affected)
```

Control-of-Flow Language Elements

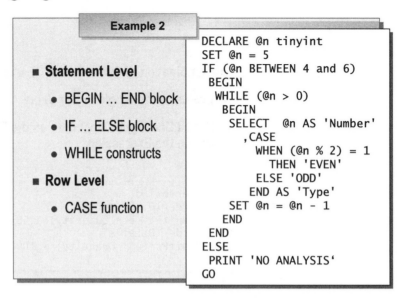

Example 2

- **Statement Level**
  - BEGIN ... END block
  - IF ... ELSE block
  - WHILE constructs
- **Row Level**
  - CASE function

```
DECLARE @n tinyint
SET @n = 5
IF (@n BETWEEN 4 and 6)
 BEGIN
  WHILE (@n > 0)
   BEGIN
    SELECT  @n AS 'Number'
      ,CASE
        WHEN (@n % 2) = 1
          THEN 'EVEN'
         ELSE 'ODD'
         END AS 'Type'
     SET @n = @n - 1
   END
 END
ELSE
 PRINT 'NO ANALYSIS'
GO
```

Transact-SQL contains several language elements that control the flow of logic within a statement. It also contains the CASE function that allows you to use conditional logic on a single row at a time within a SELECT or UPDATE statement.

Statement Level

The following language elements enable you to control the flow of logic within a script:

BEGIN ... END Blocks   These elements enclose a series of Transact-SQL statements so that they are treated as a unit.

IF ... ELSE Blocks   These elements specify that SQL Server should execute the first alternative if the certain condition is true. Otherwise, SQL Server should execute the second alternative.

WHILE Constructs   These elements execute a statement repeatedly as long as the specified condition is true. BREAK and CONTINUE statements control the operation of the statements inside a WHILE loop.

Tip   Indent Transact-SQL statements within a control-of-flow block to improve readability.

Example 1

This example determines whether a customer has any orders before deleting the customer from the customer list.

```
USE northwind
IF EXISTS (SELECT * FROM orders
            WHERE customerid = 'frank')
  PRINT '*** Customer cannot be deleted ***'
ELSE
  BEGIN
    DELETE customers WHERE customerid = 'frank'
    PRINT '*** Customer deleted ***'
  END
GO
```

Row Level

A CASE function lists predicates, assigns a value for each, and then tests each one. If the expression in the WHEN clause returns a true value, the CASE function returns the expression in the THEN clause. If the expression is false, and you have specified an ELSE clause, SQL Server returns the value in the ELSE clause. You can use a CASE function anywhere that you use an expression.

Syntax

CASE *expression*
    {WHEN *expression* THEN *result*} [,...*n*]
  [ELSE *result*]
  END

Example 2

The following example declares a local variable, checks to see whether it equals 4, 5, or 6, and if it does, counts through a WHILE loop that determines whether the current value is an odd or even number.

```
DECLARE  @n tinyint
SET   @n = 5
IF (@n BETWEEN 4 and 6)
 BEGIN
  WHILE (@n > 0)
   BEGIN
    SELECT  @n AS 'Number'
      ,CASE
         WHEN (@n % 2) = 1
           THEN 'ODD'
         ELSE 'EVEN'
         END AS 'Type'
    SET @n = @n - 1
   END
 END
ELSE
 PRINT 'NO ANALYSIS'
GO
```

Result

Number	Type
5	EVEN

(1 row(s) affected)

Number	Type
4	ODD

(1 row(s) affected)

Number	Type
3	EVEN

(1 row(s) affected)

Number	Type
2	ODD

(1 row(s) affected)

Number	Type
1	EVEN

(1 row(s) affected)

Reserved Keywords

- **Identifier Names That Have Special Meaning**
  - Transact-SQL keywords
  - ANSI SQL-92 keywords
  - ODBC reserved keywords
- **Do Not Use Reserved Keywords for Identifier Names**

SQL Server reserves certain keywords for its exclusive use. For example, using either the DUMP or BACKUP keyword in an **osql** or SQL Query Analyzer session tells SQL Server to make a backup copy of all or part of a database, or a backup copy of the log.

You cannot include reserved keywords in a Transact-SQL statement in any location except that defined by SQL Server. You should avoid naming an object with a reserved keyword. If an object name matches a keyword, whenever you refer to the object you must enclose it within delimiting identifiers, such as quotation marks or brackets [ ].

The system and database administrator roles, or the database creator, is usually responsible for checking for reserved keywords in Transact-SQL statements and database names.

Warning   It is possible to construct syntactically correct Transact-SQL statements that may parse successfully and compile, but that still return a run-time error during execution. As a best practice, do not use reserved keywords.

Lab A: Using SQL Server Books Online

Objectives

After completing this lab, you will be able to:

- View the contents, use the index, and search for information in Microsoft®
  SQL Server™ Books Online, as well as save the location of information on
  the **Favorites** tab.

Prerequisites

None.

Lab Setup

None.

For More Information

If you require help in executing files, search SQL Query Analyzer Help for
"Execute a query".

Other resources that you can use include:

- The **Northwind** database schema.
- SQL Server Books Online.

Scenario

The organization of the classroom is meant to simulate a worldwide trading
firm named Northwind Traders. Its fictitious domain name is nwtraders.msft.
The primary DNS server for nwtraders.msft is the instructor computer, which
has an Internet Protocol (IP) address of 192.168.x.200 (where x is the assigned
classroom number). The name of the instructor computer is London.

The following table provides the user name, computer name, and the IP address for each student computer in the fictitious nwtraders.msft domain. Find the user name for your computer and make a note of it.

User name	Computer name	IP address
SQLAdmin1	Vancouver	192.168.x.1
SQLAdmin2	Denver	192.168.x.2
SQLAdmin3	Perth	192.168.x.3
SQLAdmin4	Brisbane	192.168.x.4
SQLAdmin5	Lisbon	192.168.x.5
SQLAdmin6	Bonn	192.168.x.6
SQLAdmin7	Lima	192.168.x.7
SQLAdmin8	Santiago	192.168.x.8
SQLAdmin9	Bangalore	192.168.x.9
SQLAdmin10	Singapore	192.168.x.10
SQLAdmin11	Casablanca	192.168.x.11
SQLAdmin12	Tunis	192.168.x.12
SQLAdmin13	Acapulco	192.168.x.13
SQLAdmin14	Miami	192.168.x.14
SQLAdmin15	Auckland	192.168.x.15
SQLAdmin16	Suva	192.168.x.16
SQLAdmin17	Stockholm	192.168.x.17
SQLAdmin18	Moscow	192.168.x.18
SQLAdmin19	Caracas	192.168.x.19
SQLAdmin20	Montevideo	192.168.x.20
SQLAdmin21	Manila	192.168.x.21
SQLAdmin22	Tokyo	192.168.x.22
SQLAdmin23	Khartoum	192.168.x.23
SQLAdmin24	Nairobi	192.168.x.24

Estimated time to complete this lab: 15 minutes

Exercise 1
Using SQL Server Books Online

In this exercise, you will use SQL Server Books Online to retrieve information on SQL Server.

▶ **To view the contents of Getting Started in SQL Server Books Online**

In this procedure, you will view the contents of SQL Server Books Online and familiarize yourself with conventions used in the documentation.

1. Log on to the **NWTraders** classroom domain by using the information in the following table.

Option	Value
User name	**SQLAdmin**x (where x corresponds to your computer name as designated in the nwtraders.msft classroom domain)
Password	**password**

2. On the taskbar, click the **Start** button, point to **Programs**, point to **Microsoft SQL Server**, and then click **Books Online**.

    Note You can access SQL Server Books Online for SQL Server Installation topics directly from the SQL Server 2000 compact disc. Insert the SQL Server 2000 compact disc into the CD-ROM drive, and when the **Microsoft SQL Server** dialog box appears, click **Browse Setup/Upgrade Help**.

3. In the console tree, review the organization of SQL Server Books Online.

4. On the **Contents** tab, in the **Active Subset** list, click **Entire Collection**, and then review the contents of **Getting Started**.

5. In the console tree, expand **Getting Started with SQL Server Books Online**, and then click **Documentation Conventions**. Review the information in the details pane.

6. In the console tree, expand **Using SQL Server Books Online**, and then click **Finding a Topic**. Review the information in the details pane.

7. In the console tree, expand **Finding a Topic**, and then click **Using the Search tab**. Review the information in the details pane.

▶ **To use the SQL Server Books Online index to obtain information on the Northwind sample database**

In this procedure, you will use the SQL Server Books Online index to view information on the **Northwind** sample database quickly.

1. Click the **Index** tab, and then type **Northwind**

2. Double-click **Northwind sample database**.

3. In the **Topics Found** dialog box, double-click **Northwind sample database**. Review the information in the details pane.

4. Click the **Favorites** tab, and then click **Add**.

5. Click the **Contents** tab, and then in the console tree, expand **Northwind sample database** and notice the available topics.

▶ **To search SQL Server Books Online for a word or phrase**

In this procedure, you will use SQL Server Books Online to search for information about the architecture of SQL Server.

1. Click the **Search** tab, select the **Match similar words** check box; clear the **Search titles only** check box.

2. On the **Search** tab, type **sql NEAR architecture** and then click **List Topics**.

   Notice the number of topics that are found.

3. On the **Search** tab, clear the **Match similar words** check box, select the **Search titles only** check box, and then click **List Topics**.

   Notice that only two topics are found.

4. Double-click **Fundamentals of SQL Server Architecture**.

5. Click the details pane, and then press CTRL+F.

6. In the **Find** box, type **oltp** and then click **Find Next**.

Note Notice that the search finds the first instance of oltp. You may have to move the **Find** dialog box to view this selection.

---

7. Close SQL Server Books Online.

Review

- The Transact-SQL Programming Language
- Types of Transact-SQL Statements
- Transact-SQL Syntax Elements

1. Describe the basic types of Transact-SQL statements and their uses.

2. How does Transact-SQL relate to the ANSI SQL-92 specification?

Microsoft®
Training &
Certification

Module 2:
Using Transact-SQL
Querying Tools

Contents

Overview

- **SQL Query Analyzer**
- **Using the Object Browser Tool in SQL Query Analyzer**
- **Using Templates in SQL Query Analyzer**
- **Using the osql Utility**
- **Executing Transact-SQL Statements**

Microsoft® SQL Server™ 2000 provides several querying tools that you can use to execute Transact-SQL scripts. This module describes how to use SQL Query Analyzer and the **osql** command-line utility and how to execute Transact-SQL statements in a number of different ways.

At the end of this module, you will be able to:

- Describe the basic functions of SQL Query Analyzer.
- Describe how to use the Object Browser tool in SQL Query Analyzer.
- Describe how to use the templates in SQL Query Analyzer.
- Describe how to use the **osql** command-line utility.
- Execute Transact-SQL statements in a various ways.

SQL Query Analyzer

- **Free-Form Text Editor**
- **Color-Coding of Transact-SQL Syntax**
- **Multiple Query Windows with Grid or Text Output**
- **Partial Script Execution**
- **Query Execution Information**

You use SQL Query Analyzer in SQL Server to view query statements and results graphically. You also can use it for writing, modifying, and saving Transact-SQL scripts.

SQL Query Analyzer also provides tools for determining how SQL Server is interpreting and working with a Transact-SQL statement.

SQL Query Analyzer includes:

- *A free-form text editor.* This editor has advanced text-editing capabilities such as block indents, block comment or un-comment, and conversion to upper- or lower-case.

- *Color-coding.* As you write a query, SQL Query Analyzer highlights keywords, character strings, and other language elements, and you can customize how they appear by using color-coding.

- *Multiple query windows with grid or text output.* Each query window has its own connection to a SQL Server. You can view results in a text window or in a grid.

- *Partial script execution.* This capability allows you to execute portions of a script. When you can select portions of a script, SQL Server executes only those portions.

- *Query execution information.* Query execution information includes such things as client statistics, server trace information, and execution plan data. You can use this information to help tune and troubleshoot your scripts.

Using the Object Browser Tool in SQL Query Analyzer

- ■ **The Object Browser Enables Navigation of the Tree View of Objects in a Database**

- ■ **Using the Object Browser, You Can:**

  - Script objects

  - Execute stored procedures

  - Open tables

  - Alter objects in the database

  - Use Transact-SQL templates

You can use the Object Browser tool within SQL Query Analyzer to navigate the tree view of objects in a database and drill down to a specific object. The Object Browser also scripts objects, executes stored procedures, and allows you to gain access to tables and views.

Using the Object Browser, you can:

- ■ Script objects.

  The operations that the Object Browser supports vary, depending on the type of object. For example, table objects can generate scripts containing SELECT statements, data definition statements such as CREATE, or data manipulation statements such as INSERT.

- ■ Execute stored procedures.

  When you execute a stored procedure that has a parameter, the Object Browser prompts for values.

- ■ Open tables.

  The Object Browser displays query results separately. You can edit, insert, or delete rows.

- ■ Alter objects in the database.

  You can view and edit objects in a database. The Object Browser displays an ALTER statement for the selected object in the Editor pane. For example, if the selected object is a stored procedure, the Object Browser provides an ALTER PROCEDURE statement. You can use this ALTER statement to specify the changes, and then execute it.

- Use Transact-SQL templates.

  These templates contain Transact-SQL scripts that help you create objects in the database. You can use these templates to:

  - Create databases, tables, views, indexes, stored procedures, triggers, statistics, and functions.

  - Manage extended properties, linked servers, logon accounts, roles, and users.

  - Declare and use cursors.

  - Customize scripts.

Using Templates in SQL Query Analyzer

- **Templates**
  - Are starting points for creating objects in a database
  - Contain parameters to help you customize scripts
- **Format for Template Parameter Definitions**
  - <parameter_name, data_type, value>

SQL Query Analyzer includes templates that you can use as starting points for creating objects in a database.

SQL Server provides a variety of templates in the Templates\SQL Query Analyzer directory. Among the templates provided are those that create databases, tables, views, indexes, stored procedures, triggers, statistics, and functions. Other templates in this directory help you manage extended properties, linked servers, logins, roles, and users, and help you to declare and use cursors.

The template scripts provided with SQL Query Analyzer contain parameters to help you customize scripts. Template parameter definitions use this format:

```
<parameter_name, data_type, value>
```

The following table describes the format and template parameter definitions:

Format	Template parameter definition
<parameter_name>	Name of the parameter in the script
<data_type>	Data type of the parameter
<value>	Value that is to replace every occurrence of the parameter in the script

You use a dialog box to insert values into the script. For example, when you execute a function from Object Browser, the function that is written to the Edit pane contains parameter definitions for any arguments in the function. You then use the Replace Template Parameters dialog box to specify argument values.

Using the osql Utility

- **Starting the osql Command-line Utility**
- **Using the Interactive Mode**
- **Using the Script Execution Mode**
- **Using Extended osql Scripting Commands**

The *osql utility* is a command-line utility for ad hoc, interactive execution of Transact-SQL statements and scripts. To use the **osql** command-line utility, users must understand Transact-SQL and know how to execute scripts from a command prompt.

The **osql** command-line utility uses SQL Server Open Database Connectivity (ODBC) to communicate with the server and is subject to the restrictions and behaviors of the ODBC application programming interface (API).

Starting the osql Command-line Utility

You start the **osql** command-line utility directly from the operating system with the case-sensitive options listed below. You can call it from a batch file or from a command prompt. A *batch* is a set of Transact-SQL statements that are submitted together and executed as a group.

Using the Interactive Mode

The **osql** command-line utility accepts Transact-SQL statements and sends them to SQL Server interactively. The results are formatted and displayed on the screen.

Use the GO statement to execute Transact-SQL statements in the input buffer. Use the QUIT or EXIT statement to exit the **osql** command-line utility.

Using the Script Execution Mode

Users submit an **osql** batch specifying a single Transact-SQL statement to execute or pointing the utility to a text file that contains Transact-SQL statements to execute. The output is usually directed to a text file, but the output also can be displayed in the command prompt window.

Partial Syntax

osql [-**S** *server_name*] [-**E**] [-**U** *login_id*] [-**P** *password*]
[-**i** *input_file*] [-**o** *output_file*] [-**?**]

Note   Parameters in **osql** statements are case sensitive.

Remember that the dash (-) or forward slash (/) character can precede arguments. The following table describes the most commonly used arguments.

Argument	Description
-**S** *server_name*	Specifies the SQL Server to which to connect. The *server_name* is the name of the server computer on the network. This option is required if you execute **osql** from a remote computer on the network.
-**E**	Uses a trusted connection instead of requesting a password.
-**U** *login_id*	Is the user login ID. Login IDs are case sensitive. If neither the -**U** or -**P** option is used, SQL Server uses the currently logged in user account and will not prompt for a password.
-**P** *password*	Is a user-specified password. If the -**P** option is not used, **osql** prompts for a password. If the -**P** option is used at the end of the command prompt without any password, **osql** uses the default password (NULL). Passwords are case sensitive. If neither the -**U** or -**P** option is used, SQL Server uses the currently logged in user account and will not prompt for a password.
-**i** *input_file*	Identifies the file that contains a batch of Transact-SQL statements or stored procedures. The less than (<) symbol can be used in place of -**i**.
-**o** *output_file*	Identifies the file that receives output from **osql**. The greater than (>) symbol can be used in place of -**o**. If the input file is Unicode, the output file will be Unicode if -**o** is specified. If the input file is not Unicode, the output file is OEM.
-**?**	Displays the syntax summary of **osql** switches.

Using Extended osql Scripting Commands

The **osql** command-line utility can also process commands that are not Transact-SQL statements. The osql command-line utility only recognizes these commands when they occur at the beginning of a line or immediately following the **osql** prompt. Subsequent statements on the same line will cause an error.

The following table describes these additional commands.

Command	Description
GO	Executes all statements entered after the last GO
RESET	Clears any statements that you have entered
ED	Calls the editor
!! *command*	Executes an operating-system command
QUIT or EXIT( )	Exits from **osql**
CTRL+C	Ends a query without exiting from **osql**

◆ Executing Transact-SQL Statements

- **Dynamically Constructing Statements**
- **Using Batches**
- **Using Scripts**

You can execute Transact-SQL statements in a variety of ways by:

- Dynamically constructing statements at run-time.
- Using batches to group statements that should be run together.
- Using scripts to save batches to a file for later use.

Dynamically Constructing Statements

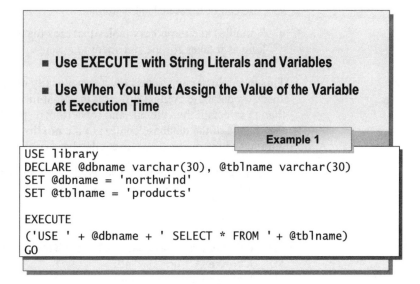

- **Use EXECUTE with String Literals and Variables**

- **Use When You Must Assign the Value of the Variable at Execution Time**

Example 1

```
USE library
DECLARE @dbname varchar(30), @tblname varchar(30)
SET @dbname = 'northwind'
SET @tblname = 'products'

EXECUTE
('USE ' + @dbname + ' SELECT * FROM ' + @tblname)
GO
```

You can build statements dynamically so that they are constructed at the same time that a script is executed.

To build a statement dynamically, use the EXECUTE statement with a series of string literals and variables that are resolved at execution time.

Dynamically constructed statements are useful when you want the value of the variable to be assigned when the statement executes. For example, you can create a dynamic statement that performs the same action on a series of database objects.

Syntax

EXECUTE ({@*str_var* | '*tsql_string*'} + [{@*str_var* | '*tsql_string*'}...])}

Consider the following facts about the EXECUTE statement:

- The EXECUTE statement executes statements composed of character strings within a Transact-SQL batch. Because these are string literals, be sure that you add spaces in the appropriate places in order to ensure proper concatenation.

- The EXECUTE statement can include a string literal, a string local variable, or a concatenation of both.

- All items within the EXECUTE string must consist of character data; you must convert all numeric data before you use the EXECUTE statement.

- You cannot use functions to build the string for execution in the EXECUTE statement.

- You can create any valid Transact-SQL statements dynamically, including functions.
- You can nest EXECUTE statements.
- Variables and temporary tables that are created dynamically last only as long as it takes for the statement to execute.

Example 1

This example demonstrates how a dynamically executed statement is used to specify a database context different than that in which you are currently and then to select all the columns and rows from a specified table. In this example, the change of the database context to the **northwind** database lasts only for the duration of the query. The current database context is unchanged.

Using a stored procedure, the user could pass the database and table information into the statement as parameters and then query a specific table within a database.

```
USE library
DECLARE @dbname varchar(30), @tablename varchar(30)
SET @dbname = 'northwind'
SET @tablename = 'products'

EXECUTE
  ('USE ' + @dbname + ' SELECT productname FROM ' +
@tablename)
GO
```

Result

productname
Chai
Chang
Aniseed Syrup

Example 2

This example demonstrates how a dynamically executed statement can be used to change a database option for the duration of the statement. The following statement does not return a count of the number of rows affected.

```
USE northwind
EXECUTE ('SET NOCOUNT ON '+ 'SELECT lastname, reportsto FROM
employees WHERE reportsto IS NULL')
GO
```

Result

lastname	reportsto
Fuller	NULL

Using Batches

- **One or More Transact-SQL Statements Submitted Together**
- **Defining a Batch with the GO Statement**
- **How SQL Server Processes Batches**
- **Statements That You Cannot Combine in a Batch**
  - CREATE PROCEDURE
  - CREATE VIEW
  - CREATE TRIGGER
  - CREATE RULE
  - CREATE DEFAULT

You can also submit one or more statements in a batch.

One or More Transact-SQL Statements Submitted Together

A *batch* is a set of Transact-SQL statements that are submitted together and executed as a group. Batches can be run interactively or as part of a script. A script can include more than one batch of Transact-SQL statements.

Defining a Batch with the GO Statement

Use a GO statement to signal the end of a batch. GO is not a universally accepted Transact-SQL statement; it is a statement accepted only by SQL Query Analyzer and the **osql** utility. Applications based on the ODBC or OLE DB APIs generate a syntax error if they attempt to execute a GO statement.

How SQL Server Processes Batches

SQL Server optimizes, compiles, and executes the statements in a batch together. However, the statements do not necessarily execute as a recoverable unit of work.

The scope of user-defined variables is limited to a batch, so a variable cannot be referenced after a GO statement.

Note If a syntax error exists in a batch, none of the statements in that batch executes. Execution begins with the next batch.

Statements That You Cannot Combine in a Batch

You must execute certain object creation statements in their own batches within a script, because of the way object creation statements are defined. These object creation statements are indicated by a pattern—an object definition header, followed by the AS keyword with one or more definition statements. In addition, each creation statement must be concluded by a **GO** command if there is more than one in a script.

You must execute these statements in separate batches:

- CREATE PROCEDURE
- CREATE VIEW
- CREATE TRIGGER
- CREATE RULE AS
- CREATE DEFAULT

Example 1

This example shows statements would fail as executed as part of a single batch, because the query improperly combines statements that cannot be combined in a batch. You must insert a GO statement before each CREATE VIEW statement to execute this statement correctly.

```
CREATE DATABASE ...
CREATE TABLE ...
CREATE VIEW ...
CREATE VIEW ...
GO
```

Example 2

This example groups the statements used in Example 1 into proper batches so that they execute correctly.

```
CREATE DATABASE ...
CREATE TABLE ...
GO

CREATE VIEW ...
GO

CREATE VIEW ...
GO
```

Using Scripts

■ **A Script Is One or More Transact-SQL Statements Saved as a File Using the .sql Extension**

■ **Scripts:**

- Contain saved statements

- Can be written using any text editor

- Can recreate database objects or execute statements repeatedly

- Execute in SQL Query Analyzer or in the **osql** utility

Scripts are one of the most common ways to execute Transact-SQL statements. They are one or more Transact-SQL statements that are saved as a file.

You can write and save scripts in SQL Query Analyzer or in any text editor such as Notepad. Save the script file with the .sql file name extension.

Saved scripts are very useful when you want to recreate databases or data objects, or when you must use a set of statements repeatedly.

You can open and execute the script file in SQL Query Analyzer or use the **osql** utility (or another query tool).

Recommended Practices

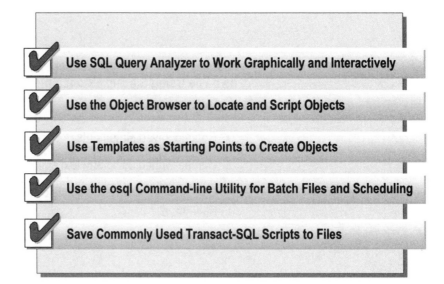

The following recommended practices should help you use Transact-SQL querying tools:

- Use SQL Query Analyzer when you want to work graphically and interactively. You can use multiple connections to SQL Server and cut and paste between windows, while leveraging the color-coding of syntax and the scripting ability of the Object Browser tool.

- Use the Object Browser tool to locate and script table and column names and to create error-free scripts that alter objects and modify data.

- Use templates in SQL Query Analyzer as starting points for creating objects in a database.

- Use the **osql** command-line utility for batch files and for the execution of repetitive tasks. Additional scripting features with the **osql** command-line utility environment can benefit automation and maintenance tasks.

- Save commonly used Transact-SQL scripts to files. These files effectively constitute a library of reusable scripts for consistency and future use.

Additional information on the following topics is available in SQL Server Books Online.

Topic	Search for
Using SQL Query Analyzer	"Overview of SQL Query Analyzer"
Using the **osql** utility	"osql utility"

Lab A: Creating and Executing Transact-SQL Scripts

Objectives

After completing this lab, you will be able to:

- Write basic SELECT statements that return ordered and limited result sets.
- Modify and execute a script by using the **osql** utility.

Prerequisites

Before working on this lab, you must have:

- Script files for this lab, which are located in C:\Moc\2071\Labfiles\L02.
- Answer files for this lab, which are located in
  C:\Moc\2071\Labfiles\L02\Answers.

For More Information

If you require help in executing files, search SQL Query Analyzer Help for
"Execute a query".

Other resources that you can use include:

- The **Northwind** database schema.
- Microsoft SQL Server Books Online.

Scenario

The organization of the classroom is meant to simulate that of a worldwide trading firm named Northwind Traders. Its fictitious domain name is nwtraders.msft. The primary DNS server for nwtraders.msft is the instructor computer, which has an Internet Protocol (IP) address of 192.168.x.200 (where x is the assigned classroom number). The name of the instructor computer is London.

The following table provides the user name, computer name, and IP address for each student computer in the fictitious nwtraders.msft domain. Find the user name for your computer, and make a note of it.

User name	Computer name	IP address
SQLAdmin1	Vancouver	192.168.x.1
SQLAdmin2	Denver	192.168.x.2
SQLAdmin3	Perth	192.168.x.3
SQLAdmin4	Brisbane	192.168.x.4
SQLAdmin5	Lisbon	192.168.x.5
SQLAdmin6	Bonn	192.168.x.6
SQLAdmin7	Lima	192.168.x.7
SQLAdmin8	Santiago	192.168.x.8
SQLAdmin9	Bangalore	192.168.x.9
SQLAdmin10	Singapore	192.168.x.10
SQLAdmin11	Casablanca	192.168.x.11
SQLAdmin12	Tunis	192.168.x.12
SQLAdmin13	Acapulco	192.168.x.13
SQLAdmin14	Miami	192.168.x.14
SQLAdmin15	Auckland	192.168.x.15
SQLAdmin16	Suva	192.168.x.16
SQLAdmin17	Stockholm	192.168.x.17
SQLAdmin18	Moscow	192.168.x.18
SQLAdmin19	Caracas	192.168.x.19
SQLAdmin20	Montevideo	192.168.x.20
SQLAdmin21	Manila	192.168.x.21
SQLAdmin22	Tokyo	192.168.x.22
SQLAdmin23	Khartoum	192.168.x.23
SQLAdmin24	Nairobi	192.168.x.24

Estimated time to complete this lab: 30 minutes

Exercise 1
Writing Basic SELECT Statements

In this exercise, you will write various statements that return rows from the **products** table in the **Northwind** database. C:\Moc\2071\Labfiles\L02\Answers contains completed scripts for this exercise.

▶ To write a SELECT statement that returns ordered data

In this procedure, you will write a statement that returns all the rows and columns from the **products** table and sorts the results in ascending order by the **productname** column. Answer_Ordered.sql is a completed script for this procedure.

1. Log on to the **NWTraders** classroom domain by using the information in the following table.

Option	Value
User name	**SQLAdmin**x (where *x* corresponds to your computer name as designated in the nwtraders.msft classroom domain)
Password	**password**

2. Open SQL Query Analyzer and, if requested, log in to the (local) server with Microsoft Windows® Authentication.

   You have permission to log in to and administer SQL Server because you are logged as **SQLAdmin**x, which is a member of the Windows 2000 local group, Administrators. All members of this group are automatically mapped to the SQL Server **sysadmin** role.

3. In the **DB** list, click **northwind**.

4. Type and execute a SELECT statement that returns all the rows and columns from the **products** table and sorts the results in ascending order by the **productname** column.

   You can execute the **sp_help** system stored procedure on the **products** table to find the correct column names.

   ```
   SELECT * FROM products ORDER BY productname
   ```

5. Click the **Execute Mode to Results in Grid** toolbar button.

6. Execute the statement again.

▶ **To write a SELECT statement that returns limited data**

In this procedure, you will write a statement that retrieves products from a specific category. Answer_Limited.sql is a completed script for this procedure.

• Type and execute a SELECT statement that retrieves all products in category (**categoryid**) 4 from the **products** table.

You can execute the **sp_help** system stored procedure on the **products** table to find the correct column names.

```
SELECT * FROM products WHERE categoryid = 4
GO
```

Tip To see more information about the SELECT statement (as well as any Transact-SQL statement and system table), select the **SELECT** keyword in the query window, press **Shift+F1**, and then double click **SELECT clause**.

Exercise 2
Modifying a Script File

In this exercise, you will modify, save, and execute a simple script file. C:\Moc\2071\Labfiles\L02\Answers contains completed scripts for this exercise.

▶ To modify a script file

In this procedure, you will execute a script that contains errors. By using the error information that is returned, you will make changes to the script so that it executes correctly. Then, you will save and execute the script.

1. Open C:\Moc\2071\Labfiles\L02\MyScript.sql, review, and then execute it. You will get errors when you run this file. These errors are intentional. Answer_MyScript.sql is a completed script for this procedure.

2. Type block comment keywords around the lines of the script name and description.

    ```
    /*
                MYSCRIPT.SQL

        This script queries the customer table and
        returns a list of customer numbers and their
        last names.
        This script should be run in the northwind database.
    */
    ```

3. Add a statement that specifies that the script will run in the context of the **Northwind** database.

    ```
    USE northwind
    ```

4. Include end of batch markers (GO statements) in the proper areas of the script.

    ```
    SELECT CompanyName FROM customers
    GO
    ```

5. Save the script and then execute it.

6. Minimize SQL Query Analyzer.

Exercise 3
Execute a Script Using the osql Utility

In this exercise, you will use the **osql** command-line utility to execute the script that you created in Exercise 2.

▶ **To display the osql command-line utility arguments**

In this procedure, you will display the **osql** command-line utility arguments. Open a command prompt window.

1. Type the following command to display the **osql** command-line arguments.

   ```
   osql -?
   ```

2. Review the arguments.

▶ **To execute a script file by using the osql utility**

In this procedure, you will execute a script file by using the **osql** utility. The -E argument specifies that a trusted connection should be made to SQL Server.

1. Open a command prompt window.

2. Type the following command to execute C:\Moc\2071\Labfiles\L02\MyScript.sql. Make sure that the path is correct.

   ```
   osql -E -i "C:\MOC\2071\labfiles\L02\MyScript.sql"
   ```

Note If the -S argument is not used to specify the SQL Server to which the **osql** utility connects, then the **osql** utility connects to the local SQL Server by default. The -E command-line parameter used specifies that a trusted connection should be made to SQL Server. Again, since no particular SQL Server was explicitly specified, then a connection is made to the local SQL Server.

---

3. Verify that the results are the same as those obtained in Exercise 2.

Review

- **SQL Server Query Analyzer**
- **Using the Object Browser Tool in SQL Query Analyzer**
- **Using Templates in SQL Query Analyzer**
- **Using the osql Utility**
- **Executing Transact-SQL Statements**

1. What is the best querying tool to use within a batch file to capture the results of a query in a text file? Why?

2. What is the best way to create and use Transact-SQL statements for future re-use?

3. How does a Transact-SQL batch differ from a Transact-SQL script?

Microsoft®
Training &
Certification

Module 3:
Retrieving Data

Contents

***Microsoft*®**

Overview

- **Retrieving Data by Using the SELECT Statement**
- **Filtering Data**
- **Formatting Result Sets**
- **How Queries Are Processed**
- **Performance Considerations**

This module provides students with the knowledge and skills to perform basic queries by using the SELECT statement, which includes sorting data, eliminating duplicates, and changing the format of the result set. The module concludes with a description of how queries are processed.

At the end of this module, students will be able to:

- Retrieve data from tables by using the SELECT statement.
- Filter data by using different search conditions to use with the WHERE clause.
- Format results sets.
- Describe how queries are processed.
- Describe performance considerations that affect retrieving data.

◆ Retrieving Data by Using the SELECT Statement

- Using the SELECT Statement
- Specifying Columns
- Using the WHERE Clause to Specify Rows

Before you can work with data, you must select the data that you want to retrieve from your tables. You can use the SELECT statement to specify the columns and rows of data that you want to retrieve from tables.

Using the SELECT Statement

- **Select List Specifies the Columns**
- **WHERE Clause Specifies the Condition Restricting the Query**
- **FROM Clause Specifies the Table**

Partial Syntax

```
SELECT [ALL | DISTINCT] <select_list>
 FROM {<table_source>} [,...n]
 WHERE <search_condition>
```

Use the SELECT statement to retrieve data.

Partial Syntax

SELECT [ALL | DISTINCT] *<select_list>*
   FROM {*<table_source>*} [*,...n*]
   [WHERE *<search_condition>*]

Use the SELECT statement to specify the columns and rows that you want to be returned from a table:

- The select list specifies the columns to be returned.

- The WHERE clause specifies the condition restricting the query. When you use search conditions in the WHERE clause, you can restrict the number of rows by using comparison operators, character strings, and logical operators as search conditions.

- The FROM clause specifies the table from which columns and rows are returned.

Specifying Columns

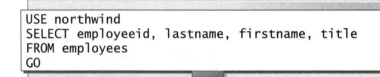

```
USE northwind
SELECT employeeid, lastname, firstname, title
FROM employees
GO
```

employeeid	lastname	firstname	title
1	Davolio	Nancy	Sales Representative
2	Fuller	Andrew	Vice President, Sales
3	Leverling	Janet	Sales Representative
4	Peacock	Margaret	Sales Representative
5	Buchanan	Steven	Sales Manager
6	Suyama	Michael	Sales Representative
7	King	Robert	Sales Representative
8	Callahan	Laura	Inside Sales Coordinator
9	Dodsworth	Anne	Sales Representative

You can retrieve particular columns from a table by listing them in the select list.

The select list contains the columns, expressions, or keywords to select or the local variable to assign. The options that can be used in the select list include:

Partial Syntax

<select_list> ::=

```
{   *
   | { table_name | view_name | table_alias }.*
   |    { column_name | expression | IDENTITYCOL | ROWGUIDCOL }
     [ [AS] column_alias ]
   | column_alias = expression
}   [,...n]
```

When you specify columns to retrieve, consider the following facts and guidelines:

- The select list retrieves and displays the columns in the specified order.

- Separate the column names with commas, except for the last column name.

- Avoid or minimize the use of an asterisk (*) in the select list. An asterisk is used to retrieve all columns from a table.

Example

This example retrieves the **employeeid**, **lastname**, **firstname**, and **title** columns of all employees from the **employees** table.

```
USE northwind
SELECT employeeid, lastname, firstname, title
FROM employees
GO
```

Result

employeeid	lastname	firstname	title
1	Davolio	Nancy	Sales Representative
2	Fuller	Andrew	Vice President, Sales
3	Leverling	Janet	Sales Representative
4	Peacock	Margaret	Sales Representative
5	Buchanan	Steven	Sales Manager
6	Suyama	Michael	Sales Representative
7	King	Robert	Sales Representative
8	Callahan	Laura	Inside Sales Coordinator
9	Dodsworth	Anne	Sales Representative

```
(9 row(s) affected)
```

Using the WHERE Clause to Specify Rows

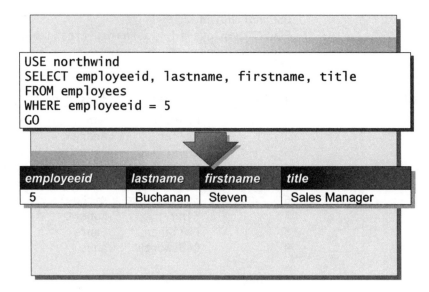

```
USE northwind
SELECT employeeid, lastname, firstname, title
FROM employees
WHERE employeeid = 5
GO
```

employeeid	lastname	firstname	title
5	Buchanan	Steven	Sales Manager

Using the WHERE clause, you can retrieve specific rows based on given search conditions. The search conditions in the WHERE clause can contain an unlimited list of predicates.

<search_condition> ::=
  { [NOT] <predicate> | (<search_condition>) }
  [{AND | OR} [NOT] {<predicate> | (<search_condition>) }]
  } [,...*n*]

The predicate placeholder lists the expressions that can be included in the WHERE clause. The options that can be contained in a predicate include:

<predicate> ::=
  {
  expression { = | <> | > | >= | < | <= } *expression*
  | *string_expression* [NOT] LIKE *string_expression*
  [ESCAPE '*escape_character*']
  | *expression* [NOT] BETWEEN *expression* AND *expression*
  | *expression* IS [NOT] NULL
  | CONTAINS
  ({*column* | * }, '<contains_search_condition>')
  | FREETEXT ({*column* | * }, '*freetext_string*')
  | *expression* [NOT] IN (*subquery* | *expression* [,...*n*])
  | *expression* { = | <> | > | >= | < | <= }
  {ALL | SOME | ANY} (*subquery*)
  | EXISTS (*subquery*)
  }

When you specify rows with the WHERE clause, consider the following facts and guidelines:

- Place single quotation marks around all **char**, **nchar**, **varchar**, **nvarchar**, **text**, **datetime**, and **smalldatetime** data.

- Use a WHERE clause to limit the number of rows that are returned when you use the SELECT statement.

Example

This example retrieves the **employeeid**, **lastname**, **firstname**, and **title** columns from the **employees** table for the employee with an **employeeid** of 5.

```
USE northwind
SELECT employeeid, lastname, firstname, title
FROM employees
WHERE employeeid = 5
GO
```

Result

employeeid	lastname	firstname	title
5	Buchanan	Steven	Sales Manager

(1 row(s) affected)

◆ Filtering Data

- **Using Comparison Operators**
- **Using String Comparisons**
- **Using Logical Operators**
- **Retrieving a Range of Values**
- **Using a List of Values as Search Criteria**
- **Retrieving Unknown Values**

You sometimes want to limit the results that a query returns. You can limit the results by specifying search conditions in a WHERE clause to filter data. There is no limit to the number of search conditions that you can include in a SELECT statement. The following table describes the type of filter and the corresponding search condition that you can use to filter data.

Type of filter	Search condition
Comparison operators	=, >, <, >=, <=, and <>
String comparisons	LIKE and NOT LIKE
Logical operators: combination of conditions	AND, OR
Logical operator: negations	NOT
Range of values	BETWEEN and NOT BETWEEN
Lists of values	IN and NOT IN
Unknown values	IS NULL and IS NOT NULL

Using Comparison Operators

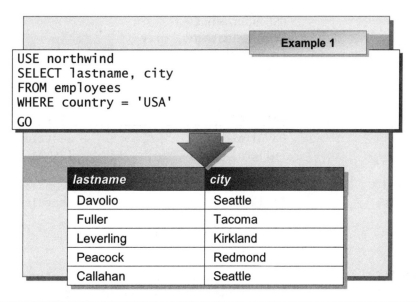

Use comparison operators to compare the values in a table to a specified value or expression. You also can use comparison operators to check for a condition. Comparison operators compare columns or variables of compatible data types. The comparison operators are listed in the following table.

Operator	Description
=	Equal to
>	Greater than
<	Less than
>=	Greater than or equal to
<=	Less than or equal to
<>	Not equal to

Note Avoid the use of NOT in search conditions. They may slow data retrieval because all rows in a table are evaluated.

Example 1

This example retrieves the last name and city of employees who reside in the United States from the **employees** table.

```
USE northwind
SELECT lastname, city
FROM employees
WHERE country = 'USA'
GO
```

Result

lastname	city
Davolio	Seattle
Fuller	Tacoma
Leverling	Kirkland
Peacock	Redmond
Callahan	Seattle

(5 row(s) affected)

Example 2

This example retrieves the **orderid** and **customerid** columns with order dates that are older than 8/1/96 from the **orders** table.

```
USE northwind
SELECT orderid, customerid
FROM orders
WHERE orderdate < '8/1/96'
GO
```

Result

orderid	customerid
10248	VINET
10249	TOMSP
10250	HANAR
10251	VICTE
10252	SUPRD
10253	HANAR
.	.
.	.
.	.

(22 row(s) affected)

Using String Comparisons

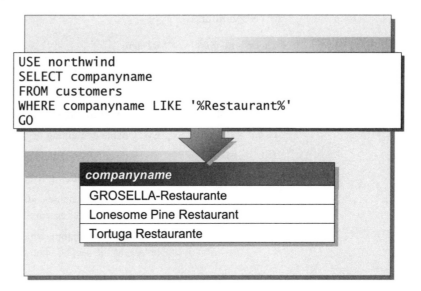

```
USE northwind
SELECT companyname
FROM customers
WHERE companyname LIKE '%Restaurant%'
GO
```

companyname
GROSELLA-Restaurante
Lonesome Pine Restaurant
Tortuga Restaurante

You can use the LIKE search condition in combination with wildcard characters to select rows by comparing character strings. When you use the LIKE search condition, consider the following facts:

- All characters in the pattern string are significant, including leading and trailing blank spaces.

- LIKE can be used only with data of the **char**, **nchar**, **varchar**, **nvarchar**, **binary**, **varbinary**, **smalldatetime** or **datetime** data types, and under certain conditions, with **text**, **ntext**, and **image** data types.

Types of Wildcard Characters

Use the following four wildcard characters to form your character string search criteria.

Wildcard	Description
%	Any string of zero or more characters
_	Any single character
[]	Any single character within the specified range or set
[^]	Any single character *not* within the specified range or set

Examples of the Use of Wildcard Characters

The following table lists examples of the use of wildcards with the LIKE search condition.

Expression	Returns
LIKE 'BR%'	Every name beginning with the letters BR
LIKE 'Br%'	Every name beginning with the letters Br
LIKE '%een'	Every name ending with the letters een
LIKE '%en%'	Every name containing the letters en
LIKE '_en'	Every three-letter name ending in the letters en
LIKE '[CK]%'	Every name beginning with the letter C or K
LIKE '[S-V]ing'	Every four-letter name ending in the letters ing and beginning with any single letter from S to V
LIKE 'M[^c]%'	Every name beginning with the letter M that does not have the letter c as the second letter

Example

This example retrieves companies from the **customers** table that have the word restaurant in their company names.

```
USE northwind
SELECT companyname
FROM customers
WHERE companyname LIKE '%Restaurant%'
GO
```

Result

companyname

```
GROSELLA-Restaurante
Lonesome Pine Restaurant
Tortuga Restaurante

(3 row(s) affected)
```

Using Logical Operators

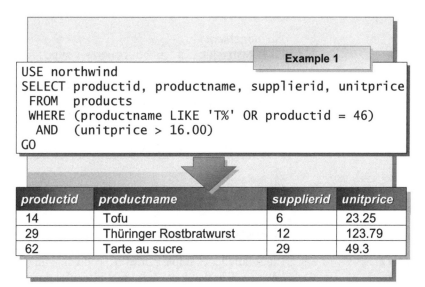

Example 1

```
USE northwind
SELECT  productid, productname, supplierid, unitprice
 FROM   products
 WHERE  (productname LIKE 'T%' OR productid = 46)
  AND   (unitprice > 16.00)
GO
```

productid	productname	supplierid	unitprice
14	Tofu	6	23.25
29	Thüringer Rostbratwurst	12	123.79
62	Tarte au sucre	29	49.3

Use the logical operators AND, OR, and NOT to combine a series of expressions and to refine query processing. The results of a query may vary depending on the grouping of expressions and the order of the search conditions.

When you use logical operators, consider the following guidelines:

- Use the AND operator to retrieve rows that meet all of the search criteria.

- Use the OR operator to retrieve rows that meet any of the search criteria.

- Use the NOT operator to negate the expression that follows the operator.

Using Parentheses

Use parentheses when you have two or more expressions as the search criteria. Using parentheses allows you to:

- Group expressions.

- Change the order of evaluation.

- Make expressions more readable.

Order of Search Conditions

When you use more than one logical operator in a statement, consider the following facts:

- Microsoft® SQL Server™ 2000 evaluates the NOT operator first, followed by the AND operator and then the OR operator.

- The precedence order is from left to right if all operators in an expression are of the same level.

Example 1

The following example retrieves all products with product names that begin with the letter T or have a product identification number of 46, and that have a price greater than $16.00.

```
USE northwind
SELECT productid, productname, supplierid, unitprice
 FROM products
 WHERE (productname LIKE 'T%' OR productid = 46)
  AND (unitprice > 16.00)
GO
```

Result

productid	productname	supplierid	unitprice
14	Tofu	6	23.25
29	Thüringer Rostbratwurst	12	123.79
62	Tarte au sucre	29	49.3

(3 row(s) affected)

Example 2

The following example retrieves products with product names that begin with the letter T or that have a product identification number of 46 and a price greater than $16.00. Compare the query in Example 1 to that in Example 2. Notice that because the expressions are grouped differently, the queries are processed differently and return different result sets.

```
USE northwind
SELECT productid, productname, supplierid, unitprice
 FROM products
 WHERE (productname LIKE 'T%')
  OR    (productid = 46 AND unitprice > 16.00)
GO
```

Result

productid	productname	supplierid	unitprice
54	Tourtière	25	7.45
62	Tarte au sucre	29	49.3
23	Tunnbröd	9	9
19	Teatime Chocolate Biscuits	8	9.2
14	Tofu	6	23.25
29	Thüringer Rostbratwurst	12	123.79

(6 row(s) affected)

Retrieving a Range of Values

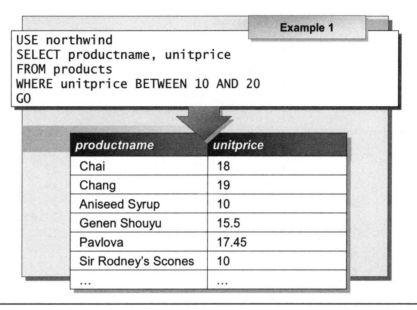

Use the BETWEEN search condition in the WHERE clause to retrieve rows that are within a specified range of values. When you use the BETWEEN search condition, consider the following facts and guidelines:

- SQL Server includes the end values in the result set.

- To simplify the syntax, use the BETWEEN search condition rather than an expression that includes the AND operator with two comparison operators ($> = x$ AND $< = y$). However, to search for an exclusive range in which the returned rows do not contain the end values, use an expression that includes the AND operator with two comparison operators ($> x$ AND $< y$).

- Use the NOT BETWEEN search condition to retrieve rows outside of the specified range. Be aware that using NOT conditions may slow data retrieval.

Example 1

This example retrieves the product name and unit price of all products with a unit price between $10.00 and $20.00. Notice that the result set includes the end values.

```
USE northwind
SELECT productname, unitprice
FROM products
WHERE unitprice BETWEEN 10 AND 20
GO
```

Result

productname	unitprice
Chai	18
Chang	19
Aniseed Syrup	10
Genen Shouyu	15.5
Pavlova	17.45
Sir Rodney's Scones	10
.	
.	
.	

```
(29 row(s) affected)
```

Example 2

This example retrieves the product name and unit price of all products with a unit price between $10 and $20. Notice that the result set excludes the end values.

```
USE northwind
SELECT productname, unitprice
FROM products
WHERE (unitprice > 10)
 AND  (unitprice < 20)
GO
```

Result

productname	unitprice
Chai	18
Chang	19
Genen Shouyu	15.5
Pavlova	17.45
.	
.	
.	

```
(25 row(s) affected)
```

Using a List of Values as Search Criteria

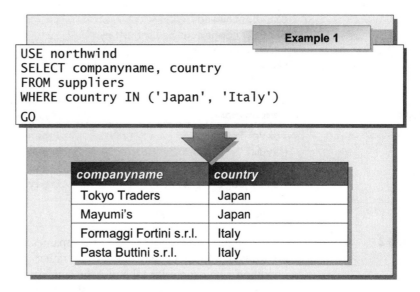

Example 1

```
USE northwind
SELECT companyname, country
FROM suppliers
WHERE country IN ('Japan', 'Italy')
GO
```

companyname	country
Tokyo Traders	Japan
Mayumi's	Japan
Formaggi Fortini s.r.l.	Italy
Pasta Buttini s.r.l.	Italy

Use the IN search condition in the WHERE clause to retrieve rows that match a specified list of values. When you use the IN search condition, consider the following guidelines:

- Use either the IN search condition or a series of comparison expressions that are connected with an OR operator—SQL Server resolves them in the same way, returning identical result sets.

- Do not include a null value in the search condition. A null value in the search condition list equates to the expression, = NULL. If ANSI_NULLS is ON, a comparison with NULL always evaluates to UNKNOWN. This may return unpredictable result sets. If ANSI_NULLS is OFF, the expression =a comparison with NULL evaluates to true or false, depending upon the contents of the column being compared. To reduce confusion, use the IS NULL or IS NOT NULL functions instead.

- Use the NOT IN search condition to retrieve rows that are not in your specified list of values. Be aware that using NOT conditions may slow data retrieval.

Example 1

This example produces a list of companies from the **suppliers** table that are located in Japan or Italy.

```
USE northwind
SELECT companyname, country
FROM suppliers
WHERE country IN ('Japan', 'Italy')
GO
```

Result

companyname	country
Tokyo Traders	Japan
Mayumi's	Japan
Formaggi Fortini s.r.l.	Italy
Pasta Buttini s.r.l.	Italy

(4 row(s) affected)

Example 2

This example also produces a list of companies from the **suppliers** table that are located in Japan or Italy. Notice that rather than using the IN search condition, two expressions that use the comparison operator are joined by the OR operator. The result set is identical to the result set in Example 1.

```
USE northwind
SELECT companyname, country
FROM suppliers
WHERE country = 'Japan' OR country = 'Italy'
GO
```

Result

companyname	country
Tokyo Traders	Japan
Mayumi's	Japan
Formaggi Fortini s.r.l.	Italy
Pasta Buttini s.r.l.	Italy

(4 row(s) affected)

Retrieving Unknown Values

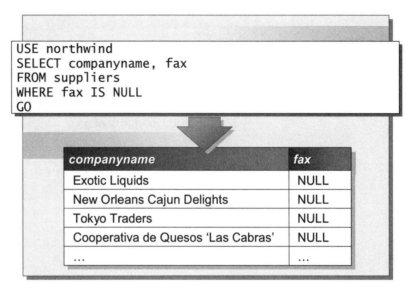

```
USE northwind
SELECT companyname, fax
FROM suppliers
WHERE fax IS NULL
GO
```

companyname	fax
Exotic Liquids	NULL
New Orleans Cajun Delights	NULL
Tokyo Traders	NULL
Cooperativa de Quesos 'Las Cabras'	NULL
...	...

A column has a null value if no value is entered during data entry and no default values are defined for that column. A null value is not the same as entries with a zero (a numerical value) or a blank (a character value).

Use the IS NULL search condition to retrieve rows in which information is missing from a specified column. When you retrieve rows that contain unknown values, consider the following facts and guidelines:

- Null values fail all comparisons because they do not evaluate equally with one another.

- You define whether columns allow null values in the CREATE TABLE statement.

- Use the IS NOT NULL search condition to retrieve rows that have known values in the specified columns.

Example

This example retrieves a list of companies from the **suppliers** table for which the **fax** column contains a null value.

```
USE northwind
SELECT companyname, fax
FROM suppliers
WHERE fax IS NULL
GO
```

Result

companyname	fax
Exotic Liquids	NULL
New Orleans Cajun Delights	NULL
Tokyo Traders	NULL
Cooperativa de Quesos 'Las Cabras'	NULL
.	
.	
.	

```
(16 row(s) affected)
```

◆ Formatting Result Sets

- **Sorting Data**
- **Eliminating Duplicate Rows**
- **Changing Column Names**
- **Using Literals**

You can improve the readability of a result set by sorting the order in which the result set is listed, eliminating any duplicate rows, changing column names to column aliases, or using literals to replace result set values. These formatting options do not change the data, only the presentation of it.

Sorting Data

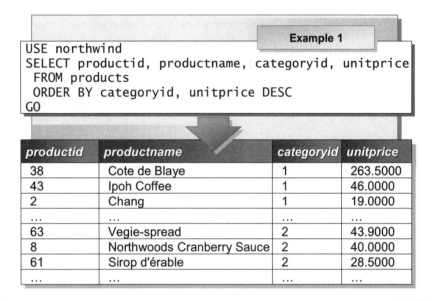

```
                                          Example 1
USE northwind
SELECT productid, productname, categoryid, unitprice
 FROM products
 ORDER BY categoryid, unitprice DESC
GO
```

productid	productname	categoryid	unitprice
38	Cote de Blaye	1	263.5000
43	Ipoh Coffee	1	46.0000
2	Chang	1	19.0000
...	...	...	...
63	Vegie-spread	2	43.9000
8	Northwoods Cranberry Sauce	2	40.0000
61	Sirop d'érable	2	28.5000
...	...	...	...

Use the ORDER BY clause to sort rows in the result set in ascending (ASC) or descending (DESC) order. When you use the ORDER BY clause, consider the following facts and guidelines:

- The sort order is specified when SQL Server is installed. Execute the **sp_helpsort** system stored procedure to determine the sort order that was defined for the database during installation.

- SQL Server does not guarantee an order in the result set unless the order is specified with an ORDER BY clause.

- SQL Server sorts in ascending order by default.

- Columns that are included in the ORDER BY clause do not have to appear in the select list.

- You can sort by column names, computed values, or expressions.

- You can refer to columns by their positions in the select list in the ORDER BY clause. The columns are evaluated in the same way and return the same result set.

- You cannot use **text**, **ntext** or **image** columns in the ORDER BY clause.

Tip   Using appropriate indexes can make ORDER BY sorts more efficient.

Example 1

This example retrieves the product identification, product name, category, and unit price of each product from the **products** table. By default, the result set is ordered by category in ascending order, and within each category the rows are ordered by unit price in descending order.

```
USE northwind
SELECT productid, productname, categoryid, unitprice
 FROM products
 ORDER BY categoryid, unitprice DESC
GO
```

Result

productid	productname	categoryid	unitprice
38	Côte de Blaye	1	263.5000
43	Ipoh Coffee	1	46.0000
2	Chang	1	19.0000
1	Chai	1	18.0000
35	Steeleye Stout	1	18.0000
39	Chartreuse verte	1	18.0000
76	Lakkalikööri	1	18.0000
70	Outback Lager	1	15.0000
34	Sasquatch Ale	1	14.0000
67	Laughing Lumberjack Lager	1	14.0000
75	Rhönbräu Klosterbier	1	7.7500
24	Guaraná Fantástica	1	4.5000
63	Vegie-spread	2	43.9000
8	Northwoods Cranberry Sauce	2	40.0000
61	Sirop d'érable	2	28.5000
6	Grandma's Boysenberry Spread	2	25.0000

.
.
.

(77 row(s) affected)

Example 2

This example is similar to Example 1. The only difference is that the numbers that follow the ORDER BY clause indicate the position of columns in the select list. SQL Server resolves both queries in the same way, returning the same result set.

```
USE northwind
SELECT productid, productname, categoryid, unitprice
 FROM products
 ORDER BY 3, 4 DESC
GO
```

Eliminating Duplicate Rows

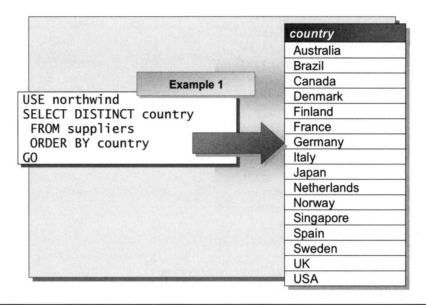

If you require a list of unique values, use the DISTINCT clause to eliminate duplicate rows in the result set. When you use the DISTINCT clause, consider the following facts:

- All rows that meet the search condition that is specified in the SELECT statement are returned in the result set unless you have specified the DISTINCT clause.

- The combination of values in the select list determines distinctiveness.

- Rows that contain any unique combination of values are retrieved and returned in the result set.

- The DISTINCT clause sorts the result set in random order unless you have included an ORDER BY clause.

- If you specify a DISTINCT clause, the ORDER BY columns must appear in the SELECT list.

Example 1

This example retrieves all rows from the **suppliers** table but displays each country name only once.

```
USE northwind
SELECT DISTINCT country
 FROM suppliers
 ORDER BY country
GO
```

Result

country
Australia
Brazil
Canada
Denmark
Finland
France
Germany
Italy
Japan
Netherlands
Norway
Singapore
Spain
Sweden
UK
USA

```
(16 row(s) affected)
```

Example 2

This example does not specify the DISTINCT clause. All rows from the **suppliers** table are retrieved and listed in descending order. Notice that each instance of a country is displayed.

```
USE northwind
SELECT country
 FROM suppliers
 ORDER BY country
GO
```

Result

country
Australia
Australia
Brazil
Canada
Canada
Denmark
Finland
France
France
France
Germany
Germany
Germany
Italy
Italy
Japan
Japan
Netherlands
Norway
Singapore
Spain
.
.
.

```
(29 row(s) affected)
```

Changing Column Names

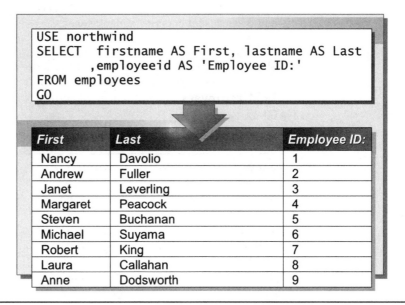

```
USE northwind
SELECT  firstname AS First, lastname AS Last
        ,employeeid AS 'Employee ID:'
FROM employees
GO
```

First	Last	Employee ID:
Nancy	Davolio	1
Andrew	Fuller	2
Janet	Leverling	3
Margaret	Peacock	4
Steven	Buchanan	5
Michael	Suyama	6
Robert	King	7
Laura	Callahan	8
Anne	Dodsworth	9

Create more readable column names by using the AS keyword to replace default column names with aliases in the select list.

Partial Syntax

SELECT *column_name* | *expression* AS *column_heading*
   FROM *table_name*

When you change column names, consider the following facts and guidelines:

- By default, the result set displays the column names that are designated in the CREATE TABLE statement.

- Include single quotation marks for column names that contain blank spaces or that do not conform to SQL Server object naming conventions.

- You can create column aliases for computed columns that contain functions or string literals.

- You can include up to 128 characters in a column alias.

Example

This example retrieves a list of employees from the **employees** table. The specified column aliases replace the **firstname**, **lastname**, and **employeeid** columns. Notice that the Employee ID: alias is enclosed in single quotation marks because it contains a blank space.

```
USE northwind
SELECT  firstname AS First, lastname AS Last
        ,employeeid AS 'Employee ID:'
FROM employees
GO
```

Result

First	Last	Employee ID:
Nancy	Davolio	1
Andrew	Fuller	2
Janet	Leverling	3
Margaret	Peacock	4
Steven	Buchanan	5
Michael	Suyama	6
Robert	King	7
Laura	Callahan	8
Anne	Dodsworth	9

(9 row(s) affected)

Using Literals

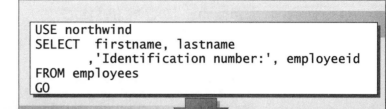

```
USE northwind
SELECT  firstname, lastname
        ,'Identification number:', employeeid
FROM employees
GO
```

First	Last	Employee ID:
Nancy	Davolio	Identification Number: 1
Andrew	Fuller	Identification Number: 2
Janet	Leverling	Identification Number: 3
Margaret	Peacock	Identification Number: 4
Steven	Buchanan	Identification Number: 5
Michael	Suyama	Identification Number: 6
Robert	King	Identification Number: 7
Laura	Callahan	Identification Number: 8
Anne	Dodsworth	Identification Number: 9

Literals are letters, numerals, or symbols that are used as specific values in a result set. You can include literals in the select list to make result sets more readable.

Partial Syntax

SELECT *column_name* | *'string literal'* [, *column_name* | *'string_literal'...*]
    FROM *table_name*

Example

This example retrieves a list of employees from the **employees** table. Notice that the Identification number: character string precedes the **employeeid** column in the result set.

```
USE northwind
SELECT  firstname, lastname
        ,'Identification number:', employeeid
FROM employees
GO
```

Result

firstname	lastname		employeeid
Nancy	Davolio	Identification number:	1
Andrew	Fuller	Identification number:	2
Janet	Leverling	Identification number:	3
Margaret	Peacock	Identification number:	4
Steven	Buchanan	Identification number:	5
Michael	Suyama	Identification number:	6
Robert	King	Identification number:	7
Laura	Callahan	Identification number:	8
Anne	Dodsworth	Identification number:	9

(9 row(s) affected)

◆ How Queries Are Processed

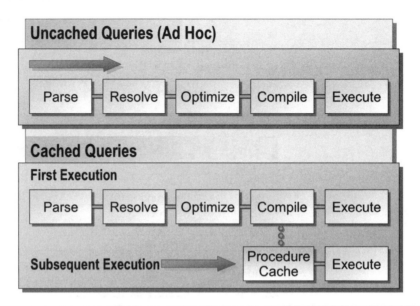

All queries follow the same process before they are executed. SQL Server can store some of the processing for subsequent execution of the same query.

Uncached Queries (Ad Hoc)

All queries are parsed, resolved, optimized, and compiled before they are executed.

Process	Description
Parse	Checks syntax for accuracy.
Resolve	Validates that the names of the objects are present; determines object ownership permission.
Optimize	Determines the indexes to use and the join strategies.
Compile	Translates the query into an executable form.
Execute	Submits compiled requests for processing.

Cached Queries

To improve performance, SQL Server can save compiled query plans for reuse. Query plans are optimized instructions on how to process queries and access the data. The query plans are stored in the *procedure cache*, a temporary storage location for the currently executing version of a specific query.

How Queries Are Cached Automatically

```
■ Ad Hoc Batches

USE northwind
SELECT * FROM products WHERE unitprice = $12.5
SELECT * FROM products WHERE unitprice = 12.5
SELECT * FROM products WHERE unitprice = $12.5
GO

■ Auto-Parameterization

USE library
SELECT * FROM member WHERE member_no = 7890
SELECT * FROM member WHERE member_no = 1234
SELECT * FROM member WHERE member_no = 7890
GO
```

Cached queries are saved in an area of memory called the *procedure cache.*
Query definitions are cached automatically under two conditions—ad hoc
batches and auto-parameterization. Automatic caching cannot be
specified directly.

Ad Hoc Batches

SQL Server caches the plans from ad hoc batches. If a subsequent batch
matches the text of the first batch, SQL Server uses the cached plan. This plan
is limited to exact textual matches.

Example 1

The same query plan would be used for the first and third statements. The
second statement would use a different query plan.

```
USE northwind
SELECT * FROM products WHERE unitprice = $12.5
SELECT * FROM products WHERE unitprice = 12.5
SELECT * FROM products WHERE unitprice = $12.5
GO
```

Auto-Parameterization

SQL Server attempts to determine the constants that are actually parameters and makes them into parameters automatically. If successful, later queries that follow the same template can use the same plan.

Example 2

Auto-parameterization uses the same query plan for all three of the following statements.

```
USE library
SELECT * FROM member WHERE member_no = 7890
SELECT * FROM member WHERE member_no = 1234
SELECT * FROM member WHERE member_no = 7890
GO
```

Performance Considerations

- **Not Search Conditions May Slow Data Retrieval**

- **LIKE Search Conditions Slow Data Retrieval**

- **Exact Matches or Ranges May Speed Data Retrieval**

- **ORDER BY Clause May Slow Data Retrieval**

You should consider some of the issues that affect the performance of SQL Server when you perform basic queries:

- Use positive rather than negative search conditions. Negative search conditions—such as NOT BETWEEN, NOT IN, and IS NOT NULL—may slow data retrieval because all rows are evaluated.

- Avoid using the LIKE search condition if you can write a more specific query. Data retrieval may be slower when you use the LIKE search condition.

- Use exact matches or ranges as search conditions when possible. Again, specific queries perform better.

- Data retrieval may decrease if you use the ORDER BY clause because SQL Server must determine and sort the result set before it returns the first row.

Recommended Practices

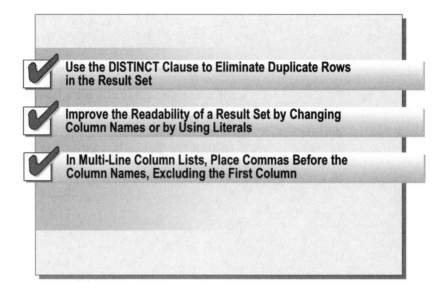

The following recommended practices should help you perform basic queries:

- Use the DISTINCT clause to eliminate duplicate rows in result sets. All rows that meet the search conditions that are specified in the SELECT statement are returned in the result set unless you use the DISTINCT clause.

- Improve the readability of result sets by changing column names to column aliases or using literals to replace result set values. These formatting options change the presentation of the data, not the data itself.

- In multi-line column lists, place commas before the column names, excluding the first column. This style allows you to comment out or cut and paste single lines easily. For example, use the following style:

```
USE .northwind
SELECT  firstname AS First
        ,lastname AS Last
        ,employeeid AS 'Employee ID:'
FROM employees
GO
```

Additional information on the following topics is available in SQL Server Books Online.

Topic	Search on
Using character strings	"pattern matching"
Sorting result sets	"sort order"

Lab A: Retrieving Data and Manipulating Result Sets

Objectives

After completing this lab, you will be able to:

- Perform queries on databases by using the SELECT statement.
- Sort the data and eliminate duplicate values in a result set.
- Format the result set by using column aliases and literals.

Prerequisites

Before working on this lab, you must have:

- Answer files for this lab, which are located in C:\Moc\2071\Labfiles\L03\Answers.
- The **library** database installed.

Lab Setup

None.

For More Information

If you require help in executing files, search Microsoft® SQL Server™ 2000 Query Analyzer Help for "Execute a query".

Other resources that you can use include:

- The **library** database schema.
- SQL Server Books Online.

Scenario

The organization of the classroom is meant to simulate a worldwide trading firm named Northwind Traders. Its fictitious domain name is nwtraders.msft. The primary DNS server for nwtraders.msft is the instructor computer, which has an Internet Protocol (IP) address of 192.168.x.200 (where x is the assigned classroom number). The name of the instructor computer is London.

The following table provides the user name, computer name, and the IP address for each student computer in the fictitious nwtraders.msft domain. Find the user name for your computer and make a note of it.

User name	Computer name	IP address
SQLAdmin1	Vancouver	192.168.x.1
SQLAdmin2	Denver	192.168.x.2
SQLAdmin3	Perth	192.168.x.3
SQLAdmin4	Brisbane	192.168.x.4
SQLAdmin5	Lisbon	192.168.x.5
SQLAdmin6	Bonn	192.168.x.6
SQLAdmin7	Lima	192.168.x.7
SQLAdmin8	Santiago	192.168.x.8
SQLAdmin9	Bangalore	192.168.x.9
SQLAdmin10	Singapore	192.168.x.10
SQLAdmin11	Casablanca	192.168.x.11
SQLAdmin12	Tunis	192.168.x.12
SQLAdmin13	Acapulco	192.168.x.13
SQLAdmin14	Miami	192.168.x.14
SQLAdmin15	Auckland	192.168.x.15
SQLAdmin16	Suva	192.168.x.16
SQLAdmin17	Stockholm	192.168.x.17
SQLAdmin18	Moscow	192.168.x.18
SQLAdmin19	Caracas	192.168.x.19
SQLAdmin20	Montevideo	192.168.x.20
SQLAdmin21	Manila	192.168.x.21
SQLAdmin22	Tokyo	192.168.x.22
SQLAdmin23	Khartoum	192.168.x.23
SQLAdmin24	Nairobi	192.168.x.24

Estimated time to complete this lab: 45 minutes

Exercise 1
Retrieving Data

In this exercise, you will select specific data from tables in the **library** database. C:\Moc\2071\Labfiles\L03\Answers contains completed scripts for this exercise.

▶ To select specific columns

In this procedure, you will write and execute a SELECT statement that retrieves the **title** and **title_no** columns from the **title** table.

1. Log on to the **NWTraders** classroom domain by using the information in the following table.

Option	Value
User name	**SQLAdminx** (where *x* corresponds to your computer name as designated in the nwtraders.msft classroom domain)
Password	**Password**

2. Open SQL Query Analyzer and, if requested, log in to the (local) server with Microsoft Windows®Authentication.

   You have permission to log in to and administer SQL Server because you are logged as **SQLAdminx**, which is a member of the Windows 2000 local group, Administrators. All members of this group are automatically mapped to the SQL Server **sysadmin** role.

3. On the **QUERY** menu point to and click **Results in Text**.

4. In the **DB** list, click **library**.

5. Write and execute a SELECT statement that retrieves the **title** and **title_no** columns from the **title** table. Answer_Columns.sql is a completed script for this step.

6. Save the SELECT statement as ANSI text with an .sql file name extension.

7. Save the result set with an .rpt file name extension.

8. On the **QUERY** menu point to and click **Results in Grid** to reset the results format.

Result

Your result should look similar to the following partial result set.

```
Title                             title_no
------------------------------    --------
Last of the Mohicans              1
The Village Watch-Tower           2
Self Help; Conduct & Perseverance 3
Songs of a Savoyard               4
.
.
.
(50 row(s) affected)
```

► **To select rows by using a comparison operator**

In this procedure, you will write and execute a SELECT statement that retrieves data from specific rows by using a WHERE clause with a comparison operator. Answer_Comparison.sql is a completed script for this procedure.

- Write and execute a SELECT statement that retrieves the title of title number 10 from the **title** table.

  You can execute the **sp_help** system stored procedure for the **title** table to find the correct column names.

Result

Your result should look similar to the following result set.

title
The Night-Born
(1 row(s) affected)

► **To select rows by using a range**

In this procedure, you will write and execute a SELECT statement that retrieves data from specific rows by using a WHERE clause with a range. Answer_Range.sql is a completed script for this procedure.

- Write and execute a SELECT statement that retrieves the member numbers and assessed fines from the **loanhist** table for all members who have had fines between $8.00 and $9.00.

  You can execute the **sp_help** system stored procedure for the **loanhist** table to find the correct column names.

Result

Your result should look similar to the following partial result set. The actual number of rows returned may vary.

member_no	fine_assessed
7399	9.0000
7399	9.0000
7399	9.0000
7399	9.0000
.	.
.	.
.	.
(312 row(s) affected)	

▶ To select rows by using a list of values

In this procedure, you will write and execute a SELECT statement that retrieves data from specific rows by using a WHERE clause that contains a list of values. Answer_InList.sql is a completed script for this procedure.

- Write and execute a SELECT statement that retrieves the title number and author from the **title** table for all books authored by Charles Dickens or Jane Austen. Use the IN operator as part of the SELECT statement.

Result

Your result should look similar to the following result set.

author	title_no
Jane Austen	27
Charles Dickens	30
Charles Dickens	31
Jane Austen	41
Jane Austen	43

(5 row(s) affected)

▶ To select rows by using a character string comparison

In this procedure, you will write and execute a SELECT statement that retrieves data from specific rows that contain a character string similar to another character string. Answer_String.sql is a completed script for this procedure.

- Write and execute a SELECT statement that retrieves the title number and title from the **title** table for all rows that contain the character string "adventures" in the title. Use the LIKE operator in your query.

Result

Your result should look similar to the following result set.

title_no	title
26	The Adventures of Robin Hood
44	Adventures of Huckleberry Finn

(2 row(s) affected)

▶ **To select rows that contain null values**

In this procedure, you will write and execute a SELECT statement that retrieves data from specific rows by using a WHERE clause that searches for null values. Answer_IsNull.sql is a completed script for this procedure.

- Write and execute a SELECT statement that retrieves the member number, assessed fine, and fine that is paid for loans that have unpaid fines from the **loanhist** table. Retrieve rows that have fines entered in the **fine_assessed** column and that have null values for the **fine_paid** column.

Result

Your result should look similar to the following result set. The number of rows returned may vary.

member_no	fine_assessed	fine_paid
4645	5.0000	NULL
4240	.0000	NULL
3821	1.0000	NULL
3389	9.0000	NULL
.		
.		
.		

(1118 row(s) affected)

Exercise 2
Manipulating Result Sets

In this exercise, you will write and execute queries that change the way that the data is displayed in the result set. You will use the DISTINCT keyword to eliminate duplicate rows and the ORDER BY keyword to sort the result set. Additionally, you will change the column names and presentation of data in result sets by using aliases and literals.

C:\Moc\2071\Labfiles\L03\Answers contains completed scripts for this exercise.

▶ To eliminate duplicate rows from the result set

In this procedure, you will write and execute a query on the **adult** table that returns only unique combinations of cities and states in your result set. Answer_Duplicates.sql is a completed script for this procedure.

- Write and execute a query that retrieves all of the unique pairs of cities and states from the **adult** table. You should receive only one row in the result set for each city and state pair.

Result

Your result should look similar to the following partial result set.

City	state
Salt Lake City	UT
Atlanta	GA
Tallahassee	FL
Washington	DC
.	
.	
.	

(23 row(s) affected)

▶ To sort data

In this procedure, you will write and execute a query that retrieves the titles from the **title** table and lists them in alphabetical order. Answer_Sort.sql is a completed script for this procedure.

- Write and execute a query that retrieves a sorted list of all titles from the **title** table.

Result

Your result should look similar to the following partial result set.

Title

A Tale of Two Cities
Adventures of Huckleberry Finn
Ballads of a Bohemian
Candide
.

.

.

(50 row(s) affected)

▶ **To compute data, return computed values, and use a column alias**

In this exercise, you will write and execute a query that returns the **member_no**, **isbn**, and **fine_assessed** columns from the **loanhist** table of all archived loans with a non-null value in the **fine_assessed** column. Then, you will create a new column in the result set that contains the computed value of the **fine_assessed** column multiplied by two, and you will use a column alias named double fine.

Answer_Computed.sql is a completed script for this procedure.

1. Write and execute a query that retrieves the **member_no**, **isbn**, and **fine_assessed** columns from the **loanhist** table of all archived loans a non-null value in the **fine_assessed** column.

2. Create a computed column that contains the value of the **fine_assessed** column multiplied by two.

3. Use the column alias 'double fine' for the computed column. Enclose the column alias within single quotation marks because it does not conform to the SQL Server object naming conventions.

Result

Your result should look similar to the following result set. The actual number of rows returned may vary.

member_no	isbn	fine_assessed	double fine
7399	101	9.0000	18.0000
6709	102	9.0000	18.0000
.			
.			
.			

(1300 row(s) affected)

▶ **To format the result set of a column by using string functions**

In this procedure, you will write and execute a query that lists all members in the **member** table with the last name Anderson. Format the result set in lowercase characters and display a single column of e-mail names that consists of the member's first name, middle initial, and first two letters of the last name.

Answer_Formatting.sql is a completed script for this procedure.

1. Write and execute a query that generates a single column that contains the **firstname**, **middleinitial**, and **lastname** columns from the **member** table for all members with the last name Anderson.

2. Use the column alias email_name.

3. Modify the query to return a list of e-mail names with the member's first name, middle initial, and first two letters of the last name in lowercase characters. Use the SUBSTRING function to retrieve part of a string column. Use the LOWER function to return the result in lowercase characters. Use the addition (+) operator to concatenate the character strings.

Result

Your result should look similar to the following partial result set. The number of rows returned may vary.

```
email_name
amyaan
angelaaan
brianaan
clairaan
 .
 .
 .
(390 row(s) affected)
```

▶ **To format the result set of a column by using literals**

In this procedure, you will format the result set of a query for readability by using the CONVERT function and string literals. Answer_Literals.sql is a completed script for this procedure.

1. Write and execute a query that retrieves the **title** and **title_no** columns from the **title** table. Your result set should be a single column with the following format:

```
The title is: Poems, title number 7
```

This query returns a single column based on an expression that concatenates four elements:

- **The title is:** string constant
- **title.title** column
- **title number** string constant
- **title.title_no** column

2. Use the CONVERT function to format the **title.title_no** column and the addition (+) operator to concatenate the character strings.

Result

Your result should look similar to the following partial result set.

```
The title is: Last of the Mohicans, title number 1
The title is: The Village Watch-Tower, title number 2
The title is: Self Help; Conduct & Perseverance, title number 3
The title is: Songs of a Savoyard, title number 4
The title is: Fall of the House of Usher, title number 5
.
.
.
(50 row(s) affected)
```

Exercise 3
Using System Functions

In this exercise, you will gather system information by using system functions. C:\Moc\2071\Labfiles\L03\Answers contains completed scripts for this exercise.

▶ **To determine the server process ID**

In this procedure, you will observe current server activity and determine the activity that your session is generating. Answer_SPID.sql is a completed script for this procedure.

1. Execute the **sp_who** system stored procedure.

   SQL Server displays all activity that is occurring on the server.

2. To determine which activity is yours, execute the following statement:

   ```
   SELECT @@spid
   GO
   ```

   The server process ID (spid) number of your process is returned in the results.

3. Execute the **sp_who** system stored procedure again, using your spid number as an additional parameter. (In the following statement, *n* represents your spid number.)

   ```
   EXEC sp_who n
   GO
   ```

   The activity related to your spid is displayed.

▶ **To retrieve environmental information**

In this procedure, you will determine which version of SQL Server that you are running and you will retrieve connection, database context, and server information. You will perform these tasks by using system functions.

Answer_Environment.sql is a completed script for this procedure.

1. Execute the following statement:

   ```
   SELECT @@version
   GO
   ```

2. Execute the following statement:

   ```
   SELECT USER_NAME(), DB_NAME(), @@servername
   GO
   ```

▶ **To retrieve metadata**

In this procedure, you will execute several queries to return the metadata from specific database objects by using information schema views. Remember that **information_schema** is a predefined database user that is the owner of the information schema views. Answer_Metadata.sql is a completed script for this procedure.

1. Execute the following statement to return a list of all the user-defined tables in a database:

```
USE library
SELECT *
 FROM information_schema.tables
 WHERE table_type = 'base table'
GO
```

2. Execute the following statement to return the primary key and foreign key columns for the **orders** table:

```
USE northwind
SELECT *
 FROM information_schema.key_column_usage
 WHERE table_name = 'orders'
GO
```

What column has a primary key defined on it?

_____

_____

Review

- Retrieving Data by Using the SELECT Statement
- Filtering Data
- Formatting Result Sets
- How Queries Are Processed
- Performance Considerations

You are the database administrator for a health care plan. The **physicians** table was created with the following statement:

```
CREATE TABLE dbo.physicians (
    physician_no int IDENTITY (100, 2) NOT NULL ,
    f_name varchar (25) NOT NULL ,
    l_name varchar (25) NOT NULL ,
    street varchar (50) NULL ,
    city varchar (255) NULL ,
    state varchar (255) NULL ,
    postal_code varchar (7) NULL ,
    co_pay money NOT NULL CONSTRAINT phys_co_pay DEFAULT (10)
    )
```

1. How would you retrieve information about physicians who have practices in the states of New York (NY), Washington (WA), Virginia (VA), or California (CA)?

2. How can you generate a list of states that does not include any duplicate states in the result set?

3. How can you generate a column in your result set that lists the co_pay value plus a service charge of $5.00 for each physician, and then alias this column as **Amt_Due**?

Microsoft®
Training &
Certification

Module 4: Grouping and Summarizing Data

Contents

Overview

- **Listing the TOP *n* Values**

- **Using Aggregate Functions**

- **GROUP BY Fundamentals**

- **Generating Aggregate Values Within Result Sets**

- **Using the COMPUTE and COMPUTE BY Clauses**

You may want to group or summarize data when you retrieve it.

This module provides students with the skills to group and summarize data by using aggregate functions. These skills include using the GROUP BY and HAVING clauses to summarize and group data and using the ROLLUP and CUBE operators with the GROUPING function to group data and summarize values for those groups. This module also introduces how to use the COMPUTE and COMPUTE BY clauses to generate summary reports and to list the TOP *n* values in a result set.

After completing this module, you will be able to:

- Use the TOP *n* keyword to retrieve a list of the specified top values in a table.

- Generate a single summary value by using aggregate functions.

- Organize summary data for a column by using aggregate functions with the GROUP BY and HAVING clauses.

- Generate summary data for a table by using aggregate functions with the GROUP BY clause and the ROLLUP or CUBE operator.

- Generate control-break reports by using the COMPUTE and COMPUTE BY clauses.

Listing the TOP *n* Values

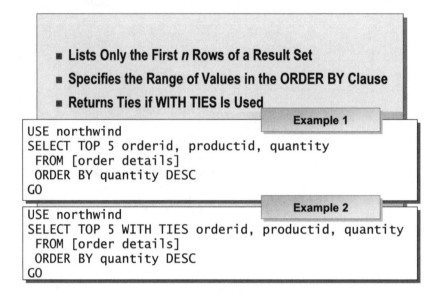

- **Lists Only the First *n* Rows of a Result Set**
- **Specifies the Range of Values in the ORDER BY Clause**
- **Returns Ties if WITH TIES Is Used**

Example 1
```
USE northwind
SELECT TOP 5 orderid, productid, quantity
 FROM [order details]
 ORDER BY quantity DESC
GO
```

Example 2
```
USE northwind
SELECT TOP 5 WITH TIES orderid, productid, quantity
 FROM [order details]
 ORDER BY quantity DESC
GO
```

Use the TOP *n* keyword to list only the first *n* rows or *n* percent of a result set. Although the TOP *n* keyword is not ANSI-standard, it is useful, for example, to list a company's top selling products.

When you use the TOP *n* or TOP *n* PERCENT keyword, consider the following facts and guidelines:

- Specify the range of values in the ORDER BY clause. If you do not use an ORDER BY clause, Microsoft® SQL Server™ 2000 returns rows that satisfy the WHERE clause in no particular order.

- Use an unsigned integer following the TOP keyword.

- If the TOP *n* PERCENT keyword yields a fractional row, SQL Server rounds to the next integer value.

- Use the WITH TIES clause to include ties in your result set. Ties result when two or more values are the same as the last row that is returned in the ORDER BY clause. Your result set may therefore include any number of rows.

Note You can use the WITH TIES clause only when an ORDER BY clause exists.

Example 1

This example uses the TOP *n* keyword to find the five products with the highest quantities that are ordered in a single order. Tied values are excluded from the result set.

```
USE northwind
SELECT TOP 5 orderid, productid, quantity
 FROM [order details]
 ORDER BY quantity DESC
GO
```

Result

orderid	productid	quantity
10764	39	130
11072	64	130
10398	55	120
10451	55	120
10515	27	120

(5 row(s) affected)

Example 2

This example uses the TOP *n* keyword and the WITH TIES clause to find the five products with the highest quantities that are ordered in a single order. The result set lists a total of 10 products, because additional rows with the same values as the last row also are included. Compare the following result set to the result set in Example 1.

```
USE northwind
SELECT TOP 5 WITH TIES orderid, productid, quantity
 FROM [order details]
 ORDER BY quantity DESC
GO
```

Result

orderid	productid	quantity
10764	39	130
11072	64	130
10398	55	120
10451	55	120
10515	27	120
10595	61	120
10678	41	120
10711	53	120
10776	51	120
10894	75	120

(10 row(s) affected)

◆ Using Aggregate Functions

Aggregate function	Description
AVG	Average of values in a numeric expression
COUNT	Number of values in an expression
COUNT (*)	Number of selected rows
MAX	Highest value in the expression
MIN	Lowest value in the expression
SUM	Total values in a numeric expression
STDEV	Statistical deviation of all values
STDEVP	Statistical deviation for the population
VAR	Statistical variance of all values
VARP	Statistical variance of all values for the population

Functions that calculate averages and sums are called *aggregate functions*. When an aggregate function is executed, SQL Server summarizes values for an entire table or for groups of columns within the table, producing a single value for each set of rows for the specified columns:

- You can use aggregate functions with the SELECT statement or in combination with the GROUP BY clause.

- With the exception of the COUNT(*) function, all aggregate functions return a NULL if no rows satisfy the WHERE clause. The COUNT(*) function returns a value of zero if no rows satisfy the WHERE clause.

Tip Index frequently aggregated columns to improve query performance. For example, if you aggregate frequently on the **quantity** column, indexing on the **quantity** column improves aggregate operations.

The data type of a column determines the functions that you can use with it. The following table describes the relationships between functions and data types.

Function	Data type
COUNT	COUNT is the only aggregate function that can be used on columns with **text**, **ntext**, or **image** data types.
MIN and MAX	You cannot use the MIN and MAX functions on columns with **bit** data types.
SUM and AVG	You can use only the SUM and AVG aggregate functions on columns with **int**, **smallint**, **tinyint**, **decimal**, **numeric**, **float**, **real**, **money**, and **smallmoney** data types.
	When you use the SUM or AVG function, SQL Server treats the **smallint** or **tinyint** data types as an **int** data type value in your result set.

Partial Syntax

```
SELECT [ ALL | DISTINCT ]
    [ TOP n [PERCENT] [ WITH TIES] ] <select_list>
    [ INTO new_table ]
    [ FROM <table_sources> ]
    [ WHERE <search_conditions> ]
    [ [ GROUP BY [ALL] group_by_expression [,...n]]
    [HAVING <search_conditions> ]
    [ WITH { CUBE | ROLLUP } ]
    ]
    [ ORDER BY { column_name [ ASC | DESC ] } [,...n] ]
    [ COMPUTE
    { { AVG | COUNT | MAX | MIN | SUM } (expression) } [,...n]
    [ BY expression [,...n]
    ]
```

Example 1

This example calculates the average unit price of all products in the **products** table.

```
USE northwind
SELECT AVG(unitprice)
 FROM products
GO
```

Result

```
28.8663

(1 row(s) affected)
```

Example 2

This example adds all rows in the **quantity** column in the **order details** table.

```
USE northwind
SELECT SUM(quantity)
 FROM [order details]
GO
```

Result

```
51317

(1 row(s) affected)
```

Using Aggregate Functions with Null Values

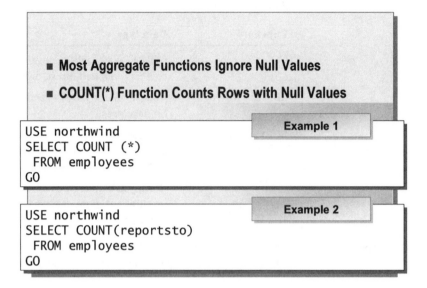

Null values can cause aggregate functions to produce unexpected results. For example, if you execute a SELECT statement that includes a COUNT function on a column that contains 18 rows, two of which contain null values, your result set returns a total of 16 rows. SQL Server ignores the two rows that contain null values.

Therefore, use caution when using aggregate functions on columns that contain null values, because the result set may not be representative of your data. However, if you decide to use aggregate functions with null values, consider the following facts:

- SQL Server aggregate functions, with the exception of the COUNT (*) function, ignore null values in columns.

- The COUNT (*) function counts all rows, even if every column contains a null value. For example, if you execute a SELECT statement that includes the COUNT (*) function on a column that contains a total of 18 rows, two of which contain null values, your result set returns a total of 18 rows.

Example 1

This example lists the number of employees in the **employees** table.

```
USE northwind
SELECT COUNT(*)
 FROM employees
GO
```

Result

```
9

(1 row(s) affected)
```

Example 2

This example lists the number of employees who do not have a null value in the **reportsto** column in the **employees** table, indicating that a reporting manager is defined for that employee.

```
USE northwind
SELECT COUNT(reportsto)
 FROM employees
GO
```

Result

8

(1 row(s) affected)

◆ GROUP BY Fundamentals

- Using the GROUP BY Clause
- Using the GROUP BY Clause with the HAVING Clause

By itself, an aggregate function produces a single summary value for all rows in a column.

If you want to generate summary values for a column, use aggregate functions with the GROUP BY clause. Use the HAVING clause with the GROUP BY clause to restrict the groups of rows that are returned in the result set.

Note Using the GROUP BY clause does not guarantee a sort order. If you want the results to be sorted, include the ORDER BY clause.

Using the GROUP BY Clause

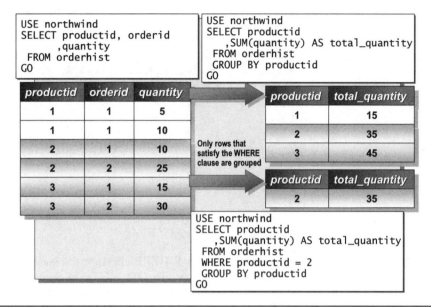

Use the GROUP BY clause on columns or expressions to organize rows into groups and to summarize those groups. For example, use the GROUP BY clause to determine the quantity of each product that was ordered for all orders.

When you use the GROUP BY clause, consider the following facts and guidelines:

- SQL Server produces a column of values for each defined group.

- SQL Server returns only single rows for each group that you specify; it does not return detail information.

- All columns that are specified in the GROUP BY clause must be included in the select list.

- If you include a WHERE clause, SQL Server groups only the rows that satisfy the WHERE clause conditions.

- The number of columns items is limited by the GROUP BY column sizes, the aggregated columns, and the aggregate values involved in the query. This originates from the limit of 8,060 bytes on the intermediate work table that is needed to hold the intermediate query results.

- Do not use the GROUP BY clause on columns that contain multiple null values because the null values are processed as a group.

- Use the ALL keyword with the GROUP BY clause to display all rows with null values in the aggregate columns, regardless of whether the rows satisfy the WHERE clause.

Note The **orderhist** table is specifically created for the examples in this module. The 2071_R04.sql script, which is included in the Batches folder on the Student Materials compact disc, can be executed to add this table to the **Northwind** database.

Example 1

This example returns information about orders from the **orderhist** table. The query groups and lists each product ID and calculates the total quantity ordered. The total quantity is calculated with the SUM aggregate function and displays one value for each product in the result set.

```
USE northwind
SELECT productid, SUM(quantity) AS total_quantity
 FROM orderhist
 GROUP BY productid
GO
```

Result

productid	total_quantity
1	15
2	35
3	45

```
(3 row(s) affected)
```

Example 2

This example adds a WHERE clause to the query in Example 1. This query restricts the rows to product ID 2 and then groups these rows and calculates the total quantity ordered. Compare this result set to that in Example 1.

```
USE northwind
SELECT productid, SUM(quantity) AS total_quantity
 FROM orderhist
 WHERE productid = 2
 GROUP BY productid
GO
```

Result

productid	total_quantity
2	35

```
(1 row(s) affected)
```

Example 3

This example returns information about orders from the **order details** table. This query groups and lists each product ID and then calculates the total quantity ordered. The total quantity is calculated with the SUM aggregate function and displays one value for each product in the result set. This example does not include a WHERE clause and, therefore, returns a total for each product ID.

```
USE northwind
SELECT productid, SUM(quantity) AS total_quantity
 FROM [order details]
 GROUP BY productid
GO
```

Result

productid	total_quantity
61	603
3	328
32	297
.	
.	
.	

```
(77 row(s) affected)
```

Using the GROUP BY Clause with the HAVING Clause

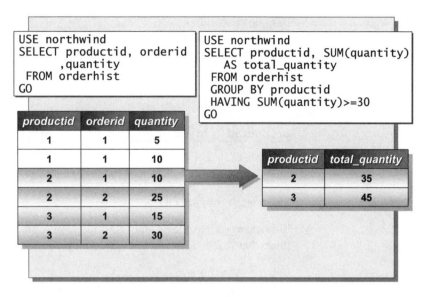

Use the HAVING clause on columns or expressions to set conditions on the groups included in a result set. The HAVING clause sets conditions on the GROUP BY clause in much the same way that the WHERE clause interacts with the SELECT statement.

When you use the HAVING clause, consider the following facts and guidelines:

- Use the HAVING clause only with the GROUP BY clause to restrict the grouping. Using the HAVING clause without the GROUP BY clause is not meaningful.

- You can reference any of the columns that appear in the select list.

- Do not use the ALL keyword with the HAVING clause because the HAVING clause overrides the ALL keyword and returns groups that satisfy only the HAVING clause.

Example 1

This example lists each group of products from the **orderhist** table that has orders of 30 or more units.

```
USE northwind
SELECT productid, SUM(quantity) AS total_quantity
 FROM orderhist
 GROUP BY productid
 HAVING SUM(quantity) >=30
GO
```

Result

productid	total_quantity
2	35
3	45

(2 row(s) affected)

Example 2

This example lists the product ID and quantity for products that have orders for more than 1,200 units.

```
USE northwind
 SELECT productid, SUM(quantity) AS total_quantity
 FROM [order details]
 GROUP BY productid
 HAVING SUM(quantity) > 1200
GO
```

Result

productid	total_quantity
59	1496
56	1263
60	1577
31	1397

(4 row(s) affected)

◆ Generating Aggregate Values Within Result Sets

- **Using the GROUP BY Clause with the ROLLUP Operator**
- **Using the GROUP BY Clause with the CUBE Operator**
- **Using the GROUPING Function**

Use the GROUP BY clause with the ROLLUP and CUBE operators to generate aggregate values within result sets. The ROLLUP or CUBE operators can be useful for cross-referencing information within a table without having to write additional scripts.

When you use the ROLLUP or CUBE operators, use the GROUPING function to identify the detail and summary values in the result set.

Using the GROUP BY Clause with the ROLLUP Operator

```
USE northwind
SELECT productid, orderid, SUM(quantity) AS total_quantity
 FROM orderhist
 GROUP BY productid, orderid
 WITH ROLLUP
 ORDER BY productid, orderid
GO
```

productid	orderid	total_quantity	Description
NULL	NULL	95	Grand total
1	NULL	15	Summarizes only rows for **productid 1**
1	1	5	Detail value for **productid 1, orderid 1**
1	2	10	Detail value for **productid 1, orderid 2**
2	NULL	35	Summarizes only rows for **productid 2**
2	1	10	Detail value for **productid 2, orderid 1**
2	2	25	Summarizes only rows for **productid 3**
3	NULL	45	Summarizes only rows for **productid 3**
3	1	15	Detail value for **productid 3, orderid 1**
3	2	30	Detail value for **productid 3, orderid 2**

Use the GROUP BY clause with the ROLLUP operator to summarize group values. The GROUP BY clause with the ROLLUP operator provides data in a standard relational format.

For example, you could generate a result set that includes the quantity that is ordered for each product for each order, the total quantity that is ordered for each product, and the grand total of all products.

When you use the GROUP BY clause with the ROLLUP operator, consider the following facts and guidelines:

- SQL Server processes data from right to left, along the list of columns that are specified in the GROUP BY clause. SQL Server then applies the aggregate function to each group.

- SQL Server adds a row to the result set that displays cumulative aggregates, such as a running sum or a running average. These cumulate aggregates are indicated with a NULL in the result set.

- You cannot use the ALL keyword with the ROLLUP operator.

- When you use the ROLLUP operator, ensure that the columns that follow the GROUP BY clause have a relationship that is meaningful in your business environment.

Example 1

This example lists all rows from the **orderhist** table and summary quantity values for each product.

```
USE northwind
SELECT productid, orderid, SUM(quantity) AS total_quantity
 FROM orderhist
 GROUP BY productid, orderid
 WITH ROLLUP
 ORDER BY productid, orderid
GO
```

Result

productid	orderid	total_quantity
NULL	NULL	95
1	NULL	15
1	1	5
1	2	10
2	NULL	35
2	1	10
2	2	25
3	NULL	45
3	1	15
3	2	30

```
(10 row(s) affected)
```

Example 2

This example returns information about orders from the **order details** table. This query contains a SELECT statement with a GROUP BY clause without the ROLLUP operator. The example returns a list of the total quantity that is ordered for each product on each order, for orders with an **orderid** less than 10250.

```
USE northwind
SELECT orderid, productid, SUM(quantity) AS total_quantity
 FROM [order details]
 WHERE orderid < 10250
 GROUP BY orderid, productid
 ORDER BY orderid, productid
GO
```

Result

orderid	productid	total_quantity
10248	11	12
10248	42	10
10248	72	5
10249	14	9
10249	51	40

```
(5 row(s) affected)
```

Example 3

This example adds the ROLLUP operator to the statement in Example 2. The result set includes the total quantity for:

- Each product for each order (also returned by the GROUP BY clause without the ROLLUP operator).

- All products for each order.

- All products for all orders (grand total).

Notice in the result set that the row that contains NULL in both the **productid** and **orderid** columns represents the grand total quantity for all orders for all products. The rows that contain NULL in the **productid** column represent the total quantity of a product for the order in the **orderid** column.

```
USE northwind
SELECT orderid, productid, SUM(quantity) AS total_quantity
 FROM [order details]
 WHERE orderid < 10250
 GROUP BY orderid, productid
 WITH ROLLUP
 ORDER BY orderid, productid
GO
```

Result

orderid	productid	total_quantity
NULL	NULL	76
10248	NULL	27
10248	11	12
10248	42	10
10248	72	5
10249	NULL	49
10249	14	9
10249	51	40

(8 row(s) affected)

Using the GROUP BY Clause with the CUBE Operator

```
USE northwind
SELECT productid, orderid, SUM(quantity) AS total_quantity
 FROM orderhist
 GROUP BY productid, orderid
 WITH CUBE
 ORDER BY productid, orderid
 GO
```

The CUBE operator produces two more summary values than the ROLLUP operator

productid	orderid	total_quantity	Description
NULL	NULL	95	Grand total
NULL	1	30	Summarizes all rows for **orderid 1**
NULL	2	65	Summarizes all rows for **orderid 2**
1	NULL	15	Summarizes only rows for **productid 1**
1	1	5	Detail value for **productid 1, orderid 1**
1	2	10	Detail value for **productid 1, orderid 2**
2	NULL	35	Summarizes only rows for **productid 2**
2	1	10	Detail value for **productid 2, orderid 1**
2	2	25	Detail value for **productid 2, orderid 2**
3	NULL	45	Summarizes only rows for **productid 3**
3	1	15	Detail value for **productid 3, orderid 1**
3	2	30	Detail value for **productid 3, orderid 2**

Use the GROUP BY clause with the CUBE operator to create and summarize all possible combinations of groups based on the GROUP BY clause. Use the GROUP BY clause with the ROLLUP operator to provide data in a standard relational format.

When you use the GROUP BY clause with CUBE operator, consider the following facts and guidelines:

- If you have n columns or expressions in the GROUP BY clause, SQL Server returns 2^n possible combinations in the result set.

- The NULLs in the result set indicate that those particular rows are created as a result of the CUBE operator.

- You cannot use the ALL keyword with the CUBE operator.

- When you use the CUBE operator, ensure that the columns that follow the GROUP BY clause have a relationship that is meaningful in your business environment.

Example

This example returns a result that provides the quantity for each product for each order, total quantity for all products for each order, total quantity for each product for all orders, and a grand total quantity for all products for all orders.

```
USE northwind
SELECT productid, orderid, SUM(quantity) AS total_quantity
 FROM orderhist
 GROUP BY productid, orderid
 WITH CUBE
 ORDER BY productid, orderid
GO
```

Result

productid	orderid	total_quantity
NULL	NULL	95
NULL	1	30
NULL	2	65
1	NULL	15
1	1	5
1	2	10
2	NULL	35
2	1	10
2	2	25
3	NULL	45
3	1	15
3	2	30

(12 row(s) affected)

Using the GROUPING Function

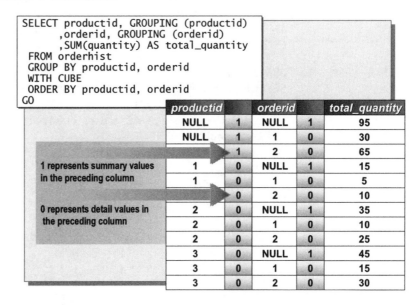

```
SELECT productid, GROUPING (productid)
      ,orderid, GROUPING (orderid)
      ,SUM(quantity) AS total_quantity
 FROM orderhist
 GROUP BY productid, orderid
 WITH CUBE
 ORDER BY productid, orderid
 GO
```

productid		orderid		total_quantity
NULL	1	NULL	1	95
NULL	1	1	0	30
	1	2	0	65
1	0	NULL	1	15
1	0	1	0	5
	0	2	0	10
2	0	NULL	1	35
2	0	1	0	10
2	0	2	0	25
3	0	NULL	1	45
3	0	1	0	15
3	0	2	0	30

1 represents summary values in the preceding column

0 represents detail values in the preceding column

Use the GROUPING function with either the ROLLUP or CUBE operator to distinguish between the detail and summary values in your result set. Using the GROUPING function helps to determine whether the NULLs that appear in your result set are actual null values in the base tables or whether the ROLLUP or CUBE operator generated the row.

When you use the GROUPING function, consider the following facts and guidelines:

- SQL Server produces new columns in the result set for each column that is specified in the GROUPING function.

- SQL Server returns a value of 1 to represent ROLLUP or CUBE summary values in the result set.

- SQL Server returns a value of 0 to represent detail values in the result set.

- You can specify the GROUPING function only on columns that exist in the GROUP BY clause.

- Use the GROUPING function to assist in referencing your result sets programmatically.

Example 1

This example returns a result that provides the quantity for each product for each order, total quantity for all products for each order, total quantity for each product for all orders, and a grand total quantity for all products for all orders. The GROUPING function distinguishes the rows in the result set that the CUBE operator generates.

```
USE northwind
SELECT productid, GROUPING (productid)
      ,orderid, GROUPING (orderid)
      ,SUM(quantity) AS total_quantity
 FROM orderhist
 GROUP BY productid, orderid
 WITH CUBE
 ORDER BY productid, orderid
GO
```

Result

productid		orderid		total_quantity
NULL	1	NULL	1	95
NULL	1	1	0	30
NULL	1	2	0	65
1	0	NULL	1	15
1	0	1	0	5
1	0	2	0	10
2	0	NULL	1	35
2	0	1	0	10
2	0	2	0	25
3	0	NULL	1	45
3	0	1	0	15
3	0	2	0	30

(12 row(s) affected)

Example 2

This example uses the GROUPING function on the **productid** and **orderid** columns that are listed in the GROUP BY clause. The result set has an additional column after the **productid** and **orderid** columns. The GROUPING function returns a 1 when the values in that particular column have been grouped together by the CUBE operator. The result set includes the total quantity for each product for each order, each product for all orders, all products for each order, and the grand total quantity for all products for all orders.

Notice in the result set that the rows that contain NULL in both the **productid** and the **orderid** columns represent the grand total quantity of all products for all orders. Rows that contain NULL in the **productid** column represent the total quantity for all products for each order. Rows that contain NULL in the **orderid** column represent the total quantity for a product for all orders.

```
USE northwind
SELECT orderid, GROUPING(orderid), productid
      ,GROUPING(productid), SUM(quantity) AS total_quantity
 FROM [order details]
 WHERE orderid < 10250
 GROUP BY orderid, productid
 WITH CUBE
 ORDER BY orderid, productid
GO
```

Result

orderid		productid		total_quantity
NULL	1	NULL	1	76
NULL	1	11	0	12
NULL	1	14	0	9
NULL	1	42	0	10
NULL	1	51	0	40
NULL	1	72	0	5
10248	0	NULL	1	27
10248	0	11	0	12
10248	0	42	0	10
10248	0	72	0	5
10249	0	NULL	1	49
10249	0	14	0	9
10249	0	51	0	40

(13 row(s) affected)

Using the COMPUTE and COMPUTE BY Clauses

COMPUTE	COMPUTE BY

``USE northwind``
``SELECT productid, orderid``
``       ,quantity``
``FROM orderhist``
``ORDER BY productid, orderid``
``COMPUTE SUM(quantity)``
``GO``
	``USE northwind``
	``SELECT productid, orderid, quantity``
	`` FROM orderhist``
	`` ORDER BY productid, orderid``
	`` COMPUTE SUM(quantity) BY productid``
	`` COMPUTE SUM(quantity)``
	``GO``

COMPUTE

productid	orderid	quantity
1	1	5
1	2	10
2	1	10
2	2	25
3	1	15
3	2	30
	sum	95

COMPUTE BY

productid	orderid	quantity
1	1	5
1	2	10
	sum	15
2	1	10
2	2	25
	sum	35
3	1	15
3	2	30
	sum	45
	sum	95

The COMPUTE and COMPUTE BY clauses generate extra summary rows of data in a non-relational format that is not ANSI-standard. While it is useful for viewing, the output is not well suited for generating result sets to use with other applications.

For example, you may want to use COMPUTE and COMPUTE BY to print basic reports quickly or to verify results of applications that you are writing. However, other tools, such as Crystal Reports or Microsoft Access, offer richer reporting capabilities.

If you use the COMPUTE and COMPUTE BY clauses, consider the following facts:

■   You cannot include **text**, **ntext**, or **image** data types in a COMPUTE or COMPUTE BY clause.

■   You cannot adjust the format of your result set. For example, if you use the SUM aggregate function, SQL Server displays the word sum in your result set. You cannot change it to read summary.

Generating a Report with Detail and Summary Values for a Column

The COMPUTE clause produces detailed rows and a single aggregate value for a column. When you use the COMPUTE clause, consider the following facts and guidelines:

■   You can use multiple COMPUTE clauses with the COMPUTE BY clause in a single statement.

■   SQL Server requires that you specify the same columns in the COMPUTE clause that are listed in the select list.

■   Do not use the SELECT INTO statement in the same statement as a COMPUTE clause because statements that include COMPUTE do not generate relational output.

Example 1

This example lists each row in the **orderhist** table and generates a grand total for all products that are ordered.

```
USE northwind
SELECT productid, orderid, quantity
 FROM orderhist
 ORDER BY productid, orderid
 COMPUTE SUM(quantity)
GO
```

Result

productid	orderid	total_quantity
1	1	5
1	2	10
2	1	10
2	2	25
3	1	15
3	2	30

```
                               sum
                               ==========
                               95
```

7 row(s) affected

Generating a Report with Detail and Summary Values for Subset of Groups

The COMPUTE BY clause generates detail rows and multiple summary values. Summary values are generated when column values change. Use COMPUTE BY for data that is easily categorized. When you use the COMPUTE BY clause, consider the following facts and guidelines:

- You should use an ORDER BY clause with the COMPUTE BY clause so that rows are grouped together.

- Specify the column names after the COMPUTE BY clause to determine which summary values that SQL Server generates.

- The columns listed after the COMPUTE BY clause must be identical to or a subset of those that are listed after the ORDER BY clause. They must be listed in the same order (left-to-right), start with the same expression, and not skip any expressions.

Example 2

This example lists each row in the **orderhist** table, generates a total that is ordered for each product, and a grand total of all products that are ordered.

```
USE northwind
SELECT productid, orderid, quantity
 FROM orderhist
 ORDER BY productid, orderid
 COMPUTE SUM(quantity) BY productid
 COMPUTE SUM(quantity)
GO
```

Result

productid	orderid	total_quantity
1	1	5
1	2	10
		sum
		==========
		15
2	1	10
2	2	25
		sum
		==========
		35
3	1	15
3	2	30
		sum
		==========
		45
		sum
		==========
		95

10 row(s) affected

Recommended Practices

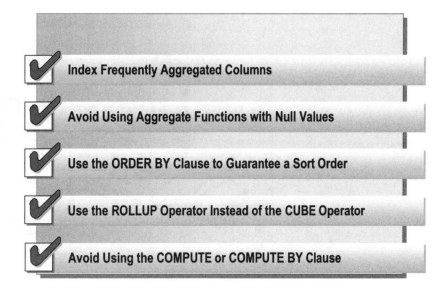

Index Frequently Aggregated Columns

Avoid Using Aggregate Functions with Null Values

Use the ORDER BY Clause to Guarantee a Sort Order

Use the ROLLUP Operator Instead of the CUBE Operator

Avoid Using the COMPUTE or COMPUTE BY Clause

When you use clauses and operators to summarize data, consider the following recommended practices:

- Index frequently aggregated columns to improve query performance. For example, adding the **quantity** column to an index improves aggregate operations, such as those in the examples in this module, even when you use the ROLLUP operator.

- Avoid using aggregate functions with columns that contain null values because the result set may not be representative of your data.

- Use the ORDER BY clause to guarantee a sort order in the result set. If you do not use the ORDER BY clause, SQL Server does not guarantee a sort order.

- Use the ROLLUP operator whenever possible because it is more efficient than the CUBE operator. The ROLLUP operator is efficient because it summarizes data as the detail data is processed. The CUBE operator can be resource intensive because of the large number of calculations that it performs.

- Use the COMPUTE or COMPUTE BY clause because it is useful for viewing and printing result sets to test your applications. However, because they generate extra summary rows of data in a non-relational format, the output is not well suited for production databases.

Additional information on the following topics is available in SQL Server Books Online.

Topic	Search on
Summarizing calculations	"aggregate system functions"

Lab A: Grouping and Summarizing Data

Objectives

After completing this lab, you will be able to:

- Use the GROUP BY and HAVING clauses to summarize data by groups.
- Use the ROLLUP and CUBE operators and GROUPING function to generate summary data.
- Use the COMPUTE and COMPUTE BY clauses to generate control-break reports, grand totals, and averages.

Prerequisites

Before working on this lab, you must have:

- Script files for this lab, which are located in C:\Moc\2071\Labfiles\L04.
- Answer files for this lab, which are located in C:\Moc\2071\Labfiles\L04\Answers.

Lab Setup

None.

For More Information

If you require help in executing files, search Microsoft SQL Server 2000 Query Analyzer Help for "Execute a query".

Other resources that you can use include:

- The **Northwind** database schema.
- SQL Server Books Online.

Scenario

The organization of the classroom is meant to simulate that of a worldwide trading firm named Northwind Traders. Its fictitious domain name is nwtraders.msft. The primary DNS server for nwtraders.msft is the instructor computer, which has an Internet Protocol (IP) address of 192.168.*x*.200 (where *x* is the assigned classroom number). The name of the instructor computer is London.

The following table provides the user name, computer name, and IP address for each student computer in the fictitious nwtraders.msft domain. Find the user name for your computer, and make a note of it.

User name	Computer name	IP address
SQLAdmin1	Vancouver	192.168.x.1
SQLAdmin2	Denver	192.168.x.2
SQLAdmin3	Perth	192.168.x.3
SQLAdmin4	Brisbane	192.168.x.4
SQLAdmin5	Lisbon	192.168.x.5
SQLAdmin6	Bonn	192.168.x.6
SQLAdmin7	Lima	192.168.x.7
SQLAdmin8	Santiago	192.168.x.8
SQLAdmin9	Bangalore	192.168.x.9
SQLAdmin10	Singapore	192.168.x.10
SQLAdmin11	Casablanca	192.168.x.11
SQLAdmin12	Tunis	192.168.x.12
SQLAdmin13	Acapulco	192.168.x.13
SQLAdmin14	Miami	192.168.x.14
SQLAdmin15	Auckland	192.168.x.15
SQLAdmin16	Suva	192.168.x.16
SQLAdmin17	Stockholm	192.168.x.17
SQLAdmin18	Moscow	192.168.x.18
SQLAdmin19	Caracas	192.168.x.19
SQLAdmin20	Montevideo	192.168.x.20
SQLAdmin21	Manila	192.168.x.21
SQLAdmin22	Tokyo	192.168.x.22
SQLAdmin23	Khartoum	192.168.x.23
SQLAdmin24	Nairobi	192.168.x.24

Estimated time to complete this lab: 45 minutes

Exercise 1
Using the TOP *n* Keyword

In this exercise, you will use the TOP *n* keyword and the WITH TIES clause to return the top number or percent of rows from a result set. C:\Moc\2071\Labfiles\L04\Answers contains completed scripts for this exercise.

▶ To use the TOP *n* keyword to list the top rows of a result set

In this procedure, you will modify a script so that it returns the first ten rows of a query. Answer_TopN1.sql is a completed script for this procedure.

1. Log on to the **NWTraders** classroom domain by using the information in the following table.

Option	Value
User name	**SQLAdmin*x*** (where *x* corresponds to your computer name as designated in the nwtraders.msft classroom domain)
Password	**Password**

2. Open SQL Query Analyzer and, if requested, log in to the (local) server with Microsoft Windows® Authentication.

   You have permission to log in to and administer SQL Server because you are logged as **SQLAdmin*x***, which is a member of the Windows 2000 local group, Administrators. All members of this group are automatically mapped to the SQL Server **sysadmin** role.

3. In the **DB** list, click **northwind**.

4. Open and review the C:\Moc\2071\Labfiles\L04\TopN.sql script, which is a query that calculates the total sale amount for each order in the **order details** table, and returns the results in descending order.

5. Modify the query described in step 4 so that the query returns the first ten rows.

6. Execute the query to verify that it returns ten rows.

Result

Your result will look similar to the following result set.

orderid	totalsale
10865	15810.0000
10981	15810.0000
10353	10540.0000
10417	10540.0000
10889	10540.0000
10424	10329.2000
10897	9903.2000
10372	8432.0000
10540	7905.0000
10816	7905.0000

(10 row(s) affected)

▶ **To list the top values of a result set using the TOP *n* keyword**

In this procedure, you will use the TOP *n* keyword to list the top values of a result set. Answer_TopN2.sql is a completed script for this procedure.

1. Modify the query described in step 5 of the previous procedure to return the top ten products (including ties) having the highest total quantity.

2. Execute the query to verify that it returns eleven rows.

Result

Your result will look similar to the following result set.

orderid	totalsale
10865	15810.0000
10981	15810.0000
10353	10540.0000
10417	10540.0000
10889	10540.0000
10424	10329.2000
10897	9903.2000
10372	8432.0000
10540	7905.0000
10816	7905.0000
10817	7905.0000

(11 row(s) affected)

3. Why were more rows returned from the query that asked for the top 10 values that included ties?

_____

_____

Exercise 2
Using the GROUP BY and HAVING Clauses

In this exercise, you will use the GROUP BY and HAVING clauses to summarize data from the **Northwind** database. C:\Moc\2071\Labfiles\L04\Answers contains completed scripts for this exercise.

▶ To use the GROUP BY clause to summarize data

In this procedure, you will open a script that contains a query that includes the GROUP BY clause. Then you will modify the query to obtain different results.

1. Open and review the C:\Moc\2071\Labfiles\L04\Groupby.sql script, which is a query that calculates the total quantity of items ordered for two different categories of items in the **order details** table.

2. Execute the query to review the results.

Result

Your result will look similar to the following result set.

categoryid	total_quantity
1	9532
2	5298

(2 row(s) affected)

▶ To calculate the total quantity for each category

Answer_Groupby1.sql is a completed script for this procedure.

1. Modify the script from step 1 of the previous procedure to summarize the quantity by category for all products, regardless of category.

2. Execute the query to review the results.

Result

Your result will look similar to the following result set.

categoryid	total_quantity
1	9532
2	5298
3	7906
4	9149
5	4562
6	4199
7	2990
8	7681

(8 row(s) affected)

▶ **To calculate the total quantity for each order**

In this procedure, you will calculate the total quantity for each order. Answer_Groupby2.sql is a completed script for this procedure.

1. Modify the script from step 1 of the previous procedure to summarize the quantity by **orderid** for all products, regardless of category.

2. Execute the query to review the results.

Result

Your result will look similar to the following partial result set.

ordered	total_quantity
10248	27
10249	49
10250	60
.	
.	
.	
11075	42
11076	50
11077	72

(830 row(s) affected)

▶ **To calculate the number of orders with more than 250 units ordered**

In this procedure, you will calculate the number of orders with more than 250 units ordered. Answer_Groupby3.sql is a completed script for this procedure.

1. Modify the script from step 1 of the previous procedure to summarize the quantity by **orderid** for all products, regardless of category, and only return orders that had more than 250 units ordered.

2. Execute the query to review the results.

Result

Your result will look similar to the following result set.

ordered	total_quantity
10515	286
10612	263
10658	255
10678	280
10847	288
10895	346
10990	256
11030	330

(8 row(s) affected)

Exercise 3
Using the ROLLUP and CUBE Operators

In this exercise, you will use the ROLLUP and CUBE operators to generate summary data. You also will use the GROUPING function to determine the result rows that are summaries. C:\Moc\2071\Labfiles\L04\Answers contains completed scripts for this exercise.

▶ **To use the ROLLUP operator to generate summary results**

In this procedure, you will use the ROLLUP operator with the GROUP BY and HAVING clauses to generate summary results. Answer_Rollup1.sql is a completed script for this procedure.

1. Open and review the C:\Moc\2071\Labfiles\L04\Rollup.sql script, which is a query that summarizes the quantity of items that were ordered by **productid** and **ordered**, and performs a rollup calculation.

2. Modify the query from step 1 to limit the result to product number 50 by using a WHERE clause, and then execute the query.

3. Execute the query to review the results. Make note of the rows that have null values.

Result

Your result will look similar to the following result set.

productid	orderid	total_quantity
NULL	NULL	235
50	NULL	235
50	10350	15
50	10383	15
50	10429	40
50	10465	25
50	10637	25
50	10729	40
50	10751	20
50	10920	24
50	10948	9
50	11072	22

(12 row(s) affected)

4. What is the significance of the null values in the **productid** and **orderid** columns?

_____

_____

▶ **To use the CUBE operator to generate summary results**

In this procedure, you will use the CUBE operator and the GROUPING function to distinguish between summary and detail rows in the result set. Answer_Cube1.sql is a completed script for this procedure.

1. Open and review the C:\Moc\2071\Labfiles\L04\Rollup.sql script, which is a query that summarizes the quantity of items that were ordered by **productid** and **ordered**, and performs a rollup calculation.

2. Modify the query from step 1 to use the CUBE operator instead of the ROLLUP operator. Also, use the GROUPING function on the **productid** and **orderid** columns to distinguish between summary and detail rows in the result set, and then execute the query.

3. Execute the query to review the results.

Result   Your result will look similar to the following result set.

productid		orderid		total_quantity
NULL	1	NULL	1	235
NULL	1	10350	0	15
NULL	1	10383	0	15
NULL	1	10429	0	40
NULL	1	10465	0	25
NULL	1	10637	0	25
NULL	1	10729	0	40
NULL	1	10751	0	20
NULL	1	10920	0	24
NULL	1	10948	0	9
NULL	1	11072	0	22
50	0	NULL	1	235
50	0	10350	0	15
50	0	10383	0	15
50	0	10429	0	40
50	0	10465	0	25
50	0	10637	0	25
50	0	10729	0	40
50	0	10751	0	20
50	0	10920	0	24
50	0	10948	0	9
50	0	11072	0	22

(22 row(s) affected)

Which rows are summaries?

_____

_____

Which rows are summaries by product? By order?

_____

_____

Exercise 4
Using the COMPUTE and COMPUTE BY Clauses

In this exercise, you will use the COMPUTE and COMPUTE BY clauses to generate control-break reports and end-of-report totals and averages.

C:\Moc\2071\Labfiles\L04\Answers contains completed scripts for this exercise.

▶ **To use the COMPUTE clause to generate reports**

In this procedure, you will modify an existing query by adding the COMPUTE and COMPUTE BY clauses to generate subtotals and grand totals. Answer_Compute1.sql is a completed script for this procedure.

1. Open and review the C:\Moc\2071\Labfiles\L04\Compute.sql script, which is a query that returns the **orderid** and **quantity** ordered for all orders with an **orderid** > 11070.

2. Modify the query from step 1 to generate a grand total for the quantity column using the COMPUTE clause.

3. Execute the query to review the results.

Result

Your result will look similar to the following partial result set.

ordered	quantity
11070	40
11070	20
11070	30
.	
.	
.	
11077	24
11077	4
11077	1
	Sum
	=========
	543

(45 row(s) affected)

▶ **To use the COMPUTE BY clause to generate reports**

In this procedure, you will modify an existing query by using the COMPUTE BY clause to generate grand totals. Answer_Compute2.sql is a completed script for this procedure.

1. Open and review the C:\Moc\2071\Labfiles\L04\Compute.sql script, which is a query that returns the **orderid** and **quantity** ordered for all orders with an **orderid** > 11070.

2. Modify the query from step 1 to generate a control-break report that provides the total quantity for order numbers 11075 and 11076.

3. Execute the query to review the results.

Result

Your result will look similar to the following result set.

ordered	quantity
11075	10
11075	30
11075	2
	Sum
	==========
	42
11076	20
11076	20
11076	10
	Sum
	==========
	50

```
(8 row(s) affected)
```

▶ **To add total quantity and average quantity to the end of the control-break report**

In this procedure, you will add total quantity and average quantity to the end of the control-break report. Answer_Compute3.sql is a completed script for this procedure.

1. Modify the query from step 1 of the previous procedure to add total quantity and average quantity to the end of the control-break report.

2. Execute the query to review the results.

Result

Your result will look similar to the following result set. Notice that this result set is similar to that of step 3 of the previous procedure, with the addition of end-of-report totals (total quantity and average quantity).

orderid	quantity
11075	10
11075	30
11075	2
	Sum
	==========
	42
11076	20
11076	20
11076	10
	Sum
	==========
	50
	Sum
	==========
	92
	Avg
	==========
	15

(10 row(s) affected

Review

■ Listing the TOP *n* Values

■ Using Aggregate Functions

■ GROUP BY Fundamentals

■ Generating Aggregate Values Within Result Sets

■ Using the COMPUTE and COMPUTE BY Clauses

1. An employee in the marketing department has asked you to provide summary data for product sales. She needs all breakfast cereals summarized by type (hot, cold, or low-fat), manufacturer, and size of the store where the product was sold (small, medium, or large). Assuming that a single table holds all this information, what clauses or operators might you use with the SELECT statement? Why?

2. Your manager has asked you to deliver a file that includes all of the data from Question 1 to another development group that is responsible for report generation and graphing tools. Would using the COMPUTE and COMPUTE BY clauses be appropriate for this task? Why or why not?

3. You are reviewing the results of a SELECT statement that used the GROUP BY clause and the CUBE operator. You see null values in the result set, and you know that null values are allowed in the tables that the SELECT statement uses. How can you distinguish between detail rows and summary rows with null values?

4. You need to provide a list of the top 100 products, as well as the products that are in the bottom five percent of sales. Can you use the SELECT TOP *n* [PERCENT] statement to answer each question? Are there other ways to answer the questions?

Microsoft®
Training &
Certification

Module 5: Joining Multiple Tables

Contents

Microsoft®

Overview

- Using Aliases for Table Names
- Combining Data from Multiple Tables
- Combining Multiple Result Sets

This module provides students with an overview of querying multiple tables by using different types of joins, combining result sets by using the UNION operator, and creating tables by using the SELECT INTO statement.

After completing this module, you will be able to:

- Use aliases for table names.

- Combine data from two or more tables by using joins.

- Combine multiple result sets into one result set by using the UNION operator.

Using Aliases for Table Names

- **Example 1 (without an alias name)**

```
USE joindb
 SELECT buyer_name, sales.buyer_id, qty
 FROM buyers   INNER JOIN sales
  ON buyers.buyer_id = sales.buyer_id
GO
```

- **Example 2 (with an alias name)**

```
USE joindb
SELECT buyer_name, s.buyer_id, qty
 FROM buyers AS b   INNER JOIN sales AS s
  ON b.buyer_id = s.buyer_id
GO
```

Using aliases for table names improves script readability, facilitates writing complex joins, and simplifies the maintenance of Transact-SQL.

You can replace a long and complex fully qualified table name with a simple, abbreviated alias name when writing scripts. You use an alias name in place of the full table name.

Partial Syntax

SELECT * FROM server.database.schema.table AS table_alias

Example 1

This example displays the names of buyers, buyer ID, and the quantity sold from the **buyers** and **sales** tables. This query does not use alias names for the tables in the JOIN syntax.

```
USE joindb
SELECT buyer_name, sales.buyer_id, qty
 FROM buyers
 INNER JOIN sales
  ON buyers.buyer_id = sales.buyer_id
GO
```

Example 2

This example displays the names of buyers, buyer ID, and the quantity sold from the **buyers** and **sales** tables. This query uses alias names for the tables in the JOIN syntax.

```
USE joindb
SELECT buyer_name, s.buyer_id, qty
 FROM buyers AS b
 INNER JOIN sales AS s
  ON b.buyer_id = s.buyer_id
GO
```

Note Sometimes complex JOIN syntax and subqueries must use aliases for table names. For example, aliases must be used when joining a table to itself.

◆ Combining Data from Multiple Tables

- ■ **Introduction to Joins**
- ■ **Using Inner Joins**
- ■ **Using Outer Joins**
- ■ **Using Cross Joins**
- ■ **Joining More Than Two Tables**
- ■ **Joining a Table to Itself**

A join is an operation that allows you to query two or more tables to produce a result set that incorporates rows and columns from each table. You can join tables on any expression that is based on any column or combination of columns from both tables.

When you join tables, Microsoft® SQL Server™ 2000 compares the values of the specified columns row by row and then uses the comparison results to combine the qualifying values into new rows.

There are three types of joins: inner joins, outer joins, and cross joins. Additionally, you can join more than two tables by using a series of joins within a SELECT statement, or you can join a table to itself by using a self-join.

Introduction to Joins

- **Selects Specific Columns from Multiple Tables**
  - JOIN keyword specifies that tables are joined and how to join them
  - ON keyword specifies join condition
- **Queries Two or More Tables to Produce a Result Set**
  - Use primary and foreign keys as join conditions
  - Use columns common to specified tables to join tables

You join tables to produce a single result set that incorporates rows and columns from two or more tables.

Partial Syntax

```
SELECT column_name [, column_name ...]
  FROM {<table_source>} [,...n]
  <join_type> ::=
  [ INNER | { { LEFT | RIGHT | FULL } [OUTER] } ]
  [ <join_hint> ]
  JOIN
  <joined_table> ::=
  <table_source> <join_type> <table_source> ON <search_condition>
  | <table_source> CROSS JOIN <table_source>
  | <joined_table>
```

Selects Specific Columns from Multiple Tables

A join allows you to select columns from multiple tables by expanding on the FROM clause of the SELECT statement. Two additional keywords are included in the FROM clause—JOIN and ON:

- The JOIN keyword specifies which tables are to be joined and how to join them.

- The ON keyword specifies which columns the tables have in common.

Queries Two or More Tables to Produce a Result Set

A join allows you to query two or more tables to produce a single result set. When you implement joins, consider the following facts and guidelines:

- Whenever possible, specify the join condition based on the primary and foreign keys; however, you may use any other columns if required.

- In order to avoid data expansion, you must reference the entire key in the ON clause when you join tables, if one of the tables has a composite primary key. In general, join all columns that uniquely identify a row to prevent data expansion.

- Use columns common to the specified tables to join the tables. These columns should have the same or compatible data types.

- Reference a table name if the column names of the joined tables are the same. Qualify each column name by using the *table_name.column_name* format.

- If possible, limit the number of tables in a join, because the more tables that you join, the longer SQL Server may take to process your query.

- You can join one or more tables within a single SELECT statement.

Using Inner Joins

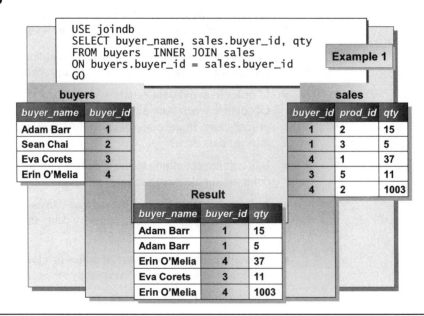

```
USE joindb
SELECT buyer_name, sales.buyer_id, qty
FROM buyers  INNER JOIN sales
ON buyers.buyer_id = sales.buyer_id
GO
```

Example 1

buyers

buyer_name	buyer_id
Adam Barr	1
Sean Chai	2
Eva Corets	3
Erin O'Melia	4

sales

buyer_id	prod_id	qty
1	2	15
1	3	5
4	1	37
3	5	11
4	2	1003

Result

buyer_name	buyer_id	qty
Adam Barr	1	15
Adam Barr	1	5
Erin O'Melia	4	37
Eva Corets	3	11
Erin O'Melia	4	1003

Inner joins combine tables by comparing values in columns that are common to both tables. SQL Server returns only rows that match the join conditions.

Note The examples in this module are from the **joindb** database—a database created specifically for teaching the different types of joins. The **joindb** database is included on the Student Materials compact disc.

Why to Use Inner Joins

Use inner joins to obtain information from two separate tables and combine that information in one result set. When you use inner joins, consider the following facts and guidelines:

- Inner joins are the SQL Server default. You can abbreviate the INNER JOIN clause to JOIN.

- Specify the columns that you want to display in your result set by including the qualified column names in the select list.

- Include a WHERE clause to restrict the rows that are returned in the result set.

- Do not use a null value as a join condition because null values do not evaluate equally with one another.

Note SQL Server does not guarantee an order in the result set unless one is specified with an ORDER BY clause.

Example 1

This example returns the **buyer_name**, **buyer_id**, and **qty** values for the buyers who purchased products. Buyers who did not purchase any products are not included in the result set. Buyers who bought more than one product are listed for each purchase.

The **buyer_id** column from either table can be specified in the select list.

```
USE joindb
SELECT buyer_name, sales.buyer_id, qty
 FROM buyers
 INNER JOIN sales
  ON buyers.buyer_id = sales.buyer_id
GO
```

Result

buyer_name	buyer_id	qty
Adam Barr	1	15
Adam Barr	1	5
Erin O'Melia	4	37
Eva Corets	3	11
Erin O'Melia	4	1003

(5 row(s) affected)

Example 2

This example returns the names of products and the companies that supply the products. Products without listed suppliers and suppliers without current products are not included in the result set.

```
USE northwind
SELECT productname, companyname
 FROM products
 INNER JOIN suppliers
  ON products.supplierid = suppliers.supplierid
GO
```

Result

productname	companyname
Chai	Exotic Liquids
Chang	Exotic Liquids
Aniseed Syrup	Exotic Liquids
Chef Anton's Cajun Seasoning	New Orleans Cajun Delights
.	
.	
.	

(77 row(s) affected)

Example 3

This example returns the names of customers who placed orders after 1/1/98. Notice that a WHERE clause is used to restrict the rows that are returned in the result set.

```
USE northwind
SELECT DISTINCT companyname, orderdate
FROM orders INNER JOIN customers
ON orders.customerid = customers.customerid
WHERE orderdate > '1/1/98'
GO
```

Result

companyname	orderdate
Alfreds Futterkiste	1998-01-15 00:00:00.000
Alfreds Futterkiste	1998-03-16 00:00:00.000
Alfreds Futterkiste	1998-04-09 00:00:00.000
Ana Trujillo Emparedados y helados	1998-03-04 00:00:00.000
.	
.	
.	

(264 row(s) affected)

Example 4

This example returns the title number of all books currently checked out and the member number of the borrower from the **copy** and **loan** tables in the **library** database. Both the **copy** and **loan** tables have a composite primary key consisting of the **isbn** and **copy_no** columns. When joining these tables, you must specify both columns as join conditions because they uniquely identify a particular copy of a book.

```
USE library
SELECT copy.title_no, loan.member_no
 FROM copy
 INNER JOIN loan
  ON copy.isbn = loan.isbn
  AND copy.copy_no = loan.copy_no
 WHERE copy.on_loan = 'Y'
GO
```

Result

title_no	member_no
1	325
1	351
2	390
2	416
.	
.	
.	

(2000 row(s) affected)

Using Outer Joins

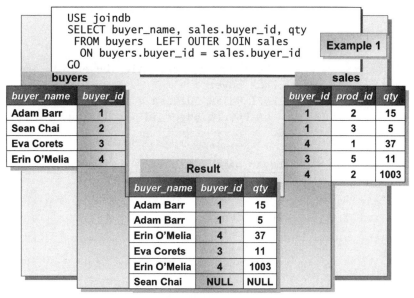

```
USE joindb
SELECT buyer_name, sales.buyer_id, qty
  FROM buyers  LEFT OUTER JOIN sales
    ON buyers.buyer_id = sales.buyer_id
  GO
```

Example 1

buyers

buyer_name	buyer_id
Adam Barr	1
Sean Chai	2
Eva Corets	3
Erin O'Melia	4

sales

buyer_id	prod_id	qty
1	2	15
1	3	5
4	1	37
3	5	11
4	2	1003

Result

buyer_name	buyer_id	qty
Adam Barr	1	15
Adam Barr	1	5
Erin O'Melia	4	37
Eva Corets	3	11
Erin O'Melia	4	1003
Sean Chai	NULL	NULL

Left or right outer joins combine rows from two tables that match the join condition, plus any unmatched rows of either the left or right table as specified in the JOIN clause. Rows that do not match the join condition display NULL in the result set. You also can use full outer joins to display all rows in the joined tables, regardless of whether the tables have any matching values.

Why to Use Left or Right Outer Joins

Use left or right outer joins when you require a complete list of data that is stored in one of the joined tables in addition to the information that matches the join condition. When you use left or right outer joins, consider the following facts and guidelines:

- Use a left outer join to display all rows from the first-named table (the table on the left of the expression). If you reverse the order in which the tables are listed in the FROM clause, the statement yields the same result as a right outer join.

- Use a right outer join to display all rows from the second-named table (the table on the right of the expression). If you reverse the order in which the tables are listed in the FROM clause, the statement yields the same result as a left outer join.

- You can abbreviate the LEFT OUTER JOIN or RIGHT OUTER JOIN clause as LEFT JOIN or RIGHT JOIN.

Example 1

This example returns the **buyer_name**, **buyer_id**, and **qty** values for all buyers and their purchases. Notice that the buyers who did not purchase any products are listed in the result set, but null values appear in the **buyer_id** and **qty** columns.

```
USE joindb
SELECT buyer_name, sales.buyer_id, qty
 FROM buyers
 LEFT OUTER JOIN sales
  ON buyers.buyer_id = sales.buyer_id
GO
```

Result

buyer_name	buyer_id	qty
Adam Barr	1	15
Adam Barr	1	5
Erin O'Melia	4	37
Eva Corets	3	11
Erin O'Melia	4	1003
Sean Chai	NULL	NULL

(6 row(s) affected)

Note   The sort order of the result set can be different because the ORDER BY clause is not used in the example.

Example 2

This example displays all customers with order dates. By using a left outer join, you retrieve one row for each customer and additional rows if the customer has placed multiple orders. NULL in the **orderdate** column is returned in the result set for customers who have not placed an order. Notice the NULL entries for customers FISSA and Paris Spécialités.

```
USE northwind
SELECT companyname, customers.customerid, orderdate
 FROM customers
 LEFT OUTER JOIN orders
  ON customers.customerid = orders.customerid
GO
```

Result

companyname	customerid	orderdate
Vins et alcools Chevalier	VINIT	1996-07-04 00:00.0
Toms Spezialitaten	TOMSP	1996-07-05 00:00.0
Hanari Carnes	HANAR	1996-07-08 00:00.0
Victuailles en stock	VICTE	1996-07-08 00:00.0
.		
.		
.		
FISSA Fabrica Inter. Salichichas S.A.	FISSA	NULL
Paris specialities	PARIS	NULL

(832 row(s) affected)

Using Cross Joins

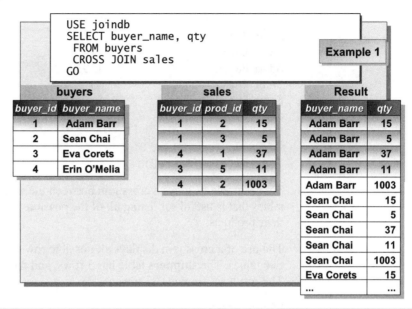

Cross joins display every combination of all rows in the joined tables. A common column is not required to use cross joins.

Why to Use Cross Joins

While cross joins are rarely used on a normalized database, you can use them to generate test data for a database or lists of all possible combinations for checklists or business templates.

When you use cross joins, SQL Server produces a Cartesian product in which the number of rows in the result set is equal to the number of rows in the first table, multiplied by the number of rows in the second table. For example, if there are 8 rows in one table and 9 rows in the other table, SQL Server returns a total of 72 rows.

Example 1

This example lists all possible combinations of the values in the **buyers.buyer_name** and **sales.qty** columns.

```
USE joindb
SELECT buyer_name, qty
 FROM buyers
 CROSS JOIN sales
GO
```

Result

buyer_name	qty
Adam Barr	15
Adam Barr	5
Adam Barr	37
Adam Barr	11
Adam Barr	1003
Sean Chai	15
Sean Chai	5

```
.

.

.
```

```
(20 row(s) affected)
```

Example 2

This example displays a cross join between the **shippers** and **suppliers** tables that is useful for listing all of the possible ways that suppliers can ship their products.

The use of a cross join displays all possible row combinations between these two tables. The **shippers** table has 3 rows, and the **suppliers** table has 29 rows. The result set contains 87 rows.

```
USE northwind
SELECT suppliers.companyname, shippers.companyname
 FROM suppliers
 CROSS JOIN shippers
GO
```

Result

companyname	companyname
Aux joyeux ecclésiastiques	Speedy Express
Bigfoot Breweries	Speedy Express
Cooperativa de Quesos 'Las Cabras'	Speedy Express
Escargots Nouveaux	Speedy Express

```
.

.

.
```

Aux joyeux ecclésiastiques	United Package
Bigfoot Breweries	United Package
Cooperativa de Quesos 'Las Cabras'	United Package
Escargots Nouveaux	United Package

```
.

.

.
```

Aux joyeux ecclésiastiques	Federal Shipping
Bigfoot Breweries	Federal Shipping
Cooperativa de Quesos 'Las Cabras'	Federal Shipping
Escargots Nouveaux	Federal Shipping

```
.

.

.
```

```
(87 row(s) affected)
```

Joining More Than Two Tables

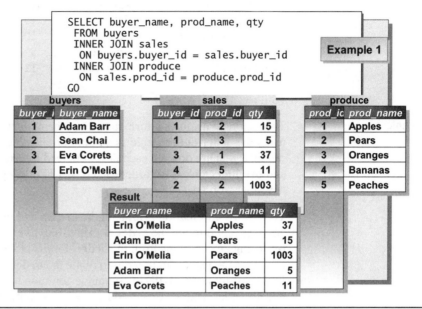

It is possible to join any number of tables. Any table that is referenced in a join operation can be joined to another table by a common column.

Why to Join More Than Two Tables

Use multiple joins to obtain related information from multiple tables. When you join more than two tables, consider the following facts and guidelines:

- You should have one or more tables with foreign key relationships to each of the tables that you want to join.

- The ON clause should reference each column that is part of a composite key.

- Include a WHERE clause to limit the number of rows that are returned.

Example 1

This example returns the **buyer_name**, **prod_name**, and **qty** columns from the **buyers**, **sales** and **produce** tables. The **buyer_id** column is common to both the **buyers** and **sales** tables and is used to join these two tables. The **prod_id** column is common to both the **sales** and **produce** tables and is used to join the **produce** table to the result of the join between **buyers** and **sales**.

```
USE joindb
SELECT buyer_name, prod_name, qty
  FROM buyers
  INNER JOIN sales
   ON buyers.buyer_id = sales.buyer_id
  INNER JOIN produce
   ON sales.prod_id = produce.prod_id
GO
```

Result

buyer_name	prod_name	qty
Erin O'Melia	Apples	37
Adam Barr	Pears	15
Erin O'Melia	Pears	1003
Adam Barr	Oranges	5
Eva Corets	Peaches	11

(5 row(s) affected)

Example 2

This example displays information from the **orders** and **products** tables by using the **order details** table as a link. For example, if you want a list of products that are ordered each day, you need information from both the **orders** and **products** tables. An order can consist of many products, and a product can have many orders.

To retrieve information from both the **orders** and **products** tables, you can use an inner join through the **order details** table. Even though you are not retrieving any columns from the **order details** table, you must include this table as part of the inner join in order to relate the **orders** table to the **products** table. In this example, the **orderid** column is common to both the **orders** and **order details** tables, and the **productid** column is common to both the **order details** and **products** tables.

```
USE northwind
SELECT orderdate, productname
 FROM orders AS O
 INNER JOIN [order details] AS OD
  ON O.orderid = OD.orderid
 INNER JOIN products AS P
  ON OD.productid = P.productid
 WHERE orderdate = '7/8/96'
```

Result

orderdate	productname
1996-07-08	Jack's New England Clam Chowder
1996-07-08	Manjimup Dried Apples
1996-07-08	Louisiana Fiery Hot Pepper Sauce
1996-07-08	Gustaf's Knakebrod
1996-07-08	Ravioli Angelo
1996-07-08	Louisiana Fiery Hot Pepper Sauce

(6 row(s) affected)

Joining a Table to Itself

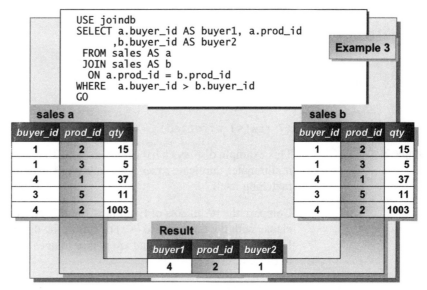

```
USE joindb
SELECT a.buyer_id AS buyer1, a.prod_id
       ,b.buyer_id AS buyer2
 FROM sales AS a
 JOIN sales AS b
  ON a.prod_id = b.prod_id
WHERE  a.buyer_id > b.buyer_id
GO
```

Example 3

sales a

buyer_id	prod_id	qty
1	2	15
1	3	5
4	1	37
3	5	11
4	2	1003

sales b

buyer_id	prod_id	qty
1	2	15
1	3	5
4	1	37
3	5	11
4	2	1003

Result

buyer1	prod_id	buyer2
4	2	1

If you want to find rows that have values in common with other rows in the same table, you can use a self-join to join a table to another instance of itself.

Why to Use Self-Joins

While self-joins are rarely used on a normalized database, you can use them to reduce the number of queries that you execute when you compare values of columns in different rows of the same table. When you use self-joins, consider the following guidelines:

- You must specify table aliases to reference two copies of the table. Remember that table aliases are different from column aliases. Table aliases are designated as the table name followed by the alias.

- When you create self-joins, each row matches itself and pairs are repeated, resulting in duplicate rows. Use a WHERE clause to eliminate these duplicate rows.

Example 1

This example displays a list of all buyers who purchased the same products. Notice that the first and third rows of the result set are rows where **buyer1** matches itself. The fourth and seventh rows are rows where **buyer4** matches itself. The second and sixth rows are rows that mirror one another.

```
USE joindb
SELECT a.buyer_id AS buyer1, a.prod_id, b.buyer_id AS buyer2
 FROM sales AS a
 INNER JOIN sales AS b
  ON a.prod_id = b.prod_id
GO
```

Result

buyer1	prod_id	buyer2
1	2	1
4	2	1
1	3	1
4	1	4
3	5	3
1	2	4
4	2	4

```
(7 row(s) affected)
```

Example 2

This example displays a list of buyers who all purchased the same products, but it eliminates duplicate rows, such as **buyer1** matching itself and **buyer4** matching itself.

Compare the result sets of Examples 1 and 2. Notice that by using a WHERE clause with the not equal to (<>) operator, the duplicate rows are eliminated. However, duplicate rows that are mirror images of one another are still returned in the result set.

```
USE joindb
SELECT a.buyer_id AS buyer1, a.prod_id, b.buyer_id AS buyer2
 FROM sales AS a
 INNER JOIN sales AS b
  ON a.prod_id = b.prod_id
 WHERE a.buyer_id <> b.buyer_id
GO
```

Result

buyer1	prod_id	buyer2
4	2	1
1	2	4

```
(2 row(s) affected)
```

Example 3

This example displays a list of buyers who all purchased the same products.

Notice that when the WHERE clause includes the greater than (>) operator, all duplicate rows are eliminated.

```
USE joindb
SELECT a.buyer_id AS buyer1, a.prod_id, b.buyer_id AS buyer2
 FROM sales AS a
 INNER JOIN sales AS b
  ON a.prod_id = b.prod_id
 WHERE a.buyer_id > b. buyer_id
GO
```

Result

buyer1	prod_id	buyer2
4	2	1

```
(1 row(s) affected)
```

Example 4

This example displays pairs of employees who have the same job title. When the WHERE clause *includes* the less than (<) operator, rows that match themselves and duplicate rows are eliminated.

```
USE northwind
SELECT a.employeeid, LEFT(a.lastname,10) AS name
    ,LEFT(a.title,10) AS title
    ,b.employeeid, LEFT(b.lastname,10) AS name
    ,LEFT(b.title,10) AS title
 FROM employees AS a
 INNER JOIN employees AS b
  ON a.title = b.title
  WHERE a.employeeid < b.employeeid
GO
```

Result

employeeid	Name	title	employeeid	name	title
1	Davolio	Sales Repr	3	Leverling	Sales Repr
1	Davolio	Sales Repr	4	Peacock	Sales Repr
1	Davolio	Sales Repr	6	Suyama	Sales Repr
1	Davolio	Sales Repr	7	King	Sales Repr
1	Davolio	Sales Repr	9	Dodsworth	Sales Repr
3	Leverling	Sales Repr	4	Peacock	Sales Repr
3	Leverling	Sales Repr	6	Suyama	Sales Repr
3	Leverling	Sales Repr	7	King	Sales Repr
3	Leverling	Sales Repr	9	Dodsworth	Sales Repr
4	Peacock	Sales Repr	6	Suyama	Sales Repr
4	Peacock	Sales Repr	7	King	Sales Repr
4	Peacock	Sales Repr	9	Dodsworth	Sales Repr
6	Suyama	Sales Repr	7	King	Sales Repr
6	Suyama	Sales Repr	9	Dodsworth	Sales Repr
7	King	Sales Repr	9	Dodsworth	Sales Repr

15 row(s) affected)

Combining Multiple Result Sets

- **Use the UNION Operator to Create a Single Result Set from Multiple Queries**
- **Each Query Must Have:**
  - Similar data types
  - Same number of columns
  - Same column order in select list

```
USE northwind
SELECT  (firstname + ' ' + lastname) AS name
        ,city, postalcode
 FROM employees
UNION
SELECT companyname, city, postalcode
 FROM customers
GO
```

The UNION operator combines the result of two or more SELECT statements into a single result set.

Use the UNION operator when the data that you want to retrieve resides in different locations and cannot be accessed with a single query. When you use the UNION operator, consider the following facts and guidelines:

- SQL Server requires that the referenced tables have similar data types, the same number of columns, and the same column order in the select list of each query.

- SQL Server removes duplicate rows in the result set. However, if you use the ALL option, all rows (including duplicates) are included in the result set.

- You must specify the column names in the first SELECT statement. Therefore, if you want to define new column headings for the result set, you must create the column aliases in the first SELECT statement.

- If you want the entire result set to be returned in a specific order, you must specify a sort order by including an ORDER BY clause at the end of the last statement affected by the UNION operator. Otherwise, the result set may not be returned in the order that you want.

- You may experience better performance if you break a complex query into multiple SELECT statements and then use the UNION operator to combine them.

Syntax

select_statement UNION [ALL] *select_statement*

Example

This example combines two result sets. The first result set returns the name, city, and postal code of each customer from the **customers** table. The second result set returns the name, city, and postal code of each employee from the **employees** table. When you use the UNION operator to combine these result sets, notice that the column alias from the first select list is returned.

```
USE northwind
SELECT (firstname + ' ' + lastname) AS name, city, postalcode
 FROM employees
UNION
SELECT companyname, city, postalcode
 FROM customers
GO
```

Result

name	city	postalcode
Alfreds Futterkiste	Berlin	12209
Ana Trujillo Emparedados y helados	México D.F.	05021
Antonio Moreno Taquería	México D.F.	05023
Around the Horn	London	WA1 1DP
B's Beverages	London	EC2 5NT
.		
.		
.		
Andrew Fuller	Tacoma	98401
Robert King	London	RG 19SP
Janet Leverling	Kirkland	98033
Anne Dodsworth	London	WG2 7LT

(100 row(s) affected)

Recommended Practices

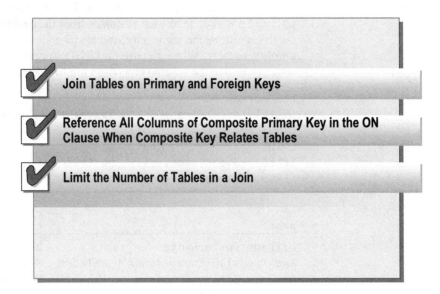

The following recommended practices should help you perform queries:

- Join tables on primary and foreign keys.
- Reference all columns of a composite primary key in the ON clause when a composite key relates tables.
- Limit the number of tables in a join because the more tables that you join, the longer SQL Server takes to process your query.

Additional information on the following topics is available in SQL Server Books Online.

Topic	Search on
Working with joins	"join fundamentals"
	"using multiple tables"

Lab A: Querying Multiple Tables

Objectives

After completing this lab, you will be able to:

- Join tables by using different join types.
- Combine result sets by using the UNION operator.

Prerequisites

Before working on this lab, you must have:

- Answer files for this lab, which are located in C:\Moc\2071\Labfiles\L05\Answers.
- The **library** database installed.

Lab Setup

None.

For More Information

If you require help in executing files, search SQL Query Analyzer Help for "Execute a query".

Other resources that you can use include:

- The **library** database schema.
- Microsoft SQL Server Books Online.

Scenario

The organization of the classroom is meant to simulate a worldwide trading firm named Northwind Traders. Its fictitious domain name is nwtraders.msft. The primary DNS server for nwtraders.msft is the instructor computer, which has an Internet Protocol (IP) address of 192.168.x.200 (where x is the assigned classroom number). The name of the instructor computer is London.

The following table provides the user name, computer name, and the IP address for each student computer in the fictitious nwtraders.msft domain. Find the user name for your computer and make a note of it.

User name	Computer name	IP address
SQLAdmin1	Vancouver	192.168.x.1
SQLAdmin2	Denver	192.168.x.2
SQLAdmin3	Perth	192.168.x.3
SQLAdmin4	Brisbane	192.168.x.4
SQLAdmin5	Lisbon	192.168.x.5
SQLAdmin6	Bonn	192.168.x.6
SQLAdmin7	Lima	192.168.x.7
SQLAdmin8	Santiago	192.168.x.8
SQLAdmin9	Bangalore	192.168.x.9
SQLAdmin10	Singapore	192.168.x.10
SQLAdmin11	Casablanca	192.168.x.11
SQLAdmin12	Tunis	192.168.x.12
SQLAdmin13	Acapulco	192.168.x.13
SQLAdmin14	Miami	192.168.x.14
SQLAdmin15	Auckland	192.168.x.15
SQLAdmin16	Suva	192.168.x.16
SQLAdmin17	Stockholm	192.168.x.17
SQLAdmin18	Moscow	192.168.x.18
SQLAdmin19	Caracas	192.168.x.19
SQLAdmin20	Montevideo	192.168.x.20
SQLAdmin21	Manila	192.168.x.21
SQLAdmin22	Tokyo	192.168.x.22
SQLAdmin23	Khartoum	192.168.x.23
SQLAdmin24	Nairobi	192.168.x.24

Estimated time to complete this lab: 45 minutes

Exercise 1
Joining Tables

In this exercise, you will write and execute queries that join tables in the **library** database. C:\Moc\2071\Labfiles\L05\Answers contains completed scripts for this exercise.

▶ **To create a mailing list by using a join**

In this procedure, you will create a mailing list of library members that includes the members' full names and complete address information. Answer_Mailing.sql is a completed script for this procedure.

1. Log on to the **NWTraders** classroom domain by using the information in the following table.

Option	Value
User name	**SQLAdmin**x (where x corresponds to your computer name as designated in the nwtraders.msft classroom domain)
Password	**Password**

2. Open SQL Query Analyzer and, if requested, log in to the (local) server with Microsoft Windows® Authentication.

   You have permission to log in to and administer SQL Server 2000 because you are logged as **SQLAdmin**x, which is a member of the Windows 2000 local group, Administrators. All members of this group are automatically mapped to the SQL Server **sysadmin** role.

3. In the **DB** list, click **library**.

4. Write a query on the **member** and **adult** tables that returns the **firstname**, **middleinitial**, **lastname**, **street**, **city**, **state**, and **zip** values. Concatenate the **firstname**, **middleinitial** and **lastname** columns into one string and alias the column as **name**.

5. Execute the query to verify that it returns the desired results.

Result

Your result will look similar to the following partial result set.

name	street	city	state	zip
Amy A Anderson	Bowery Estates	Montgomery	AL	36100
Brian A Anderson	Dogwood Drive	Sacramento	CA	94203
Daniel A Anderson	Fir Street	Washington	DC	20510-0001
Eva A Anderson	The Highlands	Atlanta	GA	30026
Gary A Anderson	James Road	Springfield	IL	62700
.				
.				
.				

5000 row(s) affected

▶ **To join several tables and order the results**

In this procedure, you will write and execute a query on the **title**, **item**, and **copy** tables that returns the **isbn**, **copy_no**, **on_loan**, **title**, **translation**, and **cover**, and values for rows in the **copy** table with an ISBN of 1 (one), 500 (five hundred), or 1000 (one thousand). Order the results by the **isbn** column.

Answer_Serveral.sql is a completed script for this procedure.

1. Write the select list of the query. Qualify the name of each column with a table alias of at least two characters (for example, **ti.title_no** for **title.title_no**).

2. Write a FROM clause that creates a inner join between the **title** and **copy** tables on the **title_no** columns. Set up the table aliases in the FROM clause that you used in the select list.

3. Add a second INNER JOIN clause to create a join between the **item** and **copy** tables on the **isbn** columns.

4. Compose a WHERE clause to restrict the rows that are retrieved from the **copy** table to those with an ISBN of 1 (one), 500 (five hundred), or 1000 (one thousand).

5. Write the ORDER BY clause to sort the result by ISBN.

6. Execute the script.

7. Execute the query to verify that it returns the desired results.

Result

Your result will look similar to the following partial result set.

isbn	copy_no	on_loan	title	translation	cover
1	1	N	Last of the Mohicans	ARABIC	HARDBACK
1	2	N	Last of the Mohicans	ARABIC	HARDBACK
1	3	N	Last of the Mohicans	ARABIC	HARDBACK
1	4	N	Last of the Mohicans	ARABIC	HARDBACK

.
.
.

(30 row(s) affected)

▶ **To join multiple tables by using an outer join**

In this procedure, you will write and execute a query to retrieve the member's full name and **member_no** from the **member** table and the **isbn** and **log_date** values from the **reservation** table for member numbers 250, 341, and 1675. Order the results by **member_no**. You should show information for these members, even if they have no books on reserve.

Answer_LeftOuter.sql is a completed script for this procedure.

1. Write the select list of the query:

   a. Create the **name** column by concatenating the **lastname**, **firstname**, and **middleinitial** for each member.

   b. Create the **date** column by converting the **log_date** to the **char(8)** data type.

2. Write a FROM clause that creates an left outer join between the **member** and **reservation** tables on the **member_no** columns.

3. Compose a WHERE clause to retrieve member numbers 250, 341, and 1675 from the **member** table.

4. Write the ORDER BY clause to sort the result by the member numbers.

5. Execute the query to verify that it returns the desired results.

   Which members have no books on reserve?

   _____

   _____

Result

Your results will look similar to the following partial result set.

member_no	Name	isbn	Date
250	Hightower, Michael A	NULL	NULL
341	Martin, Brian A	43	11/21/98
341	Martin, Brian A	330	11/21/98
341	Martin, Brian A	617	11/21/98
341	Martin, Brian A	904	11/21/98
1675	LaBrie, Joshua B	NULL	NULL

6 row(s) affected)

Exercise 2
Using the UNION Operator to Combine Result Sets

In this exercise, you will produce a single result set by using the UNION operator to concatenate the results of two similar SELECT statements. C:\Moc\2071\Labfiles\L05\Answers contains completed scripts for this exercise.

▶ **To determine which members living in Arizona have more than two children with library cards**

In this procedure, you will determine which members living in Arizona have more than two children with library cards. Answer_Union1.sql is a completed script for this procedure.

1. Write a SELECT statement that returns **member_no** and the number of juvenile records that each member has in a calculated field called **numkids**. Only return records for library members living in Arizona that have more than two kids.

2. Execute the query to verify that it returns the desired results. Note how many rows are returned.

3. Do not erase the query.

▶ **To determine which members living in California have more than three children with library cards**

In this procedure, you will determine which members living in California have more than three children with library cards. Answer_Union2.sql is a completed script for this procedure.

1. Press CTRL+N, and create a new query window.

2. Copy the query from the first procedure of this exercise and paste it into the new query window.

3. Modify the query in step 2 such so that it only returns records for library members living in California that have more than three children with library cards.

4. Execute the query to verify that it returns the desired results. Note how many rows are returned.

▶ **To combine the result sets of separate queries**

In this procedure, you will combine the result sets of separate queries. Answer_Union3.sql is a completed script for this procedure.

1. Press CTRL+N, and create a new query window.

2. Copy the query from the first procedure of this exercise and paste it into the new window.

3. Add the UNION statement on a new line at the end of the query.

4. Copy the query from the second procedure of this exercise and paste it into the new window on the line following the UNION statement that you add in step 3 in this procedure.

5. Execute the query to verify that it returns the desired results. Note how many rows are returned.

   How does the number of rows that this query returns compare to the number of rows that the queries in the first two procedures return?

   _____

   _____

Review

■ **Using Aliases for Table Names**

■ **Combining Data from Multiple Tables**

■ **Combining Multiple Result Sets**

The Duluth Mutual Life health care organization has a database that tracks information about doctors and their patients. The database includes the following tables.

Doctor table

Column	Data type and constraints
doc_id	char(9), PRIMARY KEY
fname	char(20)
lname	char(25)
specialty	char(25)
phone	char(10)

Patient table

Column	Data type and constraints
pat_id	char(9), PRIMARY KEY
fname	char(20)
lname	char(25)
insurance_company	char(25)
phone	char(10)

Casefile table

Column	Data type and constraints
admission_date	datetime, PRIMARY KEY (composite)
pat_id	char(9), PRIMARY KEY (composite), FOREIGN KEY to patient.pat_id
doc_id	char(9), FOREIGN KEY to doctor.doc_id
diagnosis	varchar(150)

Based on this table structure, answer the following questions.

1. How can you generate a list of patient names and hospital admission dates?

2. How can you generate a list of patient names for a particular doctor?

3. How can you produce a list of pairs of doctors who have the same specialty?

4. How can you produce a single list of names and phone numbers for both doctors and patients?

Microsoft®
Training & Certification

Module 6: Working with Subqueries

Contents

Microsoft®

Overview

- Introduction to Subqueries
- Using a Subquery as a Derived Table
- Using a Subquery as an Expression
- Using a Subquery to Correlate Data
- Using the EXISTS and NOT EXISTS Clauses

This module presents advanced query techniques, which include nested and correlated subqueries, and how they can be used to modify data. It describes when and how to use a subquery and how to use subqueries to break down and perform complex queries.

At the end of this module, you will be able to:

- Describe when and how to use a subquery.
- Use subqueries to break down and perform complex queries.

Introduction to Subqueries

- **Why to Use Subqueries**
  - To break down a complex query into a series of logical steps
  - To answer a query that relies on the results of an other query
- **Why to Use Joins Rather Than Subqueries**
  - SQL Server executes joins faster than subqueries
- **How to Use Subqueries**

A *subquery* is a SELECT statement nested inside a SELECT, INSERT, UPDATE, or DELETE statement or inside another subquery. Often you can rewrite subqueries as joins and use subqueries in place of an expression.

An *expression* is a combination of identifiers, values, and operators that SQL Server evaluates to obtain a result.

Why to Use Subqueries

You use subqueries to break down a complex query into a series of logical steps and, as a result, to solve a problem with a single statement. Subqueries are useful when your query relies on the results of another query.

Why to Use Joins Rather Than Subqueries

Often, a query that contains subqueries can be written as a join. Query performance may be similar with a join and a subquery. The query optimizer usually optimizes subqueries so that it uses the sample execution plan that a semantically equivalent join would use. The difference is that a subquery may require the query optimizer to perform additional steps, such as sorting, which may influence the processing strategy.

Using joins typically allows the query optimizer to retrieve data in the most efficient way. If a query does not require multiple steps, it may not be necessary to use a subquery.

How to Use Subqueries

When you decide to use subqueries, consider the following facts and guidelines:

- You must enclose subqueries in parentheses.

- You can use a subquery in place of an expression as long as a single value or list of values is returned. You can use a subquery that returns a multi-column record set in place of a table or to perform the same function as a join.

- You cannot use subqueries that retrieve columns that contain **text** and **image** data types.

- You can have subqueries within subqueries, nesting up to 32 levels. The limit varies based on available memory and the complexity of other expressions in the query. Individual queries may not support nesting up to 32 levels.

Using a Subquery as a Derived Table

- Is a Recordset Within a Query That Functions as a Table
- Takes the Place of a Table in the FROM Clause
- Is Optimized with the Rest of the Query

```
USE northwind
SELECT T.orderid, T.customerid
 FROM ( SELECT orderid, customerid
         FROM orders ) AS T
GO
```

You create a *derived table* by using a subquery in place of a table in a FROM clause. A derived table is a special use of a subquery in a FROM clause to which an alias or user-specified name refers. The result set of the subquery in the FROM clause forms a table that the outer SELECT statement uses.

Example

This example uses a subquery to create a derived table in the inner part of the query that the outer part queries. The derived table itself is functionally equivalent to the whole query, but it is separated for illustrative purposes.

```
USE northwind
SELECT T.orderid, T.customerid
 FROM ( SELECT orderid, customerid
         FROM orders ) AS T
GO
```

When used as a derived table, consider that a subquery:

- Is a recordset within a query that functions as a table.
- Takes the place of a table in the FROM clause.
- Is optimized with the rest of the query.

Using a Subquery as an Expression

- **Is Evaluated and Treated as an Expression**

- **Is Executed Once for the Query**

```
USE pubs
SELECT title, price
     ,( SELECT AVG(price) FROM titles) AS average
     ,price-(SELECT AVG(price) FROM titles) AS difference
 FROM titles
 WHERE type='popular_comp'
GO
```

In Transact-SQL, you can substitute a subquery wherever you use an expression. The subquery must evaluate to a scalar value, or to a single column list of values. Subqueries that return a list of values replace an expression in a WHERE clause that contains the IN keyword.

When used as an expression, consider that a subquery:

- Is evaluated and treated as an expression. The query optimizer often evaluates an expression as equivalent to a join connecting to a table that has one row.

- Is executed once for the entire statement.

Example

This example returns the price of a popular computer book, the average price of all books, and the difference between the price of the book and the average price of all books.

```
USE pubs
SELECT title, price
     ,(SELECT AVG(price) FROM titles) AS average
     ,price-(SELECT AVG(price) FROM titles) AS difference
 FROM titles
 WHERE type='popular_comp'
GO
```

◆ Using a Subquery to Correlate Data

- **Evaluating a Correlated Subquery**
- **Mimicking a JOIN Clause**
- **Mimicking a HAVING Clause**

You can use a correlated subquery as a dynamic expression that changes for each row of an outer query.

The query processor performs the subquery for each row in the outer query, one row at a time, which is in turn evaluated as an expression for that row and passed to the outer query. The correlated subquery is effectively a JOIN between the dynamically executed subquery and the row from the outer query.

You can typically rewrite a query in a number of ways and still obtain the same results. Correlated subqueries break down complex queries into two or more simple, related queries.

Tip You can easily recognize correlated subqueries. A column from a table inside the subquery is compared to a column from a table outside the subquery.

Evaluating a Correlated Subquery

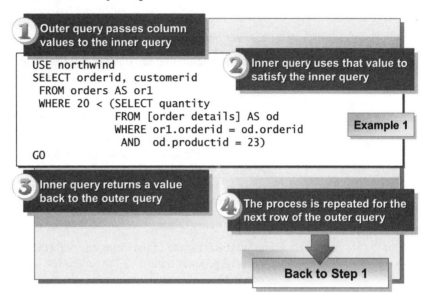

When you create a correlated subquery, the inner subqueries are evaluated repeatedly, once for each row of the outer query:

- SQL Server executes the inner query for each row that the outer query selects.

- SQL Server compares the results of the subquery to the results outside the subquery.

Example 1

This example returns a list of customers who ordered more than 20 pieces of product number 23.

```
USE northwind
SELECT orderid, customerid
 FROM orders AS or1
 WHERE 20 < (SELECT quantity
             FROM [order details] AS od
             WHERE or1.orderid = od.orderid
             AND od.productid = 23)
GO
```

Result

orderid	customerid
10337	FRANK
10348	WANDK
10396	FRANK
10402	ERNSH
10462	CONSH
.	
.	
.	

(11 row(s) affected)

Correlated subqueries return a single value or a list of values for each row specified by the FROM clause of the outer query. The following steps describe how the correlated subquery is evaluated in example 1:

1. The outer query passes a column value to the inner query.

    The column value that the outer query passes to the inner query is the **orderid**. The outer query passes the first **orderid** in the **orders** table to the inner query.

2. The inner query uses the values that the outer query passes.

    Each **orderid** in the **orders** table is evaluated to determine whether an identical **orderid** is found in the **order details** table. If the first **orderid** matches an **orderid** in the **order details** table and that **orderid** purchased product number 23, then the inner query returns that **orderid** to the outer query.

3. The inner query returns a value back to the outer query.

    The WHERE clause of the outer query further evaluates the **orderid** that purchased product number 23 to determine whether the quantity ordered exceeds 20.

4. The process is repeated for the next row of the outer query.

    The outer query passes the second **orderid** in the **orders** table to the inner query, and SQL Server repeats the evaluation process for that row.

Example 2

This example returns a list of products and the largest order ever placed for each product in the **order details** table. Notice that this correlated subquery references the same table as the outer query; the optimizer will generally treat this as a self-join.

```
USE northwind
SELECT DISTINCT productid, quantity
 FROM [order details] AS ord1
 WHERE quantity = ( SELECT MAX(quantity)
                      FROM [order details] AS ord2
                      WHERE ord1.productid = ord2.productid )
GO
```

Result

productid	quantity
50	40
67	40
4	50
9	50
11	50
.	
.	
.	

(77 row(s) affected)

Mimicking a JOIN Clause

- ■ **Correlated Subqueries Can Produce the Same Result as a JOIN Clause**

- ■ **Joins Let the Query Optimizer Determine How to Correlate Data Most Efficiently**

Example 1

```
USE pubs
SELECT DISTINCT t1.type
 FROM titles AS t1
 WHERE t1.type IN
   (SELECT t2.type
     FROM titles AS t2
     WHERE t1.pub_id <> t2.pub_id)
GO
```

You can use a correlated subquery to produce the same results as a JOIN, for example, selecting data from a table referenced in the outer query.

Note You usually can rephrase correlated subqueries as joins. Using joins rather than correlated subqueries allows the query optimizer to determine the most efficient way to correlate the data.

Example 1

This example uses a correlated subquery to find the types of books published by more than one publisher. To prevent ambiguity, aliases are required to distinguish the two different roles in which the **titles** table appears.

```
USE pubs
SELECT DISTINCT t1.type
 FROM titles AS t1
 WHERE t1.type IN
   (SELECT t2.type
     FROM titles AS t2
     WHERE t1.pub_id <> t2.pub_id)
GO
```

Result

Type
business
psychology

(2 row(s) affected)

Example 2

This example returns the same results as example 1 by using a self-join instead of a correlated subquery.

```
USE pubs
SELECT DISTINCT t1.type
 FROM titles AS t1
 INNER JOIN titles AS t2
  ON t1.type = t2.type
 WHERE t1.pub_id <> t2.pub_id
GO
```

Mimicking a HAVING Clause

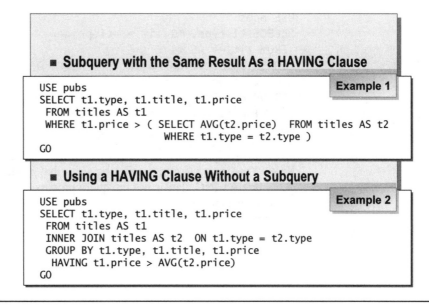

- **Subquery with the Same Result As a HAVING Clause**

```
USE pubs
SELECT t1.type, t1.title, t1.price                    Example 1
 FROM titles AS t1
  WHERE t1.price > ( SELECT AVG(t2.price)  FROM titles AS t2
                       WHERE t1.type = t2.type )
 GO
```

- **Using a HAVING Clause Without a Subquery**

```
USE pubs
SELECT t1.type, t1.title, t1.price                    Example 2
 FROM titles AS t1
  INNER JOIN titles AS t2  ON t1.type = t2.type
  GROUP BY t1.type, t1.title, t1.price
   HAVING t1.price > AVG(t2.price)
 GO
```

You can use a correlated subquery to produce the same results as a query that uses the HAVING clause.

Example 1

This example finds all titles that have a price greater than the average price for books of the same type. For each possible value of **t1**, SQL Server evaluates the subquery and includes the row in the results if the price value of that row is greater than the calculated average. It is not necessary to group by type explicitly, because the rows for which average price is calculated are restricted by the WHERE clause in the subquery.

```
USE pubs
SELECT t1.type, t1.title, t1.price
 FROM titles AS t1
  WHERE t1.price > ( SELECT AVG(t2.price)
                      FROM titles AS t2
                      WHERE t1.type = t2.type )
GO
```

Resulttype	title
Business	The Busy Executive's Database Guide
Business	Straight Talk About Computers
mod_cook	Silicon Valley Gastronomic Treats
popular_comp	But Is It User Friendly?
Psychology	Computer Phobic AND Non-Phobic Individuals: Behavior Variations
Psychology	Prolonged Data Deprivation: Four Case Studies
trad_cook	Onions, Leeks, and Garlic: Cooking Secrets of the Mediterranean

(7 row(s) affected)

Example 2

This example produces the same result set as example 1, but uses a self-join with GROUP BY and HAVING clauses.

```
USE pubs
SELECT t1.type, t1.title, t1.price
 FROM titles AS t1
 INNER JOIN titles AS t2
  ON t1.type = t2.type
 GROUP BY t1.type, t1.title, t1.price
  HAVING t1.price > AVG(t2.price)
GO
```

Note You can write correlated subqueries that produce the same results as a JOIN or HAVING clause, but the query processor may not implement them in the same manner.

Using the EXISTS and NOT EXISTS Clauses

- **Use with Correlated Subqueries**

- **Determine Whether Data Exists in a List of Values**

- **SQL Server Process**

  - Outer query tests for the existence of rows

  - Inner query returns TRUE or FALSE

  - No data is produced

Example 1

```
USE northwind
SELECT lastname, employeeid
 FROM employees AS e
 WHERE EXISTS (SELECT * FROM orders AS o
                  WHERE e.employeeid = o.employeeid
                  AND   o.orderdate = '9/5/97')
GO
```

You can use the EXISTS and NOT EXISTS operators to determine whether data exists in a list of values.

Use with Correlated Subqueries

Use the EXISTS and NOT EXISTS operators with correlated subqueries to restrict the result set of an outer query to rows that satisfy the subquery. The EXISTS and NOT EXISTS operators return TRUE or FALSE, based on whether rows are returned for subqueries.

Determine Whether Data Exists in a List of Values

When a subquery is introduced with the EXISTS operator, SQL Server tests whether data that matches the subquery exists. No rows are actually retrieved. SQL Server terminates the retrieval of rows when it knows that at least one row satisfies the WHERE condition in the subquery.

SQL Server Process

When SQL Server processes subqueries that use the EXISTS or NOT EXISTS operator:

- The outer query tests for the existence of rows that the subquery returns.

- The subquery returns either a TRUE or FALSE value based on the given condition in the query.

- The subquery does not produce any data.

Partial Syntax

WHERE [NOT] EXISTS (*subquery*)

Example 1

This example uses a correlated subquery with an EXISTS operator in the WHERE clause to return a list of employees who took orders on 4/10/2000.

```
USE northwind
SELECT lastname, employeeid
 FROM employees AS e
 WHERE EXISTS ( SELECT * FROM orders AS o
                     WHERE e.employeeid = o.employeeid
                     AND o.orderdate = '9/5/1997' )
GO
```

Result

lastname	employeeid
Peacock	4
King	7

(2 row(s) affected)

Example 2

This example returns the same result set as example 1 and shows that you could use a join operation rather than a correlated subquery. Note that the query needs the DISTINCT keyword to return only a single row for each employee.

```
USE northwind
SELECT DISTINCT lastname, e.employeeid
 FROM orders AS o
 INNER JOIN employees AS e
  ON o.employeeid = e.employeeid
 WHERE o.orderdate = '9/5/1997'
GO
```

Result

lastname	employeeid
Peacock	4
King	7

(2 row(s) affected)

Recommended Practices

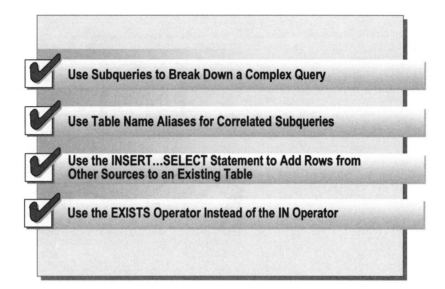

- Use Subqueries to Break Down a Complex Query
- Use Table Name Aliases for Correlated Subqueries
- Use the INSERT...SELECT Statement to Add Rows from Other Sources to an Existing Table
- Use the EXISTS Operator Instead of the IN Operator

The following recommended practices should help you perform advanced queries:

- Use subqueries to break down a complex query. You can solve a problem with a single statement by using subqueries. Subqueries are useful when your query relies on the results of another query.

- Use table name aliases for correlated subqueries. SQL Server requires that aliases be used to reference the ambiguous table names in order to distinguish between the inner and outer tables.

- Use the INSERT...SELECT statement to add rows from other sources to an existing table. Using the INSERT...SELECT statement is more efficient than writing multiple, single-row INSERT statements.

- Use the EXISTS operator instead of the IN operator wherever possible so that it is not necessary to retrieve the full result set of the subquery.

Additional information on the following topics is available in SQL Server Books Online.

Topic	Search on
Using subqueries	"creating subqueries"
Correlating tables	"using table aliases"
	"creating table aliases"
Using a subquery instead of an expression	"subqueries used in place of an expression"

Lab A: Working with Subqueries

Objectives

After completing this lab, you will be able to:

- Use a subquery as a derived table.
- Use a subquery as an expression.
- Use a subquery to correlate data.

Prerequisites

Before working on this lab, you must have:

- Script files for this lab, which are located in C:\Moc\2071\Labfiles\L06.
- Answer files for this lab, which are located in C:\Moc\2071\Labfiles\L06\Answers.
- The **library** database installed.

Lab Setup

None.

For More Information

If you require help in executing files, search SQL Query Analyzer Help for "Execute a query".

Other resources that you can use include:

- The **library** database schema.
- SQL Server Books Online.

Scenario

The organization of the classroom is meant to simulate that of a worldwide trading firm named Northwind Traders. Its fictitious domain name is nwtraders.msft. The primary DNS server for nwtraders.msft is the instructor computer, which has an Internet Protocol (IP) address of 192.168.x.200 (where x is the assigned classroom number). The name of the instructor computer is London.

The following table provides the user name, computer name, and IP address for each student computer in the fictitious nwtraders.msft domain. Find the user name for your computer, and make a note of it.

User name	Computer name	IP address
SQLAdmin1	Vancouver	192.168.x.1
SQLAdmin2	Denver	192.168.x.2
SQLAdmin3	Perth	192.168.x.3
SQLAdmin4	Brisbane	192.168.x.4
SQLAdmin5	Lisbon	192.168.x.5
SQLAdmin6	Bonn	192.168.x.6
SQLAdmin7	Lima	192.168.x.7
SQLAdmin8	Santiago	192.168.x.8
SQLAdmin9	Bangalore	192.168.x.9
SQLAdmin10	Singapore	192.168.x.10
SQLAdmin11	Casablanca	192.168.x.11
SQLAdmin12	Tunis	192.168.x.12
SQLAdmin13	Acapulco	192.168.x.13
SQLAdmin14	Miami	192.168.x.14
SQLAdmin15	Auckland	192.168.x.15
SQLAdmin16	Suva	192.168.x.16
SQLAdmin17	Stockholm	192.168.x.17
SQLAdmin18	Moscow	192.168.x.18
SQLAdmin19	Caracas	192.168.x.19
SQLAdmin20	Montevideo	192.168.x.20
SQLAdmin21	Manila	192.168.x.21
SQLAdmin22	Tokyo	192.168.x.22
SQLAdmin23	Khartoum	192.168.x.23
SQLAdmin24	Nairobi	192.168.x.24

Estimated time to complete this lab: 30 minutes

Exercise 1
Using a Subquery as a Derived Table

In this exercise, you will write a query that uses a derived table and joins the derived table to another table. You will also separate the query into individual steps to show how a derived table is processed. C:\Moc\2071\Labfiles\L06\Answers contains completed scripts for this exercise.

▶ **To execute a query that uses a derived table**

In this procedure, you will write and execute a query that uses a derived table and returns the **juvenile.adult_member_no** column and the number of juveniles for each adult member who has more than three juvenile members.

Answer_DerivedTab.sql is a completed script for this procedure.

1. Log on to the **NWTraders** classroom domain by using the information in the following table.

Option	Value
User name	**SQLAdminx** (where *x* corresponds to your computer name as designated in the nwtraders.msft classroom domain)
Password	**Password**

2. Open SQL Query Analyzer and, if requested, log in to the (local) server with Microsoft Windows® Authentication.

   You have permission to log in to and administer SQL Server because you are logged as **SQLAdminx**, which is a member of the Windows 2000 local group, Administrators. All members of this group are automatically mapped to the SQL Server **sysadmin** role.

3. In the **DB** list, click **library**.

4. Type the following query that uses a derived table.

```
USE library
SELECT d.adult_member_no, a.expr_date, d.No_Of_Children
 FROM adult AS a
 INNER JOIN (
         SELECT adult_member_no, COUNT(*) AS No_Of_Children
          FROM juvenile
          GROUP BY adult_member_no
          HAVING COUNT(*) > 3
          ) AS d
   ON a.member_no = d.adult_member_no
GO
```

5. Execute the query to verify that it returns the desired results.

Result

Your result will look similar to the following result set. The number of rows returned may vary.

adult_member_no	expr_date	No_Of_Children
1	2000-06-22 12:43:51.800	4
3	2000-06-24 12:43:51.800	4
67	2000-06-27 12:43:51.800	4

(248 row(s) affected)

Note When you answer questions later in this exercise, remember that this is the result set of the original derived table query.

▶ **To write the derived table query as two separate queries**

In this procedure, you will rewrite and execute the previous query as two separate queries to show how the query that uses a derived table is processed.

1. Type the following query that returns the **adult_member_no** column data, calculates the number of children that each adult member has, and returns only the rows containing adult members that have more than three children from the **juvenile** table.

```
USE library
SELECT adult_member_no, COUNT(*) AS No_Of_Children
 FROM juvenile
 GROUP BY adult_member_no
 HAVING COUNT(*) > 3
GO
```

2. Execute the query to verify that it returns the desired results.

Result

Your result will look similar to the following result set. The number of rows returned may vary.

Adult_member_no	No_Of_Children
1	4
3	4
5	4

(248 row(s) affected)

3. Compare the results of the query in step 1 of this procedure and the original derived table query from the previous procedure.

What are the similarities between the two results?

_____

_____

4. Type the following query that retrieves the **expr_date** column data from the **adult** table.

```
USE library
SELECT a.expr_date
 FROM adult AS a
GO
```

5. Execute the query to verify that it returns the desired results.

Result

Your result will look similar to the following result set.

```
expr_date
2000-06-22 12:43:51.800
2000-06-24 12:43:51.800
2000-06-26 12:43:51.800

(5000  row(s) affected)
```

6. Compare the results of the query in step 4 of this procedure and the original derived table query.

What are the similarities between the two results?

_____

_____

What are the differences between the two results?

_____

_____

▶ **To rewrite the derived table query by using a join**

In this procedure, you will rewrite and execute the original derived table query as a join of two separate queries to show that you can obtain the same results as using a derived table.

1. Type the following query.

```
USE library
SELECT j.adult_member_no, a.expr_date
       ,COUNT(*) AS No_Of_Children
 FROM adult AS a
 INNER JOIN juvenile AS j
  ON a.member_no = j.adult_member_no
 GROUP BY adult_member_no, expr_date
 HAVING COUNT(*) > 3
GO
```

2. Execute the query to verify that it returns the desired results.

Result

Your result will look similar to the following result set. The number of rows returned may vary.

adult_member_no	expr_date	No_Of_Children
1	2000-06-22 12:43:51.800	4
3	2000-06-24 12:43:51.800	4
5	2000-06-27 12:43:51.800	4

```
(248 row(s) affected)
```

3. Compare the results of the query in step 1 of this procedure and the results of the original derived table query.

   Do both queries return the same results?

   _____

   _____

Exercise 2
Using a Subquery as an Expression

In this exercise, you will write queries that use single values and multiple values to restrict the result sets of the outer query and to combine multiple processing steps into one SELECT statement. C:\Moc\2071\Labfiles\L06\Answers contains completed scripts for this exercise.

▶ To use a single-value subquery

In this procedure, you will write and execute a query that returns **member.firstname, member.lastname, loanhist.isbn**, and **loanhist.fine_paid** for members who have paid the highest recorded fines for all books. Answer_Highpay.sql is a completed script for this procedure.

1. Write a query that returns the largest recorded value in the **loanhist.fine_paid** column.

2. Execute the query to verify that it returns the desired results.

Result

Your result will look similar to the following result set.

```
8.0000

(1 row(s) affected)

Warning: Null value is eliminated by an aggregate or
other SET operation.
```

▶ To use a single-value subquery as part of a search condition

In this procedure, you will use a single-value subquery as part of a search condition.

1. Write a query that joins the **member** and **loanhist** tables and returns the **firstname, lastname, isbn**, and **fine_paid** for each row.

2. Use the query from step 1 of the previous procedure as selection criteria in the WHERE clause to return only those rows from the join in which the fine that is paid equals the largest value that was ever recorded for all books.

3. Include the DISTINCT keyword in your query to eliminate entries for members who have paid this fine on several occasions.

4. Execute the query to verify that it returns the desired results.

Result

Your result will look similar to the following result set. The number of rows returned may vary.

Firstname	lastname	isbn	fine_paid
Michael	Nash	883	8.0000
Robert	Rothenberg	330	8.0000

(2 row(s) affected)

Warning: Null value is eliminated by an aggregate or other SET operation.

▶ **To use a query to make a list of values**

In this procedure, you will write and execute a query on the **title**, **loan**, and **reservation** tables that returns four columns: **title_no**, **title**, **isbn**, and **Total Reserved**. The **Total Reserved** column is the per-isbn (book) count of books on reserve with more than 50 reservations and less than five copies of the book. Group the results by **title_no**, **title**, and **isbn**. Answer_SubqIn.sql is a completed script for this procedure.

1. Write a query that returns the isbn numbers of books from the **reservations** table that have more than fifty reservations.

2. Execute the query to verify that it returns the desired results.

Result

Your result will look similar to the following partial result set. The number of rows returned may vary.

Isbn
1
43
246
288
330
.
.
.

(11 row(s) affected)

▶ **To use a multiple-value subquery**

1. Write an outer query that returns the **title_no**, **title**, **isbn**, and **Total Reserved** columns in which the **Total Reserved** column is the number of records for each group of **title_no**, **title**, and **isbn**. To do this:

   a. Restrict the rows that form the groups in the outer query by specifying books that have less than five copies.

   b. Use the IN keyword as part of the WHERE clause against the list of values generated by the query in step 1 of the previous procedure.

2. Execute the query to verify that it returns the desired results.

Result

Your result will look similar to the following partial result set. The number of rows returned may vary.

title_no	Title	isbn	Total Reserved
1	Last of the Mohicans	1	197
25	The Black Tulip	246	196
33	The First 100,000 Prime Numbers	330	196
.			
.			
.			

8 row(s) affected)

Exercise 3
Using a Subquery to Correlate Data

In this exercise, you will write queries that use correlated subqueries to restrict the result set of the outer query and to combine multiple processing steps into one SELECT statement. C:\Moc\2071\Labfiles\L06\Answers contains completed scripts for this exercise.

▶ **To use a correlated subquery**

In this procedure, you will create a query that uses a correlated subquery to calculate a value, based on data from the outer query, and then uses that value as part of a comparison. You will query the **member** and **loanhist** tables to return a list of library members who have fines that total more than $5.00. A correlated subquery calculates the fines for each member. Answer_Fineof5.sql is a completed script for this procedure.

Note   You also can write this query with a join and a GROUP BY or HAVING clause instead of a correlated subquery. Answer_Finejoin.sql is a completed script for this alternate solution.

---

1. Write a query that returns the **member_no** and **lastname** columns of the **member** table, by using a table alias for the **member** table.

2. Execute the query to verify that it returns the desired results.

3. Write a query that calculates the total fines for each member as recorded in the **loanhist** table. To do this:

   a. Use an alias for the **loanhist** table.

   b. Correlate the **member.member_no** column of the outer query to the **loanhist.member_no** column of the inner query in a subquery.

   c. Use a comparison operator in the WHERE clause of the outer query to select those members who have fines that total more than $5.00.

4. Execute the query to verify that it returns the desired results.

Result

Your result will look similar to the following partial result set. The number of rows returned may vary.

member_no	lastname
204	Graff
372	Miksovsky
1054	Miksovsky
1094	O'Brian
.	
.	
.	

```
(41 row(s) affected)
```

```
Warning: Null value is eliminated by an aggregate or other
SET operation.
```

Review

■ Introduction to Subqueries

■ Using a Subquery as a Derived Table

■ Using a Subquery as an Expression

■ Using a Subquery to Correlate Data

■ Using the EXISTS and NOT EXISTS Clauses

Ask students whether they need clarification on any topic. The Duluth Mutual Life health care organization has a database that tracks information about doctors and their patients. The database includes the following tables.

Doctor table

Column	Data type and constraints
doc_id	char(9), PRIMARY KEY
fname	char(20)
lname	char(25)
specialty	char(25)
phone	char(10)

Patient table

Column	Data type and constraints
pat_id	char(9), PRIMARY KEY
fname	char(20)
lname	char(25)
insurance_company	char(25)
phone	char(10)

Casefile table

Column	Data type and constraints
admission_date	datetime, PRIMARY KEY (composite)
pat_id	char(9), PRIMARY KEY (composite), FOREIGN KEY to patient.pat_id
doc_id	char(9), FOREIGN KEY to doctor.doc_id
diagnosis	varchar(150)

Based on this table structure, answer the following questions.

1. How, with a single query, can you produce a list of all cases that were admitted on the first chronological date in the database?

2. You want to know the total number of hospital admissions, listed by patient name. How can you determine this? What are the advantages or disadvantages of your method?

Microsoft®
Training &
Certification

Module 7:
Module 7:
Modifying Data

Contents

Microsoft®

Overview

- **Using Transactions**
- **Inserting Data**
- **Deleting Data**
- **Updating Data**
- **Performance Considerations**

This module describes how transactions work and discusses how to write INSERT, DELETE, and UPDATE statements to modify data in tables.

At the end of this module, you will be able to:

- Describe how transactions work.

- Write INSERT, DELETE, and UPDATE statements to modify data in tables.

- Describe performance considerations related to modifying data.

Using Transactions

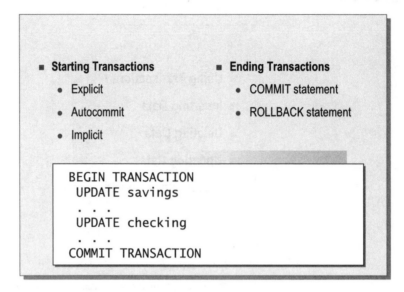

A *transaction* is a sequence of operations performed as a single logical unit of work. SQL programmers are responsible for starting and ending transactions at points that enforce the logical consistency of the data. The programmer must define the sequence of data modifications that leave the data in a consistent state relative to the organization's business rules.

Starting Transactions

You can start transactions in Microsoft® SQL Server™ 2000 in one of three modes—*explicit*, *autocommit*, or *implicit*.

- *Explicit* transactions start by issuing a BEGIN TRANSACTION statement.

- *Autocommit* transactions are the default for SQL Server. Each individual Transact-SQL statement is committed when it completes. You do not have to specify any statements to control transactions.

- *Implicit* transactions mode is set by an application programming interface (API) function or the Transact-SQL SET IMPLICIT_TRANSACTIONS ON statement. Using this mode, the next statement automatically starts a new transaction. When that transaction completes, the next Transact-SQL statement starts a new transaction.

The transaction mode is set on a session basis. If one session changes from one transaction mode to another, the change has no effect on the transaction mode session.

Ending Transactions

You can end transactions by using a COMMIT or ROLLBACK statement.

The COMMIT statement indicates that if a transaction is successful, SQL Server should commit it. A COMMIT statement guarantees that all of the transaction's modifications are permanently part of the database. A COMMIT statement also frees resources, such as locks, that the transaction uses.

The ROLLBACK statement cancels a transaction. It backs out all modifications made in the transaction by returning the data to the state in which it was at the start of the transaction. A ROLLBACK statement also frees resources held by the transaction. If a fatal error such as a deadlock occurs within a transaction, SQL Server automatically performs a ROLLBACK of the transaction in progress. Non-fatal errors, such as the violation of a CHECK constraint on UPDATE, will not cause an automatic ROLLBACK. For non-fatal errors, the developer must check @@ERROR after each statement, and issue an explicit ROLLBACK, and branch to the end of the transaction in this case.

Example

This example transfers $100 from a savings account to a checking account for a customer, by using a transaction. It will undo any data changes if there is an error at any point during the transaction.

```
BEGIN TRANSACTION

  UPDATE savings
   SET balance = balance - 100
   WHERE custid = 78910

  IF @@ERROR <> 0
   BEGIN
     RAISERROR ('Error, transaction not completed!', 16, -1)
     ROLLBACK TRANSACTION
   END

  UPDATE checking
   SET balance = balance + 100
   WHERE custid = 78910

  IF @@ERROR <> 0
   BEGIN
     RAISERROR ('Error, transaction not completed!', 16, -1)
     ROLLBACK TRANSACTION
   END

COMMIT TRANSACTION
```

Note This example is for illustration only, and will not produce results.

◆ Inserting Data

- **Inserting a Row of Data by Values**

- **Using the INSERT...SELECT Statement**

- **Creating a Table Using the SELECT INTO Statement**

- **Inserting Partial Data**

- **Inserting Data by Using Column Defaults**

You can insert data through a transaction by specifying a set of values or inserting the results of a SELECT statement. You can create a table and insert data simultaneously. You do not have to insert values into all data fields within a row.

Inserting a Row of Data by Values

- **Must Adhere to Destination Constraints or the INSERT Transaction Fails**

- **Use a Column List to Specify Destination Columns**

- **Specify a Corresponding List of Values**

```
USE northwind
INSERT customers
      (customerid, companyname, contactname, contacttitle
      ,address, city, region, postalcode, country, phone
      ,fax)

VALUES ('PECOF', 'Pecos Coffee Company', 'Michael Dunn'
        ,'Owner', '1900 Oak Street', 'Vancouver', 'BC'
        ,'V3F 2K1', 'Canada', '(604) 555-3392'
        ,'(604) 555-7293')
GO
```

The INSERT statement adds rows to a table.

Partial Syntax

INSERT [INTO]
  { *table_name* | *view_name*}
  { [(*column_list*)]
  { VALUES ({ DEFAULT | NULL| *expression*}[,...*n*])
  | DEFAULT VALUES

Use the INSERT statement with the VALUES clause to add rows to a table. When you insert rows, consider the following facts and guidelines:

- Must adhere to destination constraints or the INSERT transaction fails.

- Use the *column_list* to specify columns that will store each incoming value. You must enclose the *column_list* in parentheses and delimit it by commas. If you are supplying values for all columns, using the *column_list* is optional.

- Specify the data that you want to insert by using the VALUES clause. The VALUES clause is required for each column in the table or *column_list*.

  The column order and data type of new data must correspond to the table column order and data type. Many data types have an associated entry format. For example, character data and dates must be enclosed in single quotation marks.

Example

The following example adds Pecos Coffee Company as a new customer.

```
USE northwind
INSERT customers
      (customerid, companyname, contactname, contacttitle
      ,address, city, region, postalcode, country, phone
      ,fax)
VALUES ('PECOF', 'Pecos Coffee Company','Michael Dunn'
      ,'Owner', '1900 Oak Street', 'Vancouver', 'BC'
      ,'V3F 2K1', 'Canada', '(604) 555-3392'
      ,'(604) 555-7293')
GO
```

You can verify that Pecos Coffee Company has been added to the **customers** table by executing the following statement.

```
USE northwind
SELECT companyname, contactname
 FROM customers
 WHERE customerid = 'PECOF'
GO
```

Result

Companyname	contactname
Pecos Coffee Company	Michael Dunn

(1 row(s) affected)

Using the INSERT...SELECT Statement

- **All Rows That Satisfy the SELECT Statement Are Inserted**
- **Verify That the Table That Receives New Row Exists**
- **Ensure That Data Types Are Compatible**
- **Determine Whether Default Values Exist or Whether Null Values Are Allowed**

```
USE northwind
INSERT customers
 SELECT substring(firstname, 1, 3)
        + substring (lastname, 1, 2)
      ,lastname, firstname, title, address, city
      ,region, postalcode, country, homephone, NULL
  FROM employees
GO
```

The INSERT...SELECT statement adds rows to a table by inserting the result set of a SELECT statement.

Use the INSERT...SELECT statement to add rows to an existing table from other sources. Using the INSERT...SELECT statement is more efficient than writing multiple, single-row INSERT statements. When you use the INSERT...SELECT statement, consider the following facts and guidelines:

- All rows that satisfy the SELECT statement are inserted into the outermost table of the query.

- You must verify that the table that receives the new rows exists in the database.

- You must ensure that the columns of the table that receives the new values have data types compatible with the columns of the table source.

- You must determine whether a default value exists or whether a null value is allowed for any columns that are omitted. If null values are not allowed, you must provide values for these columns.

Syntax

INSERT *table_name*
    SELECT *column_list*
    FROM *table_list*
    WHERE *search_conditions*

Example

This example adds new customers to the **customers** table. Employees of Northwind Traders are eligible to buy company products. This query contains an INSERT statement with a SELECT clause that adds employee information to the **customers** table.

The new **customerid** column consists of the first three letters of the employee's first name, concatenated with the first two letters of the last name. The employee's last name is used as the new company name, and the first name is used as the contact name.

```
USE northwind
INSERT customers
 SELECT substring (firstname, 1, 3)
        + substring (lastname, 1, 2)
       ,lastname, firstname, title, address, city
       ,region, postalcode, country, homephone, NULL
 FROM employees
GO
```

Creating a Table Using the SELECT INTO Statement

- **Use to Create a Table and Insert Rows into the Table in a Single Operation**
- **Create a Local or Global Temporary Table**
- **Create Column Alias or Specify Column Names in the Select List for New Table**

```
USE northwind
SELECT productname AS products
       ,unitprice AS price
       ,(unitprice * 1.1) AS tax
 INTO #pricetable
 FROM products
GO
```

You can place the result set of any query into a new table by using the SELECT INTO statement.

Use the SELECT INTO statement to populate new tables in a database with imported data. You also can use the SELECT INTO statement to break down complex problems that require a data set from various sources. If you first create a temporary table, the queries that you execute on it are simpler than those you would execute on multiple tables or databases.

When you use the SELECT INTO statement, consider the following facts and guidelines:

- You can use the SELECT INTO statement to create a table and to insert rows into the table in a single operation.

  Ensure that the table name that is specified in the SELECT INTO statement is unique. If a table exists with the same name, the SELECT INTO statement fails.

- You can create a local or global temporary table.

  Create a local temporary table by preceding the table name with a number sign (#), or create a global temporary table by preceding the table name with a double number sign (##).

  A local temporary table is visible in the current session only. A global temporary table is visible to all sessions:

  - Space for a local temporary table is reclaimed when the user ends the session.

  - Space for a global temporary table is reclaimed when the session that created the table ends ,and the last Transact-SQL statement that referenced the table at that time completes.

- You must create column aliases or specify the column names of the new table in the select list.

Partial Syntax

SELECT *<select_list>*
  INTO *new_table*
  FROM {*<table_source>*}[,...*n*]
  WHERE *<search_condition>*

Example

This example creates a local temporary table based on a query made on the **products** table. Notice that you can use string and mathematical functions to manipulate the result set.

```
USE northwind
SELECT productname AS products
      ,unitprice AS price
      ,(unitprice * 1.1) AS tax
  INTO #pricetable
  FROM products
GO
```

To view your result set, you must execute the following query.

```
USE northwind
SELECT * FROM #pricetable
GO
```

Result

products	price	tax
Chai	18	19.8
Chang	19	20.9
Aniseed Syrup	10	11
Chef Anton's Cajun Seasoning	22	24.2
Chef Anton's Gumbo Mix	21.35	23.485
Grandma's Boysenberry Spread	27.5	30.25
Uncle Bob's Organic Dried Pears	33	36.3
Northwoods Cranberry Sauce	44	48.4
Mishi Kobe Niku	97	106.7
Ikura	31	34.1
Queso Cabrales	21	23.1
Queso Manchego La Pastora	38	41.8
Konbu	6	6.6
Tofu	23.25	25.575
Genen Shouyu	15.5	17.05

```
.

.

.
(77 row(s) affected)
```

Inserting Partial Data

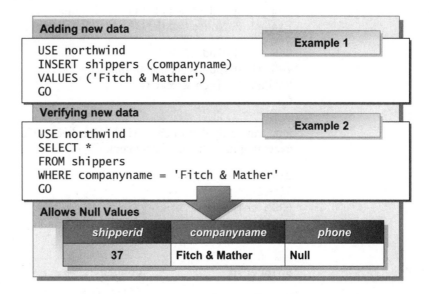

Adding new data

Example 1

```
USE northwind
INSERT shippers (companyname)
VALUES ('Fitch & Mather')
GO
```

Verifying new data

Example 2

```
USE northwind
SELECT *
FROM shippers
WHERE companyname = 'Fitch & Mather'
GO
```

Allows Null Values

shipperid	companyname	phone
37	Fitch & Mather	Null

If a column has a default value or accepts null values, you can omit the column from an INSERT statement. SQL Server automatically inserts the values.

When you insert partial data, consider the following facts and guidelines:

- List only the column names for the data that you are supplying in the INSERT statement.

- Specify the columns for which you are providing a value in the *column_list*. The data in the VALUES clause corresponds to the specified columns. Unnamed columns are filled in as if they had been named and a default value had been supplied.

- Do not specify columns in the *column_list* that have an IDENTITY property or that allow default or null values.

- Enter a null value explicitly by typing Null without single quotation marks.

Example 1

This example adds the company Fitch & Mather as a new shipper in the **shippers** table. Data is not entered for columns that have an IDENTITY property or that allow default or null values. Compare this example with Example 2. Notice that the DEFAULT keyword is omitted.

```
USE northwind
INSERT shippers (companyname)
VALUES ('Fitch & Mather')
GO
```

You can verify that Fitch & Mather has been added to the **shippers** table by executing the following statement.

```
USE northwind
SELECT *
FROM shippers
WHERE companyname = 'Fitch & Mather'
GO
```

Result

shipperid	companyname	phone
37	Fitch & Mather	NULL

(1 row(s) affected)

Example 2

This example also adds Fitch & Mather as a new shipper in the **shippers** table. Notice that the DEFAULT keyword is used for columns that allow default or null values. Compare this example to Example 1.

```
USE northwind
INSERT shippers (companyname, Phone)
VALUES ('Fitch & Mather', DEFAULT)
GO
```

Result

shipperid	companyname	phone
37	Fitch & Mather	NULL

(1 row(s) affected)

Inserting Data by Using Column Defaults

- **DEFAULT Keyword**
  - Inserts default values for specified columns
  - Columns must have a default value or allow null values

```
USE northwind
INSERT shippers (companyname, phone)
 VALUES ('Kenya Coffee Co.', DEFAULT)
GO
```

- **DEFAULT VALUES Keyword**
  - Inserts default values for all columns
  - Columns must have a default value or allow null values

When you insert rows into a table, you can save time when entering values by using the DEFAULT or DEFAULT VALUES keywords with the INSERT statement.

DEFAULT Keyword

When a table has default constraints, or when a column has a default value, use the DEFAULT keyword in the INSERT statement to have SQL Server supply the default value for you.

When you use the DEFAULT keyword, consider the following facts and guidelines:

- SQL Server inserts a null value for columns that allow null values and do not have default values.

- If you use the DEFAULT keyword, and the columns do not have default values or allow null values, the INSERT statement fails.

- You cannot use the DEFAULT keyword with a column that has the IDENTITY property (an automatically assigned, incremented value). Therefore, do not list columns with an IDENTITY property in the *column_list* or VALUES clause.

- SQL Server inserts the next appropriate value for columns that are defined with the **rowversion** data type.

Example

This example inserts a new row for the Kenya Coffee Company without using a *column_list*. The **shippers.shipperid** column has an IDENTITY property and is not included in the column list. The **phone** column allows null values.

```
USE northwind
INSERT shippers (companyname, phone)
 VALUES ('Kenya Coffee Co.', DEFAULT)
GO
```

You can verify that Kenya Coffee Co. has been added to the **shippers** table by executing the following statement.

```
USE northwind
SELECT *
 FROM shippers
 WHERE companyname = 'Kenya Coffee Co.'
GO
```

Result

shipperid	companyname	Phone
10	Kenya Coffee Co.	NULL

```
(1 row(s) affected)
```

DEFAULT VALUES Keyword

Use the DEFAULT VALUES keyword to insert an entire row into a table. When you use the DEFAULT VALUES keyword, consider the following facts and guidelines:

- SQL Server inserts a null value for columns that allow null values and do not have a default value.

- If you use the DEFAULT VALUES keyword, and the columns do not have default values or allow null values, the INSERT statement fails.

- SQL Server inserts the next appropriate value for columns with an IDENTITY property or a **rowversion** data type.

- Use the DEFAULT VALUES keyword to generate sample data and populate tables with default values.

◆ Deleting Data

- Using the DELETE Statement
- Using the TRUNCATE TABLE Statement
- Deleting Rows Based on Other Tables

You can specify the data that you want to delete.

The DELETE statement removes one or more rows from a table or view by using a transaction. You can specify which rows SQL Server deletes by filtering on the targeted table, or by using a JOIN clause or a subquery. The TRUNCATE TABLE statement is used to remove all rows from a table without using a transaction.

Using the DELETE Statement

- **The DELETE statement removes one or more rows in a table according to the WHERE clause condition, if specified**

- **Each Deleted Row Is Logged in the Transaction Log**

```
USE northwind
DELETE orders
 WHERE DATEDIFF(MONTH, shippeddate, GETDATE()) >= 6
GO
```

The DELETE statement removes rows from tables. Use the DELETE statement to remove one or more rows from a table.

Partial Syntax

DELETE [*from*] {*table_name*|*view_name*}
    WHERE *search_conditions*

Example

This example deletes all order records that are equal to or greater than six months old.

```
USE northwind
DELETE orders
 WHERE DATEDIFF(MONTH, shippeddate, GETDATE()) >= 6
GO
```

Note   This will not execute on the Northwind database, when the condition is true because it will violates the foreign key constraint between Orders and Order Details. Under normal circumstances, it is not possible to delete rows from a table or issue a truncate table statement on a table which has a foreign key constraint on it.

When you use the DELETE statement, consider the following facts:

- The DELETE statement removes one or more rows in a table, according to the WHERE clause condition, if specified; otherwise, DELETE removes all rows.

- Each deleted row is logged in the transaction log.

Using the TRUNCATE TABLE Statement

- **The TRUNCATE TABLE Statement Deletes All Rows in a Table**

- **SQL Server Retains Table Structure and Associated Objects**

- **Only Deallocation of Data Pages Is Logged in the Transaction Log**

```
USE northwind
TRUNCATE TABLE orders
GO
```

THE TRUNCATE TABLE removes all data from a table. Use the TRUNCATE TABLE statement to perform a nonlogged deletion of all rows.

Syntax

TRUNCATE TABLE [[*database.*]*owner.*]*table_name*

Example

This example removes all data from the **orders** table.

```
USE northwind
TRUNCATE TABLE orders
GO
```

Note This example is an illustration and will produce an error, due to the existence of a foreign key constraint between Orders and Order Details..

When you use the TRUNCATE TABLE statement, consider the following facts:

- SQL Server deletes all rows but retains the table structure and its associated objects.

- The TRUNCATE TABLE statement executes more quickly than the DELETE statement because SQL Server logs only the deallocation of data pages.

- If a table has an IDENTITY column, the TRUNCATE TABLE statement resets the seed value.

Deleting Rows Based on Other Tables

■ **Using an Additional FROM Clause**

  ● First FROM clause indicates table to modify

  ● Second FROM clause specifies restricting criteria for the DELETE statement

■ **Specifying Conditions in the WHERE Clause**

  ● Subqueries determine which rows to delete

Use the DELETE statement with joins or subqueries to remove rows from a table based on data stored in other tables. This is more efficient than writing multiple, single-row DELETE statements.

Using an Additional FROM Clause

In a DELETE statement, the WHERE clause references values in the table itself and is used to decide which rows to delete. If you use an additional FROM clause, you can reference other tables to make this decision. When you use the DELETE statement with an additional FROM clause, consider the following facts:

■ The first FROM clause indicates the table from which the rows are deleted.

■ The second FROM clause may introduce a join and acts as the restricting criteria for the DELETE statement.

Syntax

```
DELETE [FROM] {table_name | view_name}
  [FROM {<table_source>} [,...n]]
  [WHERE search_conditions ]
```

Example 1

This example uses a join operation with the DELETE statement to remove rows from the **order details** table for orders taken on 4/14/1998.

```
USE northwind
DELETE FROM [order details]
 FROM orders AS o
 INNER JOIN [order details] AS od
  ON o.orderid = od.orderid
 WHERE orderdate = '4/14/1998'
GO
```

Specifying Conditions in the WHERE Clause

You also can use subqueries to determine which rows to delete from a table based on rows of another table. You can specify the conditions in the WHERE clause rather than using an additional FROM clause. Use a nested or correlated subquery in the WHERE clause to determine which rows to delete.

Example 2

This example removes the same rows in the **order details** table as Example 1 and shows that you can convert a join operation to a nested subquery.

```
USE northwind
DELETE FROM [order details]
 WHERE orderid IN (
                    SELECT orderid
                     FROM orders
                     WHERE orderdate = '4/14/1998'
                  )
GO
```

◆ Updating Data

- **Updating Rows Based on Data in the Table**
- **Updating Rows Based on Other Tables**

The UPDATE statement can change data values in single rows, groups of rows, or all rows in a table or view. You can update a table based on data in the table or on data in other tables.

Updating Rows Based on Data in the Table

- **WHERE Clause Specifies Rows to Change**

- **SET Keyword Specifies the New Data**

- **Input values must have compatible data types with the columns**

- **Updates Do Not Occur in Rows That Violate Any Integrity Constraints**

```
USE northwind
UPDATE products
 SET unitprice = (unitprice * 1.1)
GO
```

The UPDATE statement modifies existing data.

Partial Syntax

UPDATE {*table_name* | *view_name*}
  SET { *column_name* = {*expression* | DEFAULT | NULL} |
  @*variable=expression*}[,...*n*]
  WHERE {*search_conditions*}

Use the UPDATE statement to change single rows, groups of rows, or all of the rows in a table. When you update rows, consider the following facts and guidelines:

- Specify the rows to update with the WHERE clause.

- Specify the new values with the SET clause.

- Verify that the input values have compatible data types with the data types that are defined for the columns.

- SQL Server does not update rows that violate any integrity constraints. The changes do not occur, and the statement is rolled back.

- You can change the data in only one table at a time.

- You can set one or more columns or variables to an expression. For example, an expression can be a calculation (like **price** * 2) or the addition of two columns.

Example

The following example adds 10 percent to the current prices of all Northwind Traders products.

```
USE northwind
UPDATE products
 SET unitprice = (unitprice * 1.1)
GO
```

Updating Rows Based on Other Tables

- **How the UPDATE Statement Works**
  - Never updates the same row twice
  - Requires table prefixes on ambiguous column names
- **Specifying Rows to Update Using Joins**
  - Uses the FROM clause
- **Specifying Rows to Update Using Subqueries**
  - Correlates the subquery with the updated table

Use the UPDATE statement with a FROM clause to modify a table based on values from other tables.

Using the UPDATE Statement

When you use joins and subqueries with the UPDATE statement, consider the following facts and guidelines:

- SQL Server never updates the same row twice in a single UPDATE statement. This is a built-in restriction that minimizes the amount of logging that occurs during updates.

- Use the SET keyword to introduce the list of columns or variable names to be updated. Columns referenced by the SET keyword must be unambiguous. For example, you can use a table prefix to eliminate ambiguity.

Partial Syntax

```
UPDATE {table_name | view_name}
  SET
  { column_name={expression | DEFAULT | NULL}
  |@variable=expression}[,...n]
  [FROM {  <table_source>
  ]
  [WHERE search_conditions]
```

Specifying Rows to Update Using Joins

When you use joins to update rows, use the FROM clause to specify joins in the UPDATE statement.

Example 1

This example uses a join to update the **products** table by adding $2.00 to the **unitprice** column for all products supplied by suppliers in the United States (USA).

```
UPDATE products
 SET unitprice = unitprice + 2
 FROM products
 INNER JOIN suppliers
  ON products.supplierid = suppliers.supplierid
 WHERE suppliers.country = 'USA'
GO
```

Specifying Rows to Update Using Subqueries

When you use subqueries to update rows, consider the following facts and guidelines:

- If the subquery does not return a single value, you must introduce the subquery with the IN, EXISTS, ANY or ALL keyword.

- Consider using aggregate functions with correlated subqueries, because SQL Server never updates the same row twice in a single UPDATE statement.

Example 2

This example uses a subquery to update the **products** table by adding $2.00 to the **unitprice** column for all products supplied by suppliers in the in the United States (USA). Notice that each product has only one supplier.

```
UPDATE products
 SET unitprice = unitprice + 2
 WHERE supplierid IN (
                      SELECT supplierid
                       FROM suppliers
                       WHERE country = 'USA'
                      )
GO
```

Example 3

This example updates the total sales for all orders of each product in the **products** table. Many orders for each product may exist. Because SQL Server never updates the same row twice, you must use an aggregate function with a correlated subquery to update the total number of sales-to-date of each product. If you want to execute the following example, you must add a **todatesales** column with a default value of 0 to the **products** table.

```
USE northwind
UPDATE products
 SET todatesales = (
                    SELECT SUM(quantity)
                     FROM [order details] AS od
                     WHERE products.productid = od.productid
                    )
GO
```

Performance Considerations

- ■ **All Data Modifications Occur Within a Transaction**
- ■ **Data Page Allocation May Occur**
- ■ **Modifying Indexed Data Incurs Additional Overhead**
- ■ **Indexes Can Assist Search Criteria**

Data modifications that occur within transactions can affect the performance of SQL Server. When modifying data, remember that:

- ■ Data locking during a single transaction can prevent other transactions and queries from running until the transaction completes.

- ■ Modifying tables can change the way data is physically stored, leading to data page allocations that must occur within the transaction.

- ■ When modifying data columns that are indexed, the indexes on those columns change as part of the transaction.

- ■ Placing indexes on columns used in the WHERE clause of a data modification statement improves performance.

Recommended Practices

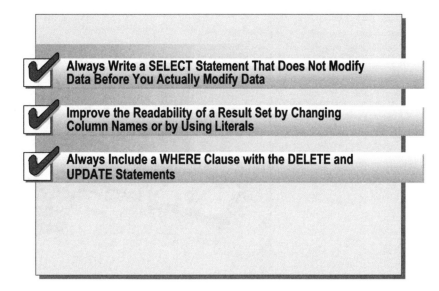

The following recommended practices should help you perform basic queries:

- Always write a SELECT statement that does not modify data before you actually modify data. This test verifies which rows your INSERT, UPDATE, or DELETE statement affects.

- Improve the readability of result sets by changing column names to column aliases or using literals to replace result set values. These formatting options change the presentation of the data, not the data itself.

- SQL Server deletes or updates all rows in a table unless you include a WHERE clause in the DELETE or UPDATE statements.

Additional information on the following topics is available in SQL Server Books Online.

Topic	Search on
Using character strings	"LIKE comparisons"
Sorting result sets	"sort order"

Lab A: Modifying Data

Objectives

After completing this lab, you will be able to:

- Modify data in tables by using the INSERT, DELETE, and UPDATE statements.
- Insert rows into a table by using the DEFAULT and DEFAULT VALUES keywords.
- Modify data based on data in other tables.

Prerequisites

Before working on this lab, you must have:

- The script files for this lab, which are located in C:\Moc\2071\Labfiles\L07.
- Answer files for this lab, which are located in C:\Moc\2071\Labfiles\L07\Answers.
- The **library** database installed.

Lab Setup

None.

For More Information

If you require help in executing files, search SQL Query Analyzer Help for "Execute a query".

Other resources that you can use include:

- The **library** database schema.
- Microsoft® SQL Server™ Books Online.

Scenario

The organization of the classroom is meant to simulate a worldwide trading firm named Northwind Traders. Its fictitious domain name is nwtraders.msft. The primary DNS server for nwtraders.msft is the instructor computer, which has an Internet Protocol (IP) address of 192.168.x.200 (where x is the assigned classroom number). The name of the instructor computer is London.

The following table provides the user name, computer name, and the IP address for each student computer in the fictitious nwtraders.msft domain. Find the user name for your computer and make a note of it.

User name	Computer name	IP address
SQLAdmin1	Vancouver	192.168.x.1
SQLAdmin2	Denver	192.168.x.2
SQLAdmin3	Perth	192.168.x.3
SQLAdmin4	Brisbane	192.168.x.4
SQLAdmin5	Lisbon	192.168.x.5
SQLAdmin6	Bonn	192.168.x.6
SQLAdmin7	Lima	192.168.x.7
SQLAdmin8	Santiago	192.168.x.8
SQLAdmin9	Bangalore	192.168.x.9
SQLAdmin10	Singapore	192.168.x.10
SQLAdmin11	Casablanca	192.168.x.11
SQLAdmin12	Tunis	192.168.x.12
SQLAdmin13	Acapulco	192.168.x.13
SQLAdmin14	Miami	192.168.x.14
SQLAdmin15	Auckland	192.168.x.15
SQLAdmin16	Suva	192.168.x.16
SQLAdmin17	Stockholm	192.168.x.17
SQLAdmin18	Moscow	192.168.x.18
SQLAdmin19	Caracas	192.168.x.19
SQLAdmin20	Montevideo	192.168.x.20
SQLAdmin21	Manila	192.168.x.21
SQLAdmin22	Tokyo	192.168.x.22
SQLAdmin23	Khartoum	192.168.x.23
SQLAdmin24	Nairobi	192.168.x.24

Estimated time to complete this lab: 60 minutes

Exercise 1
Using the INSERT Statement

In this exercise, you will use the INSERT statement to add rows to tables in the **library** database. Then, you will execute a query to verify that the new rows are added to the tables. C:\Moc\2071\Labfiles\L07\Answers contains completed scripts for this exercise.

▶ **To insert values into the item table**

In this procedure, you will insert rows into the **item** table to represent a book in the library collection.

1. Log on to the **NWTraders** classroom domain by using the information in the following table.

Option	Value
User name	**SQLAdmin***x* (where *x* corresponds to your computer name as designated in the nwtraders.msft classroom domain)
Password	**Password**

2. Open SQL Query Analyzer and, if requested, log in to the (local) server with Microsoft Windows® Authentication.

   You have permission to log in to and administer SQL Server because you are logged as **SQLAdmin***x*, which is a member of the Windows 2000 local group, Administrators. All members of this group are automatically mapped to the SQL Server **sysadmin** role.

3. In the **DB** list, click **library**.

4. Insert two rows into the **item** table for title number 8, *The Cherry Orchard*. Specify the column names for which you are supplying values. Make the first item a hardback and the second item a paperback, and use the following values. Answer_InsValues1.sql is a completed script for this step.

Column name	Data
Isbn	10001 for HARDBACK; 10101 for SOFTBACK
title_no	8
Cover	HARDBACK and SOFTBACK
Loanable	Y
Translation	ENGLISH

5. Execute the query and verify that two rows are inserted.

▶ **To insert values into the copy table**

In this procedure, you will insert rows into the **copy** table to represent a book in the library collection.

1. Add a row into the **copy** table for the hardback item that you added in step 4, and use the following values. Answer_InsValues2.sql is a completed script for this step.

Column name	Data
Isbn	10001 (the ISBN number for the hardback item that you added in step 1)
copy_no	1
title_no	8 (the title number of *The Cherry Orchard*)
On_loan	N

2. Execute the query and verify that a single row is inserted.

▶ **To determine the translation language of an item**

In this procedure, you will write a query that returns the language that an item has been translated into.

1. Write a query that returns the translation of one of the items that you inserted in step 4 from the **item** table. Answer_Translate.sql is a completed script for this step.

2. Execute the query to verify that it returns the desired results.

Exercise 2
Using the INSERT Statement with the DEFAULT Keyword

In this exercise, you will use the INSERT statement with the DEFAULT keyword to add two rows to the **title** table and to provide partial data for columns that allow null values or have default values. C:\Moc\2071\Labfiles\L07\Answers contains completed scripts for this exercise.

▶ **To determine which columns allow null values**

In this procedure, you will determine which columns allow null values.

1. Execute the **sp_help** system stored procedure to determine which columns in the **title** table allow null values. You do not have to supply values for columns that allow null values or have default values or have the IDENTITY property. Answer_WhichNull.sql is a completed script for this step.

2. Review the second results returned to determine which columns allow null values.

▶ **To insert values into the title table**

In this procedure, you will insert values into the **title** table.

1. Insert a row into the **title** table for the book, *The Art of Lawn Tennis*, by William T. Tilden. Use the DEFAULT keyword for columns that allow null values or that have default values. Do not supply a value for the **title_no** column because this column has the IDENTITY property. Answer_InsDefault1.sql is a completed script for this step.

2. Execute the query and verify that a single row is inserted.

▶ **To determine the last identity value used**

In this procedure, you will determine the last identity value used.

1. Write query to determine the **title_no** of the title that you added in step 1 of the previous procedure. Answer_Identity.sql is a completed script for this step.

2. Execute the query and make note of the value that is returned.

▶ **To retrieve the last row inserted into the title table**

In this procedure, you will retrieve the last row inserted into the **title** table.

1. Write a query to verify that the new title was added to the **title** table. Use the value that you obtained in step 1 of the previous procedure for the **title_no** column. Answer_LastRow.sql is a completed script for this step.

2. Execute the query to verify that it returns the desired results.

▶ **To insert more values into the title table**

In this procedure, you will insert more values into the **title** table.

1. Insert a row into the **title** table for the title, *Riders of the Purple Sage*, by Zane Grey. Specify a *column_list* and values for columns that do not allow null values or have default values. Answer_InsValues3.sql is a completed script for this step.

2. Execute the query and verify that a single row is inserted.

▶ **To verify that values were inserted into the title table**

In this procedure, you will verify that values were inserted into the **title** table.

1. Write and execute a query to verify that the new title and author are added to the **title** table. Answer_ChkValues3.sql is a completed script for this step.

2. Execute the query to verify that it returns the desired results.

Exercise 3
Using the INSERT Statement with the DEFAULT VALUES Keyword

In this exercise, you will use the INSERT statement with the DEFAULT VALUES keyword to add rows to a table without providing values. First you will create and work with a sample table in the **library** database. C:\Moc\2071\Labfiles\L07\Answers contains completed scripts for this exercise.

▶ **To create the sample1 table**

In this procedure, you will create a new table in the **library** database that allows null values and that specifies default values for some columns.

1. Execute the C:\Moc\2071\Labfiles\L07\ MakeSample1.sql script to create a new table called **sample1** in the **library** database with the following characteristics.

Column name	Datatype	IDENTITY property?	Allows NULL?
Cust_id	**Int**	Yes (100,5)	No
Name	**char(10)**	No	Yes

2. Execute the query to verify that it creates the **sample1** table.

▶ **To insert a row of default values into the sample1 table**

In this procedure, you will insert a row into the **sample1** table by using the DEFAULT VALUES keyword. Then, you will write and execute a query to verify that the new row was added to the table. Answer_InsDefault2.sql is a completed script for this procedure.

1. Write a query that would insert a new row into the **sample1** table without specifying the column names. Use the DEFAULT VALUES keyword with the INSERT statement.

2. Execute the query and verify that a single row is inserted.

▶ **To verify that values that were inserted into the sample1 table**

In this procedure, you will verify that values that were inserted into the
sample1 table.

1. Write a query to verify that the new row was added to the **sample1** table.
   Answer_ChkDefault2.sql is a completed script for this procedure.

2. Execute the query and compare the results to the default values defined for
   the table.

Result

Your result should look similar to the following result set.

cust_id	name
100	NULL

(1 row(s) affected)

Exercise 4
Using the DELETE Statement

In this exercise, you will use the DELETE statement to remove a book with an ISBN of 10101 and a title number of 8 from the **item** table in the **library** database. C:\Moc\2071\Labfiles\L07\Answers contains completed scripts for this exercise.

▶ To retrieve a row of data that you intend on deleting from the item table

In this procedure, you will retrieve a row of data that you want to delete from the **item** table. Answer_SelDelete1.sql is a completed script for this procedure.

1. Write a query that returns the row from the **item** table that represents a paperback copy (**isbn** 10101) of *The Cherry Orchard* (**title_no** 8).

2. Execute the query to verify that it returns the desired results.

▶ To delete a specific row of data from the item table

In this procedure, you will delete a specific row of data from the **item** table. Answer_Delete1.sql is a completed script for this procedure.

1. Modify the query from step 1 in the previous procedure so that it deletes the row from the **item** table that represents a paperback copy (**isbn** 10101) of *The Cherry Orchard* (**title_no** 8).

2. Execute the query and confirm that it one row is deleted from the **item** table.

Exercise 5
Using the UPDATE Statement

In this exercise you will modify the last name of member number 507 in the **member** table of the **library** database. C:\Moc\2071\Labfiles\L07\Answers contains completed scripts for this exercise.

▶ To retrieve a row of data that you intend on updating from the member table

In this procedure, you will retrieve a row of data that you want to update from the **member** table. Answer_SelUpdate1.sql is a completed script for this procedure.

1. Write a query that retrieves the last name of member number 507 in the **member** table.

2. Execute the query to verify that it returns the desired results.

▶ To update a specific row of data from the member table

In this procedure, you will update a specific row of data from the **member** table. Answer_Update1.sql is a completed script for this procedure.

1. Write a query that changes the last name of member number 507 in the **member** table to a different one of your choice.

2. Execute the query and confirm that it updates one row in the **member** table.

Exercise 6
Modifying Tables Based on Data in Other Tables

In this exercise, you will write queries that insert values from one or more tables in the database into an existing table, and you will delete or update rows in a table based on criteria in other tables. C:\Moc\2071\Labfiles\L07\Answers contains completed scripts for this exercise.

▶ To add a new juvenile member to the database

In this procedure, you will add a new juvenile member to the **library** database.

1. Review and execute the C:\Moc\2071\Labfiles\L07\AddJuvenile.sql script file to add a new juvenile member to the **library** database.

   Because the process of adding a new juvenile member requires two INSERT statements, this action is treated as a transaction. The SET IDENTITY_INSERT statement is used to supply a specific value for the **member.member_no** column rather than using the value that the IDENTITY property supplied.

2. Execute the query and verify that a single row was inserted into each of two tables.

▶ To determine which records should be moved from the juvenile table to the adult table

In this procedure, you will retrieve data from the **adult** and **juvenile** tables for all juvenile members over age 18. Answer_SelNewAdult.sql is a completed script for this procedure.

1. Write a SELECT statement that returns the **member_no** column from the **juvenile** table and the **street**, **city**, **state**, **zip**, and **phone_no** columns from the **adult** table. Also include in the query today's date plus one year by using the following expression:

   DATEADD(YY, 1, GETDATE())

   This last column will be used later to provide a value for the **adult.expr_date** column. This SELECT statement joins the **juvenile** table with the **member** table, such that **juvenile.adult_member_no** = **adult.member_no**.

   Include a WHERE clause to limit the rows that are added to those members in the **juvenile** table who are over age 18 by using the DATEADD function in an expression. Search Books Online for "DATEADD" if you need further assistance.

2. Execute the query to verify that it returns the desired results. Note the **member_no** values that are returned.

▶ **To insert new rows into the adult table from the juvenile table**

1. Write an INSERT statement that incorporates the SELECT statement that you created in step 1 of the previous procedure in order to add rows to the **adult** table. Answer_InsNewAdult.sql is a completed script for this procedure.

2. Execute the query and verify that one row is inserted.

▶ **To verify that a certain juvenile record was added to the adult table**

1. Write a query to verify that juvenile member number 16101 was added to the **adult** table. Answer_ChkNewAdult.sql is a completed script for this procedure.

2. Execute the query to verify that it returns the desired results.

Result

Your result will look similar to the following partial result set.

member_no	street	city	state	zip	phone_no	expr_date
16101	Bowery Estates	Montgomery	AL	36100	null	Feb 7 1998 2:58PM

(1 row(s) affected)

▶ **To determine which rows in the juvenile table should be removed**

In this procedure, you will create a query that deletes rows from the **juvenile** table that have matching rows in the **adult** table. After juvenile members are converted to adult members, those members must be deleted from the **juvenile** table. Answer_SelOldJuvenile.sql is a completed script for this procedure.

1. Write a SELECT statement that joins the **adult** and **juvenile** tables so that **juvenile.member_no = adult.member_no**.

2. Execute the query to verify that it returns the desired results.

▶ **To delete rows in the juvenile table that have matches in the adult table**

1. Write a DELETE statement that uses the SELECT statement that you created in step 1 of the previous procedure to delete these rows from the **juvenile** table. Answer_DelOldJuvenile.sql is a completed script for this procedure.

2. Execute the query and verify that one row is deleted.

▶ **To verify that a certain records were removed from the juvenile table**

1. Write a SELECT statement to verify that member number 16101 was removed from the **juvenile** table. Answer_ChkOldJuvenile.sql is an example of this query.

2. Execute the query and verify that no records are returned.

Review

- **Using Transactions**
- **Inserting Data**
- **Deleting Data**
- **Updating Data**
- **Performance Considerations**

You are the database administrator for a health care plan. The **physicians** table was created by using the following statement:

```
CREATE TABLE dbo.physicians (
    physician_no int IDENTITY (100, 2) NOT NULL
    ,f_name varchar (25) NOT NULL
    ,l_name varchar (25) NOT NULL
    ,street varchar (50) NULL
    ,city varchar (255) NULL
    ,state varchar (255) NULL
    ,postal_code varchar (7) NULL
    ,co_pay money NOT NULL CONSTRAINT phys_co_pay DEFAULT (10)
    )
GO
```

1. What is the minimum number of column values that you must supply to add a new row to the table?

2. The participating physicians have increased their costs of services. How can you increase the **co_pay** value for all doctors by 12 percent?

3. How can you remove all rows from the **physicians** table?

Microsoft®
Training &
Certification

Module 8: Querying
Full-Text Indexes

Contents

Overview

- ■ **Introduction to Microsoft Search Service**
- ■ **Microsoft Search Service Components**
- ■ **Getting Information About Full-Text Indexes**
- ■ **Writing Full-Text Queries**

You can issue full-text queries against plain-text data in tables in Microsoft® SQL Server™ 2000, including words, phrases, and multiple forms of a word or phrase. You implement the full-text search capability in SQL Server by using Microsoft Search service.

At the end of this module, the student will be able to:

- ■ Describe Microsoft Search service function and components.
- ■ Get information about full-text indexes.
- ■ Write full-text queries.

Introduction to Microsoft Search Service

- **Provides Text-based Searches in SQL Server**
  - Complex searches on unstructured text data for words and phrases
  - More powerful than LIKE operator and wildcards
- **Available in Other Microsoft Products**
  - Indexing Service, Exchange 2000, Commerce Server

With Microsoft Search service, you now can query character-based data in tables by using full-text search. A *full-text query* searches for words, phrases, or multiple forms of a word or phrase in the character-based columns (**char**, **varchar**, **text**, **ntext**, **nchar**, or **nvarchar**).

Provides Text-based Searches in SQL Server 2000

SQL Server has always had the capability to retrieve text, based on pattern matching using the LIKE operator and wildcards.

Now, by using Microsoft Search service, you can create more complex searches. With a full-text query, you can perform a linguistic search of character data in tables. A linguistic search operates on words and phrases, allowing you to search for similar words or phrases and different forms of a word, or to target words that approximate one another.

Available in Other Microsoft Products

Microsoft Search service is also included with these products:

- Microsoft Indexing Service
- Microsoft Exchange 2000
- Microsoft Commerce Server

Microsoft Search Service Components

- **Search Service Structures**
  - Full-text index
    Keeps track of significant words used in a table
    Requires unique key column or primary key
  - Full-text catalog
    Is a collection of full-text indexes
- **Microsoft Search Service Functions**
  - Indexing
  - Querying

Microsoft Search service stores information about full-text data in structures outside of SQL Server.

Search Service Structures

SQL Server uses two structures to track columns that are full-text search enabled. These structures are used to communicate with Microsoft Search service for building indexes and processing queries.

Microsoft Search service uses two structures to implement full-text searching: full-text index and full-text catalog.

Full-Text Index

A *full-text index* is an index that keeps track of the significant words used in a table and where they are located. This index structure supports an efficient search for all items containing indexed words, and advanced search operations such as phrase searches and proximity searches.

The principal design requirement for full-text indexing, querying, and synchronization is the presence of a unique key column (or single-column primary key) on all tables that are registered for full-text search.

Note Full-text indexes differ from SQL Server indexes, which are controlled by the SQL Server database in which they are defined.

Full-Text Catalog

The full-text catalog is the location where full-text indexes reside. This is an NTFS file system directory that is accessible only by Microsoft Windows NT® Administrator and Microsoft Search service. The full-text indexes are organized into full-text catalogs. Typically, the full-text index data for an entire database is placed into a single full-text catalog. However, administrators have the flexibility to partition the full-text index data for a database across more than one full-text catalog. This is particularly useful if one or more of the tables being full-text indexed contains a large number of rows.

Search Service Functions

Microsoft Search service has two primary functions: building and maintaining full-text indexes, and using the indexes to process queries.

Indexing

Microsoft Search service builds and maintains full-text indexes for tables set up for full-text indexing. It goes through the rows of the table and extracts key words from the columns specified for full-text searching. These values are stored in operating system files and are organized into full-text catalogs. A table must have a unique index defined on it in order for you to build a full-text index on it.

Querying

Microsoft Search service processes full-text search queries. It determines which entries in the index meet the full-text selection criteria. For each entry that meets the selection criteria, it returns the identity of the row plus a ranking value to the SQL Server service, where this information is used to construct the query result set.

When processing a full-text query, the search engine returns to SQL Server the key values of the rows that match the search criteria.

Getting Information About Full-Text Indexes

- **Using System Stored Procedures**
  - **sp_help_fulltext_catalogs**
  - **sp_help_fulltext_tables**
  - **sp_help_fulltext_columns**
- **Using Transact-SQL Functions**
  - Use Transact-SQL functions to obtain information about full-text properties

```
USE northwind
SELECT
 DATABASEPROPERTY('Northwind','IsFullTextEnabled')
GO
```

You can gather information about full-text search by using full-text system stored procedures, Transact-SQL functions, and SQL Server Enterprise Manager. You can retrieve metadata and status information for each level— database, catalog, table, and column.

Using System Stored Procedures

You can use the full-text system stored procedures in the following table to obtain information about full-text indexes.

Stored procedure	Function
sp_help_fulltext_catalogs	Returns the ID, name, root directory, status, and number of full-text indexed tables for the specified full-text catalog
sp_help_fulltext_tables	Returns a list of tables that are enabled for full-text indexing
sp_help_fullltext_columns	Returns the columns that are enabled for full-text indexing

Using Transact-SQL Functions

You also can use Transact-SQL functions to obtain the values of full-text properties.

The following table lists frequently used property values that you can use to get information about full-text search.

Function	Property value	Description of Property
COLUMNPROPERTY	IsFullTextIndexed	Indicates that a column is enabled for full-text search
DATABASEPROPERTY	IsFullTextEnabled	Indicates that a database is enabled for full-text search
INDEXPROPERTY	IsFulltextKey	Indicates that the index is used by Microsoft Search services
OBJECTPROPERTY	TableHasActiveFulltextIndex	Indicates that a table is enabled for full-text search
FULLTEXTCATALOGPROPERTY	PopulateStatus	Returns the in-process state of a Microsoft Search catalog
	ItemCount	Returns the number of entries contained in a Microsoft Search catalog
	IndexSize	Returns the size of the full-text index, in megabytes
	UniqueKeyCount	Returns an approximate number of non-noise words that are able to be uniquely addressed in a Microsoft Search catalog
	LogSize	Returns the size of the last full-text index, in megabytes
	PopulateCompletionAge	Returns the most recent date and time at which an update was made to the referenced Microsoft Search catalog
FULLTEXTSERVICEPROPERTY	ResourceUsage	Specifies a relative operating system execution priority setting for the Microsoft Search service
	IsFullTextInstalled	Indicates a successful installation on an organization server running SQL Server

Example

The **IsFullTextEnabled** property is also used to determine whether full-text querying is enabled for the **Northwind** database.

```
USE northwind
SELECT DATABASEPROPERTY('Northwind', 'IsFullTextEnabled')
GO
```

If a value of 1 is returned, the **Northwind** database is enabled for full-text querying. A value of 0 indicates that the **Northwind** database is not enabled for full-text querying.

◆ Writing Full-Text Queries

- **CONTAINS Predicate**
- **FREETEXT Predicate**
- **CONTAINSTABLE and FREETEXTTABLE Functions**
- **Using Full-Text Keywords**

With a full-text query, you can perform a linguistic search of character data in tables enabled for full-text search.

Microsoft Search service supports additional search predicates and functions that extend the functionality of Transact-SQL. These syntax elements are the same as those used for Microsoft Search service in the OLE DB providers for Microsoft Index Server version 2.0 and Microsoft Site Server version 3.0.

The full-text Transact-SQL extensions follow the International Standards Organization (ISO) SQL-3 functional methodology for full-text syntax extensions. The syntax elements are:

- The CONTAINS predicate.
- The FREETEXT predicate.
- The CONTAINSTABLE function.
- The FREETEXTTABLE function.

Note Search predicates are Transact-SQL statements that act to restrict the result set of a query. An example is the search conditions applied in a WHERE clause of a SELECT statement.

CONTAINS Predicate

- **Inflectional Form of a Specific Word**

- **Word or Phrase Beginning with Specific Text**

- **Word or Phrase near Another Word or Phrase**

- **One or More Specific Words and Phrases**

- **Words or Phrases with Weighted Values**

Example 1

```
SELECT plant_id, common_name, price
 FROM plants
 WHERE CONTAINS( *, ' "English Thyme" ' )
GO
```

You can use the CONTAINS predicate to search for a specific term.

Partial Syntax

The CONTAINS predicate uses functional notation in which the first parameter is the name of the column being searched, and the second parameter is a full-text search condition.

…WHERE CONTAINS ({*column*}, '<contains_search_condition>')

<contains_search_condition> ::=
  {| <generation_term>| <prefix_term>| <proximity_term>
  | <simple_term>| <weighted_term>}

Search Conditions Syntax Elements

The CONTAINS predicate supports complex syntax to search character-based columns for:

- Inflectional form of a specific word (*generation term*).

  For example, you want to search for the inflectional form of the word drive. If various rows in the table include the words drive, drives, drove, driving, and driven, all would be in the result set, because each of these can be inflectionally generated from the word drive.

- A word or a phrase in which words begin with specified text (*prefix term*).

  In a phrase, each word within the phrase is considered to be a prefix, such as the term auto tran* that matches both automatic transmission and automobile transducer.

- A word or phrase is near another word or phrase (*proximity term*).

  For example, you want to find the rows in which the word ice is near the word hockey, or in which the phrase ice skating is near the phrase ice hockey.

- One or more specific words and phrases (*simple term*).

  A word is one or more characters without spaces or punctuation. A valid phrase can consist of multiple words with spaces with or without punctuation between them. For example, ice is a word, and ice skating is a phrase. Words and phrases such as these are called *simple terms*. SQL Server discards noise words from the search criteria.

- Words or phrases with weighted values (*weighted term*).

  You can rank the results of a search by specifying the weighted value of the words or phrases. Those query results that contain the higher-valued words or phrases are presented before others.

A CONTAINS predicate can combine several of these terms by using AND and OR, for example, to find all rows with latte and New York-style bagel in the same full-text enabled database column. Furthermore, terms can be negated by the use of AND NOT, for example bagel and not cream cheese.

Note A CONTAINS search is always case insensitive.

Example 1

The following query returns the **plant_id**, **common_name**, and **price** for all rows in which the phrase English Thyme is present in either of the full-text-enabled columns. An asterisk (*) used in place of a column name searches all full-text-enabled columns for the table.

```
SELECT plant_id, common_name, price
 FROM plants
 WHERE CONTAINS( *, ' "English Thyme" ' )
GO
```

Example 2

The following query returns such items as "Jean LeDuc has always loved ice hockey" and "Jean Leduc on Ice—Hockey at Its Best" from the **description** column.

```
SELECT article_id
 FROM hockey_articles
 WHERE CONTAINS(description, '"Jean LeDuc" AND "ice hockey"' )
GO
```

Note These examples are provided as illustration only and will not produce results.

FREETEXT Predicate

- **Searches on Words, Phrases, and Sentences Extracted from Initial Query**

- **Less Precise Than the CONTAINS Predicate**

```
SELECT *
FROM news_table
WHERE FREETEXT( description,
'"The Fulton County Grand Jury said Friday an
investigation of Atlanta's recent primary
election produced no evidence that any
irregularities took place."')
GO
```

When you use the FREETEXT predicate, you can enter any set of words or phrases, or even a complete sentence. The full-text query engine examines this text, identifies all the significant words and noun phrases, and internally constructs a query with those terms. The FREETEXT predicate is less precise than the CONTAINS predicate.

Syntax

…WHERE FREETEXT ({*column* | * }, '*free_text*')

Example

The following example uses a FREETEXT predicate against a column named **description**.

```
SELECT *
FROM news_table
WHERE FREETEXT( description,
'"The Fulton County Grand Jury said Friday an investigation
of Atlanta's recent primary election produced no evidence that
any irregularities took place."')
GO
```

Note   This example is provided as an illustration only and will not produce results.

In the example, the search engine identifies the following words and noun phrases:

- Words—Fulton, county, grand, jury, Friday, investigation, Atlanta, recent, primary, election, produce, evidence, irregularities

- Phrases—Fulton county grand jury, primary election, grand jury, Atlanta's recent primary election

The words and phrases are combined internally into a query and weighted for proper ranking before the actual search is performed.

CONTAINSTABLE and FREETEXTTABLE Functions

- **Using CONTAINSTABLE and FREETEXTTABLE**
  - Return a table
  - Return column that contains full-text key values
  - *top_n_by_rank* argument
- **Choosing Which Search Condition or Function to Use**
  - Use the CONTAINS and FREETEXT predicates in any search condition
  - Use the CONTAINSTABLE and FREETEXTTABLE functions in the FROM clause

The CONTAINSTABLE and FREETEXTTABLE functions differ slightly from the CONTAINS and FREETEXT predicates. The CONTAINSTABLE and FREETEXTTABLE functions essentially create a derived table.

Using CONTAINSTABLE and FREETEXTTABLE

The CONTAINSTABLE and FREETEXTTABLE functions operate similarly to their counterpart search conditions, CONTAINS and FREETEXT. However, the functions return a table of zero, one, or more rows for those columns containing character-based data types. In addition, the CONTAINSTABLE and FREETEXTTABLE functions can be referenced in the FROM clause of a SELECT statement as though they were regular table names.

Partial Syntax

CONTAINSTABLE (*table* , { *column* | * } , ' < contains_search_condition > '
    [, *top_n_by_rank*])

The CONTAINSTABLE function uses the same search conditions as the CONTAINS predicate.

Partial Syntax

FREETEXTTABLE (*table* , { *column* | * } , '*freetext_string*' [, *top_n_by_rank*])

When you work with these functions, consider the following facts and guidelines:

- CONTAINSTABLE and FREETEXTTABLE both return a table of zero, one, or more rows, so they must always be specified in a FROM clause.
- CONTAINSTABLE and FREETEXTTABLE also are used to specify selection criteria. The table returned has a column named **key** that contains full-text key values.

  Each full-text-enabled table has a column whose values are guaranteed to be unique. The values returned in the **key** column are the full-text key values of the rows that match the selection criteria that are specified in the full-text search condition.

- The table produced by CONTAINSTABLE and FREETEXTTABLE has a column named **rank**, which contains values between 0 and 1,000. These values are used to relatively rank the rows returned according to how well they met the selection criteria, and have no comparison value outside the result set.

Tip   Specify an integer for the *top_n_by_rank* argument to specify that only the *n* highest ranked matches, in descending order, be returned.

Choosing Which Full-Text Search Method to Use

Although the Transact-SQL statement used to specify the full-text search condition is the same in both the predicates and the functions, there are major differences in the way that you should use them.

- Use CONTAINS and FREETEXT predicates in any search condition (including a WHERE clause) of a SELECT statement.

- Use CONTAINSTABLE and FREETEXTTABLE functions in the FROM clause of a SELECT statement.

Queries that use the CONTAINSTABLE and FREETEXTTABLE functions are more complex than those that use the CONTAINS and FREETEXT keywords. You must explicitly join the qualifying rows returned by the functions with the rows in the original SQL Server table.

Using Full-Text Keywords

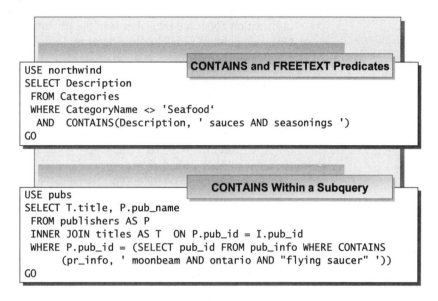

CONTAINS and FREETEXT Predicates

```
USE northwind
SELECT Description
 FROM Categories
 WHERE CategoryName <> 'Seafood'
  AND  CONTAINS(Description, ' sauces AND seasonings ')
GO
```

CONTAINS Within a Subquery

```
USE pubs
SELECT T.title, P.pub_name
 FROM publishers AS P
 INNER JOIN titles AS T  ON P.pub_id = I.pub_id
 WHERE P.pub_id = (SELECT pub_id FROM pub_info WHERE CONTAINS
        (pr_info, ' moonbeam AND ontario AND "flying saucer" '))
GO
```

You can combine the CONTAINS and FREETEXT predicates with any of the other Transact-SQL predicates, such as LIKE and BETWEEN. You also can use them in a subquery.

Example 1

This example searches for descriptions in which the category is not Seafood, and in which the description contains the word sauces and the word seasonings.

```
USE northwind
GO
 SELECT Description
 FROM Categories
 WHERE CategoryName <> 'Seafood'
  AND  CONTAINS(Description, ' sauces AND seasonings ')
GO
```

Example 2

This example uses CONTAINS within a subquery. Using the **pubs** database, the query obtains the title value of all the books in the **titles** table for the publisher that is near the flying saucer landmark in Moonbeam, Ontario. (This information about the publisher is in the **pr_info** column in the **pub_info** table. Only one publisher matches this description.)

```
USE pubs
SELECT T.title, P.pub_name
 FROM publishers AS P
 INNER JOIN titles AS T  ON P.pub_id = T.pub_id
 WHERE P.pub_id = (
         SELECT pub_id
           FROM pub_info
           WHERE CONTAINS (pr_info,
                   'moonbeam AND ontario AND "flying saucer"')
                 )
GO
```

Note   These examples are provided as illustrations only and will not produce results.

Recommended Practices

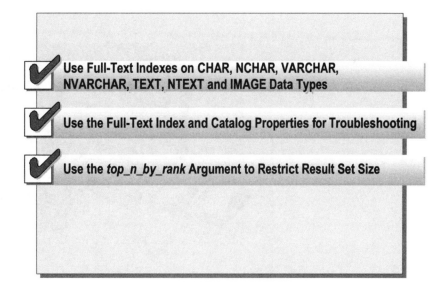

The following recommended practices should help you query full-text indexes:

- Use full-text indexes on tables with columns that contain textual data that you want to query, including those with CHAR, NCHAR, NVARCHAR, VARCHAR, TEXT, NTEXT, and IMAGE data types.

- Check the full-text index and catalog properties by using system functions and stored procedures to troubleshoot questionable query results or errors. Check that full-text search is enabled on the server, the database, and the table that you query.

- Use the *top_n_by_rank* argument when using CONTAINSTABLE and FREETEXTTABLE functions to restrict the number of returned rows.

Additional information on the following topics is available in SQL Server Books Online.

Topic	Search on
Using full-text search	"full-text query architecture"
	"full-text catalogs and indexes"
Querying full-text	"full-text query Transact-SQL components"
Using noise words	"indexing service"

Lab A: Querying Full-Text Indexes

Objectives

After completing this lab, you will be able to:

- Check the status of a full-text index.

- Write full-text queries.

Prerequisites

Before working on this lab, you must have:

- Answer files for this lab, which are located in
  C:\Moc\2071\Labfiles\L08\Answers.

Lab Setup

To complete this lab, you must have:

- Executed the C:\Moc\2071\Batches\2071B_R08.sql script file. This file is
  normally executed as part of the classroom setup. This script enables
  Microsoft Search service and creates a full-text index on the
  Products.productname column of the **Northwind** database.

For More Information

If you require help in executing files, search SQL Query Analyzer Help for
"Execute a query".

Other resources that you can use include:

- The **Northwind** database schema.

- SQL Server Books Online.

Scenario

The organization of the classroom is meant to simulate that of a worldwide trading firm named Northwind Traders. Its fictitious domain name is nwtraders.msft. The primary DNS server for nwtraders.msft is the instructor computer, which has an Internet Protocol (IP) address of 192.168.*x*.200 (where *x* is the assigned classroom number). The name of the instructor computer is London.

The following table provides the user name, computer name, and IP address for each student computer in the fictitious nwtraders.msft domain. Find the user name for your computer, and make a note of it.

User name	Computer name	IP address
SQLAdmin1	Vancouver	192.168.x.1
SQLAdmin2	Denver	192.168.x.2
SQLAdmin3	Perth	192.168.x.3
SQLAdmin4	Brisbane	192.168.x.4
SQLAdmin5	Lisbon	192.168.x.5
SQLAdmin6	Bonn	192.168.x.6
SQLAdmin7	Lima	192.168.x.7
SQLAdmin8	Santiago	192.168.x.8
SQLAdmin9	Bangalore	192.168.x.9
SQLAdmin10	Singapore	192.168.x.10
SQLAdmin11	Casablanca	192.168.x.11
SQLAdmin12	Tunis	192.168.x.12
SQLAdmin13	Acapulco	192.168.x.13
SQLAdmin14	Miami	192.168.x.14
SQLAdmin15	Auckland	192.168.x.15
SQLAdmin16	Suva	192.168.x.16
SQLAdmin17	Stockholm	192.168.x.17
SQLAdmin18	Moscow	192.168.x.18
SQLAdmin19	Caracas	192.168.x.19
SQLAdmin20	Montevideo	192.168.x.20
SQLAdmin21	Manila	192.168.x.21
SQLAdmin22	Tokyo	192.168.x.22
SQLAdmin23	Khartoum	192.168.x.23
SQLAdmin24	Nairobi	192.168.x.24

Estimated time to complete this lab: 60 minutes

Exercise 1
Obtaining Information About Full-Text Indexes

In this exercise, you will create a full-text catalog and full-text indexes so that you can use Microsoft Search service on one or more columns. C:\Moc\2071\Labfiles\L08\Answers contains completed scripts for this exercise.

▶ To use Transact-SQL to retrieve information about full-text indexes

In this procedure, you will set up Microsoft Search service on the **Northwind** database by using the Full-Text Indexing Wizard. Answer_FullText1.sql is a completed script for this procedure.

1. Log on to the **NWTraders** classroom domain by using the information in the following table.

Option	Value
User name	**SQLAdmin***x* (where *x* corresponds to your computer name as designated in the nwtraders.msft classroom domain)
Password	**Password**

2. Open SQL Query Analyzer and, if requested, log on to the (local) server with Microsoft Windows Authentication.

   You have permission to log on to and administer SQL Server because you are logged as **SQLAdmin***x*, which is a member of the Windows 2000 local group, Administrators. All members of this group are automatically mapped to the SQL Server **sysadmin** role.

3. Execute the following statement to determine whether full-text searching capability is installed on the SQL Server computer:

```
USE northwind
SELECT fulltextserviceproperty('IsFullTextInstalled')
GO
```

4. Execute the following statement to determine whether full-text searching is enabled on the **Northwind** database:

```
USE northwind
SELECT databaseproperty('Northwind', 'IsFullTextEnabled')
GO
```

5. Execute the following system stored procedure to list the tables that have full-text search enabled:

```
USE northwind
EXEC sp_help_fulltext_tables
GO
```

6. Execute the following system stored procedure to list the columns that have full-text search indexes built on them:

```
USE northwind
EXEC sp_help_fulltext_columns
GO
```

Exercise 2
Writing Full-Text Queries

In this exercise, you will write and execute full-text queries against a full-text index in order to search for specific words and phrases in the **Northwind** database. C:\Moc\2071\Labfiles\L08\Answers contains completed scripts for this exercise.

▶ To check for the words St. Andrews near the word Scotland in the employee notes

In this procedure, you will write and execute full-text queries with SELECT statements that use the CONTAINS and FREETEXT search functions. Answer_FullText2.sql is a completed script for this procedure.

1. Write a SELECT statement with the CONTAINS search function that selects the **LastName**, **Title**, **HireDate**, and **Notes** columns from the **Employees** table, where the **Employees.notes** column contains the word St. Andrews and is near the word Scotland.

2. Execute the query to verify that it returns a single row.

▶ To check for any form of the word sale in the employee notes

In this procedure, you will check for any form of the word sale in the employee notes. Answer_FullText3.sql is a completed script for this procedure.

1. Write a SELECT statement with the CONTAINS search function that selects the **LastName**, **Title**, **HireDate**, and **Notes** columns from the **Employees** table, where the **Employees.notes** column contains any form of the word sale. Answer_FullText3.sql is a completed script for this procedure.

2. Execute the query to verify that it returns four rows.

► **To check for the words cold and toast in the employee notes**

In this procedure, you will check for the words cold and toast in the employee notes. Answer_FullText4.sql is a completed script for this procedure.

1. Write and execute a SELECT statement with the FREETEXT search function that selects the **LastName**, **Title**, **HireDate**, and **Notes** columns from the **Employees** table, where the **Employees.notes** column contains the words cold and toast.

2. Execute the query to verify that it returns a single row.

► **To check for the words french and university in the employee notes of records that had orders shipped to London**

In this procedure, you will check for the words french and university in the employee notes that had order shipped to London. Answer_FullText5.sql is a completed script for this procedure.

1. Write a SELECT statement with the CONTAINS search function that selects the unique rows displaying the **LastName**, **Title**, and **HireDate** columns from the **Employees** table, where the **Employees.notes** column columns contains the words French and university, and the employee took orders that were destined for London.

2. Execute the query to verify that it returns four rows.

▶ **To join a derived table that checks for the word sales near the word manager of records that had orders shipped to London**

In this procedure, you will join a derived table that checks for the word sales near the word manager of records that had orders shipped to London. Answer_FullText6.sql is a completed script for this procedure.

1. Write a SELECT statement that displays **OrderID** and **EmployeeID** from the **Orders** table, ranking in descending order the best free-text search results for the word sales that is near the word manager in the **notes** column of the **Employees** table.

2. Execute the query to verify that it returns six rows.

Review

- **Introduction to Microsoft Search Service**
- **Microsoft Search Service Components**
- **Getting Information About Full-Text Indexes**
- **Writing Full-Text Queries**

1. Why should you use the full-text search extensions instead of standard Transact-SQL syntax to query text data?

2. You issue a full-text search query and return an empty record set back for results. You know that the table contains data that should match. What should you do?

3. You want to search the contents of the garden description column for any forms of "cultivate" that are near the word "roses." Which keywords would you need to use in your SELECT statement to create this search?

4. In your result set you would like to create a ranking. Which form of CONTAINS would you use?

5. When you create a new project and load the database structure or insert a new table into an existing project, what table characteristic is required in order to define the semantic relationships for a table?

Microsoft®
Training &
Certification

Module 9: Introduction to Programming Objects

Contents

Overview

- **Displaying the Text of a Programming Object**
- **Introduction to Views**
- **Advantages of Views**
- **Creating Views**
- **Introduction to Stored Procedures**
- **Introduction to Triggers**
- **Introduction to User-defined Functions**

This module describes how to create programming objects that enable the user to view and manipulate data without awareness of the complexity of the underlying database structure. The module introduces these programming objects—views, stored procedures, triggers, and user-defined functions—and describes the advantages of using them.

At the end of this module, you will be able to:

- Display the text of a programming object.
- Describe the concept of views.
- List the advantages of using views.
- Create views.
- Describe stored procedures.
- Describe triggers.
- Describe user-defined functions.

Displaying the Text of a Programming Object

■ **EXEC sp_helptext [@objectname =] 'name'**

```
USE library
EXEC sp_helptext 'dbo.OverdueView'
GO
```

■ **Not Every Programming Object Has Associated Text**

You can use system stored procedures to perform many administrative and informational activities in Microsoft SQL Server 2000. For example, you can use the **sp_helptext** system stored procedure to retrieve the text associated with a programming object.

Syntax

```
EXEC sp_helptext [ @objname = ] 'name'
```

The *parameter* is the name of the object in the current database for which SQL Server will display the text of the definition information.

The **sp_helptext** system stored procedure prints out the text used to create an object in multiple rows, each with 255 characters of the Transact-SQL definition. The definition resides in the text in the **syscomments** table of the current database only.

Example

This example returns the text that defines the **dbo.OverdueView** view.

```
USE library
EXEC sp_helptext 'dbo.OverdueView'
GO
```

Result

```
Text
-----------------------------------------------------------------

/*
OverdueView: Queries OnloanView. (3 table join.)
Lists the member, title, and loan information of a copy on
loan that is overdue.
*/

CREATE VIEW dbo.OverdueView
AS
SELECT *
FROM OnloanView
WHERE OnloanView.due_date < GETDATE()
```

Tip Use **EXEC sp_helptext** to verify the definition of newly created programming objects.

Introduction to Views

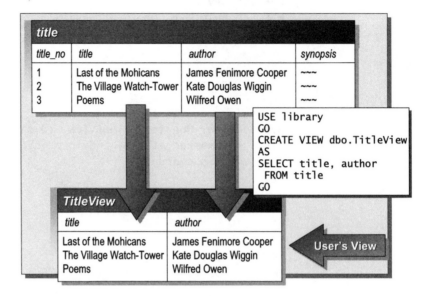

A *view* is an alternate way of looking at data from one or more tables.

A view can be thought of as either a virtual table or a stored query. The data accessible through a view is not stored in the database as a distinct object. What is stored in the database is a SELECT statement. The result set of the SELECT statement forms the virtual table returned by the view. You can use this virtual table by referencing the view name in Transact-SQL statements the same way that you reference a table.

You can use a view to do any or all of these functions:

- Restrict a user to specific rows in a table.

  For example, allow an employee to see only the rows recording his or her work in a labor-tracking table.

- Restrict a user to specific columns.

  For example, allow employees who do not work in payroll to see the name, office, work phone, and department columns in an employee table, but do not allow them to see any columns with salary information or personal information.

- Join columns from multiple tables so that they look like a single table.

- Aggregate information instead of supplying details.

  For example, present the sum of a column, or the maximum or minimum value from a column.

Example

This example creates the **titleview** view in the **library** database. The view displays two columns in the **title** table.

```
USE library
GO

CREATE VIEW dbo.TitleView
AS
SELECT title, author
 FROM title
GO
```

Query

```
SELECT * from TitleView
GO
```

Result

Title	author
Last of the Mohicans	James Fenimore Cooper
The Village Watch-Tower	Kate Douglas Wiggin
Self Help; Conduct & Perseverance	Samuel Smiles
.	
.	
.	

(50 row(s) affected)

Advantages of Views

- **Focus the Data for Users**
  - Focus on important or appropriate data only
  - Limit access to sensitive data
- **Mask Database Complexity**
  - Hide complex database design
  - Simplify complex queries, including distributed queries to heterogeneous data
- **Simplify Management of User Permissions**
- **Organize Data for Export to Other Applications**

Views offer several advantages, including focusing data for users, masking data complexity, simplifying permission management, and organizing data for export to other applications.

Focus the Data for Users

Views create a controlled environment that allows access to specific data and conceals other data. Data that is unnecessary, sensitive, or inappropriate can be left out of a view. Users can manipulate the display of data in a view, similar to a table. In addition, with the proper permissions and a few restrictions, users can modify the data that a view produces.

Mask Database Complexity

Views shield the complexity of the database design from the user. This provides developers with the ability to change the design without affecting user interaction with the database. In addition, users can see a friendlier version of the data by using names that are easier to understand than the cryptic names that are often used in databases.

Complex queries, including distributed queries to heterogeneous data, can also be masked through views. The user queries the view instead of writing the query or executing a script.

Simplify Management of User Permissions

Instead of granting permission for users to query specific columns in base tables, database owners can grant permission for users to query data through views only. This also protects changes in the design of the underlying base tables. Users can continue to query the view without interruption.

Organize Data for Export to Other Applications

You can create a view based on a complex query that joins two or more tables and then export the data to another application for further analysis.

◆ Creating Views

- Defining Views

- Restrictions on Creating Views

- Example: Viewing Information from Multiple Tables

This section describes how to create views and discusses restrictions to consider when creating views. It also provides an example of how to view information from two or more joined tables in one central location.

Defining Views

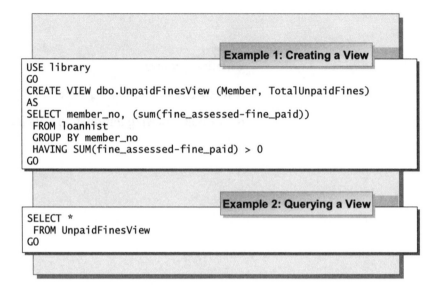

```
                                              Example 1: Creating a View
USE library
GO
CREATE VIEW dbo.UnpaidFinesView (Member, TotalUnpaidFines)
AS
SELECT member_no, (sum(fine_assessed-fine_paid))
 FROM loanhist
 GROUP BY member_no
 HAVING SUM(fine_assessed-fine_paid) > 0
GO
```

```
                                              Example 2: Querying a View
SELECT *
 FROM UnpaidFinesView
GO
```

When you create a view, SQL Server verifies the existence of objects that are referenced in the view definition. Your view name must follow the rules for identifiers. Specifying a view owner name is optional. You should develop a consistent naming convention to distinguish views from tables. For example, you could add the word View as a suffix to each view object that you create. This allows similar objects (tables and views) to be easily distinguished when you query the **INFORMATION_SCHEMA.TABLES** view.

Syntax

CREATE VIEW *owner.view_name* [(*column*[, *n.*])]
　[WITH ENCRYPTION]
　AS
　　select_statement

　[WITH CHECK OPTION]

To execute the CREATE VIEW statement, you must be a member of the system administrators (**sysadmin**) role, database owner (**db_owner**) role, or the data definition language administrator (**db_ddladmin**) role, or you must have been granted the CREATE VIEW permission. You must also have SELECT permission on all tables or views that are referenced within the view.

To avoid situations in which the owner of a view and the owner of the underlying tables differ, it is recommended that the **dbo** user own all objects in a database. Always specify the **dbo** user as the owner name when you create the object; otherwise, the object will be created with your user name as the object owner.

The contents of a view are specified with a SELECT statement. With a few limitations, views can be as complex as you like. You must specify column names if:

- Any of the columns of the view are derived from an arithmetic expression, built-in function, or constant.

- Any columns in tables that will be joined share the same name.

Important When you create views, it is important to test the SELECT statement that defines the view in order to ensure that SQL Server returns the expected result set. After you have written and tested the SELECT statement and verified the results, create the view.

Example 1

Here is an example of a view that creates a column (**TotalUnpaidFines**) that contains the values that are calculated by subtracting the value of the **fine_paid** column from the **fine_assessed** column.

```
USE library
GO

CREATE VIEW dbo.UnpaidFinesView (Member, TotalUnpaidFines)
AS
SELECT member_no, (sum(fine_assessed-fine_paid))
 FROM loanhist
 GROUP BY member_no
 HAVING SUM(fine_assessed-fine_paid) > 0
GO
```

Example 2

This example queries the view to see the results.

```
SELECT *
 FROM UnpaidFinesView
GO
```

The results should be similar to the following:

Result

Member	TotalUnpaidFines
7744	83.2

```
(1 row(s) affected)
```

```
Warning: Null value eliminated from aggregate
```

Restrictions on Creating Views

- **Can Reference a Maximum of 1024 Columns**
- **Cannot Include COMPUTE or COMPUTE BY clauses**
- **Cannot Include ORDER BY Clause, Unless Used in Conjunction with a TOP Clause**
- **Cannot Include the INTO Keyword**
- **Cannot Reference a Temporary Table**
- **Must Be Expressed as a Single Transact-SQL Batch**

When you create views, consider the following restrictions:

- Views cannot reference more than 1024 columns.
- The CREATE VIEW statement cannot include the COMPUTE or COMPUTE BY clauses.
- The CREATE VIEW statement cannot include the ORDER BY clause, unless used with a TOP clause in the SELECT statement.
- The CREATE VIEW statement cannot include the INTO keyword.
- Views cannot reference temporary tables.
- The CREATE VIEW statement cannot be combined with other Transact-SQL statements in a single batch.

Example: Viewing Information from Multiple Tables

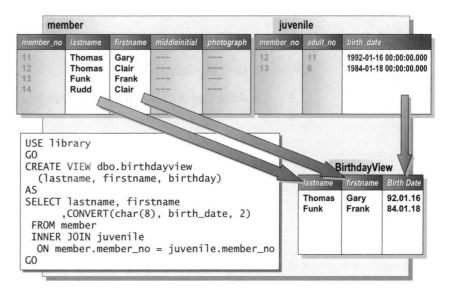

You often create views to view information from two or more joined tables in one central location.

Example

In this example, **birthdayview** that joins the **member** and **juvenile** tables is created.

```
USE library
GO

CREATE VIEW dbo.birthdayview
  (lastname, firstname, birthday)
AS
SELECT lastname, firstname
     ,CONVERT(char(8), birth_date, 2)
 FROM member
 INNER JOIN juvenile
  ON member.member_no = juvenile.member_no
GO
```

If we query the view to determine whether there are any null values in the **birthday** column, it correctly returns no rows.

```
SELECT *
 FROM birthdayview
 WHERE birthday is null
GO
```

Result

lastname	firstname	birthday

```
(0 row(s) affected)
```

◆ Introduction to Stored Procedures

- **Defining Stored Procedures**
- **Advantages of Using Stored Procedures**

This section introduces stored procedures and lists some of the advantages of using stored procedures.

Defining Stored Procedures

- **A Stored Procedure Is a Precompiled Collection of Transact-SQL Statements**
- **A Stored Procedure Encapsulates Repetitive Tasks**
- **Stored Procedures Can:**
    - Contain statements that perform operations
    - Accept input parameters
    - Return status value to indicate success or failure
    - Return multiple output parameters

A *stored procedure* is a named collection of precompiled Transact-SQL statements that is stored on the server. Using a stored procedure is a method of encapsulating repetitive tasks that executes efficiently. Stored procedures support user-declared variables, control-of-flow execution, and other advanced programming features.

Stored procedures in SQL Server are similar to procedures in other programming languages in that they can:

- Contain statements that perform operations in the database, including the ability to call other stored procedures.
- Accept input parameters.
- Return a status value to a calling stored procedure or batch to indicate success or failure (and the reason for failure).
- Return multiple values to the calling stored procedure or batch in the form of output parameters.

Example

This example shows the creation of a simple stored procedure with a complex SELECT statement. This stored procedure returns all authors (first and last names supplied), their titles, and their publishers from a four-table join in the **pubs** database. This stored procedure does not use any parameters.

```
USE pubs
GO

CREATE PROCEDURE au_info_all
AS
SELECT au_lname, au_fname, title, pub_name
 FROM authors AS a
 INNER JOIN titleauthor AS ta  ON a.au_id = ta.au_id
 INNER JOIN titles AS t  ON t.title_id = ta.title_id
 INNER JOIN publishers AS p  ON t.pub_id = p.pub_id
GO
```

Advantages of Using Stored Procedures

- **Share Application Logic**
- **Shield Database Schema Details**
- **Provide Security Mechanisms**
- **Improve Performance**
- **Reduce Network Traffic**

Stored procedures offer numerous advantages. Stored procedures significantly reduce resource and time requirements for execution. They can:

- Share application logic with other applications, thereby ensuring consistent data access and modification.

  Stored procedures can encapsulate business functionality. Business rules or policies encapsulated in stored procedures can be changed in a single location. All clients can use the same stored procedures to ensure consistent data access and modification.

- Shield users from exposure to the details of the tables in the database. If a set of stored procedures supports all of the business functions that users must perform, users never have to access the tables directly.

- Provide security mechanisms. Users can be granted permission to execute a stored procedure even if they do not have permission to access the tables or views that are referred to in the stored procedure.

- Improve performance. Stored procedures implement many tasks as a series of Transact-SQL statements. Conditional logic can be applied to the results of the first Transact-SQL statements to determine which subsequent Transact-SQL statements will be executed. All of these Transact-SQL statements and conditional logic become part of a single execution plan on the server.

- Reduce network traffic. Rather than sending hundreds of Transact-SQL statements over the network, users can perform a complex operation by sending a single statement, which reduces the number of requests that pass between the client and server.

Introduction to Triggers

- **A Trigger Is a Special Type of Stored Procedure**
- **A Trigger Is:**
  - Associated with a table
  - Invoked automatically
  - Not called directly
  - Treated as part of the transaction that fired it

A *trigger* is a special type of stored procedure that executes whenever an attempt is made to modify data in a table that the trigger protects.

Triggers are best used to maintain low-level data integrity, *not* to return query results. The primary benefit of triggers is that they can contain complex processing logic. A trigger is:

Associated with a Table   Triggers are defined on a specific table, which is referred to as the *trigger table*.

Invoked Automatically   When an attempt is made to insert, update, or delete data in a table and a trigger for that particular action has been defined on the table, the trigger executes automatically. It cannot be circumvented.

Not Called Directly   Unlike standard system stored procedures, triggers cannot be called directly and do not pass or accept parameters.

Treated as Part of the Transaction That Fired It   The trigger and the statement that fires it are treated as a single transaction that can be rolled back from anywhere within the trigger. The statement that invokes the trigger is considered the beginning of an implicit transaction, unless an explicit BEGIN TRANSACTION statement is included. The user that invoked the trigger must also have permission to perform all of the statements on all of the tables. If the trigger fails, then the transaction that called it also fails.

◆ Introduction to User-defined Functions

- **What Is a User-defined Function?**
- **Creating a User-defined Function**

Functions are subroutines made up of one or more Transact-SQL statements that you can use to encapsulate code for reuse. In addition to a number of system-defined functions that are built-in, SQL Server allows users to create their own user-defined functions.

What Is a User-defined Function?

- **Scalar Functions**
  - Similar to a built-in function
  - Returns a single data value built by a series of statements
- **Multi-Statement Table-valued Functions**
  - Content like a stored procedure
  - Referenced like a view
- **In-line Table-valued Functions**
  - Similar to a view with parameters
  - Returns a table as the result of single SELECT statement

With SQL Server, you can design your own functions to supplement and extend the system-supplied (built-in) functions. You can use user-defined functions as part of a Transact-SQL query, in the same way that you use system-supplied functions.

A user-defined function takes zero or more input parameters and returns either a scalar value or a table. Input parameters can be any data type except **timestamp**, **cursor**, or **table**. User-defined functions do not support output parameters.

SQL Server 2000 supports three types of user-defined functions:

Scalar Functions

This type of user-defined function returns a single data value of the type defined in a RETURNS clause. The body of the function, defined in a BEGIN-END block, contains the series of Transact-SQL statements that return the value. The return type can be any data type except **text**, **ntext**, **image**, **cursor**, or **timestamp**.

Multi-Statement Table-valued Functions

This type of user-defined function returns a table built by one or more Transact-SQL statements. The function body is defined in a BEGIN-END block and is similar to a stored procedure. Unlike a stored procedure, though, a multi-statement table-valued function can be referenced in the FROM clause of a SELECT statement as if it were a view.

In-line Table-valued Functions

This type of user-defined function returns a table that is the result of a single SELECT statement. An in-line table-valued function provides a representation of data similar to a view. This type of function offers more flexibility than views in the use of parameters and extends the features of indexed views.

Creating a User-defined Function

■ Creating a User-defined Function

```
USE northwind
GO
CREATE FUNCTION fn_NewRegion ( @myinput nvarchar(30) )
  RETURNS nvarchar(30)
BEGIN
  IF @myinput IS NULL
    SET @myinput = 'Not Applicable'

  RETURN @myinput
END
GO
```

■ Restrictions on User-defined Functions

You create a user-defined function in much the same way that you create a view or stored procedure.

Creating a User-defined Function

You create user-defined functions by using the CREATE FUNCTION statement. Each fully qualified user-defined function name (database_name.owner_name.function_name) must be unique. The statement specifies the input parameters with their data types, the processing instructions, and the value returned with each data type.

Syntax

CREATE FUNCTION [owner_name.] function_name
([{ @parameter_name scalar_parameter_data_type [= default] } [,...n]])
RETURNS scalar_return_data_type
[WITH < function_option> [,...n]]
[AS]
BEGIN
function_body
RETURN scalar_expression
END

Example

This example creates a user-defined function to replace a null value with the words Not Applicable.

```
USE northwind
GO

CREATE FUNCTION fn_NewRegion ( @myinput nvarchar(30) )
  RETURNS nvarchar(30)
BEGIN
  IF @myinput IS NULL
    SET @myinput = 'Not Applicable'

  RETURN @myinput
END
GO
```

When referencing a scalar user-defined function, specify both the function owner and the function name in two-part syntax.

```
SELECT LastName, City
      ,dbo.fn_NewRegion(Region) AS Region
      ,Country
 FROM Employees
GO
```

Result

LastName	City	Region	Country
Davolio	Seattle	WA	USA
Fuller	Tacoma	WA	USA
Leverling	Kirkland	WA	USA
Peacock	Redmond	WA	USA
Buchanan	London	Not Applicable	UK
Suyama	London	Not Applicable	UK
King	London	Not Applicable	UK
Callahan	Seattle	WA	USA
Dodsworth	London	Not Applicable	UK

Restrictions on User-defined Functions

Nondeterministic functions are functions such as GETDATE() that could return different result values each time that they are called with the same set of input values. Built-in nondeterministic functions are not allowed in the body of user-defined functions. These built-in functions from other categories are always nondeterministic:

@@ERROR	FORMATMESSAGE	IDENTITY	USER_NAME
@@IDENTITY	GETANSINULL	NEWID	@@ERROR
@@ROWCOUNT	GETDATE	PERMISSIONS	@@IDENTITY
@@TRANCOUNT	GetUTCDate	SESSION_USER	@@ROWCOUNT
APP_NAME	HOST_ID	STATS_DATE	@@TRANCOUNT
CURRENT_TIMESTAMP	HOST_NAME	SYSTEM_USER	
CURRENT_USER	IDENT_INCR	TEXTPTR	
DATENAME	IDENT_SEED	TEXTVALID	

Recommended Practices

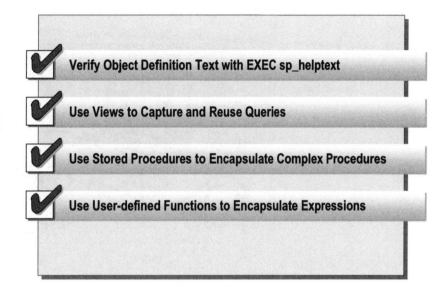

- Verify Object Definition Text with EXEC sp_helptext
- Use Views to Capture and Reuse Queries
- Use Stored Procedures to Encapsulate Complex Procedures
- Use User-defined Functions to Encapsulate Expressions

The following recommended practices should help you use programming objects:

- Verify object definitions by displaying the text associated with the object by using the **EXEC sp_helptext** system stored procedure.

- Use views to capture and reuse common queries for consistency and efficiency.

- Use stored procedures to encapsulate complex multi-statement procedures.

- Use user-defined functions to encapsulate common expressions.

Additional information on the following topics is available in SQL Server Books Online.

Topic	Search on
Using stored procedures	"effects of stored procedures on application performance"
Using views	"comparison of queries and views"
Using triggers	"enforcing business rules with triggers"

Lab A: Working with Views

Objectives

After completing this lab, you will be able to:

- Generate a view by using a SQL Query Analyzer template.
- Alter a view by using the Object Browser in SQL Query Analyzer.

Prerequisites

Before working on this lab, you must have:

- Script files for this lab, which are located in C:\Moc\2071\Labfiles\L09.
- Answer files for this lab, which are located in
  C:\Moc\2071\Labfiles\L09\Answers.
- The **library** database installed.

For More Information

If you require help, search SQL Query Analyzer Help for "Using Templates in
SQL Query Analyzer."

Other resources that you can use include:

- The **library** database schema.
- Microsoft SQL Server Books Online.

Scenario

The organization of the classroom is meant to simulate that of a worldwide trading firm named Northwind Traders. Its fictitious domain name is nwtraders.msft. The primary DNS server for nwtraders.msft is the instructor computer, which has an Internet Protocol (IP) address of 192.168.*x*.200 (where *x* is the assigned classroom number). The name of the instructor computer is London.

The following table provides the user name, computer name, and IP address for each student computer in the fictitious nwtraders.msft domain. Find the user name for your computer, and make a note of it.

User name	Computer name	IP address
SQLAdmin1	Vancouver	192.168.x.1
SQLAdmin2	Denver	192.168.x.2
SQLAdmin3	Perth	192.168.x.3
SQLAdmin4	Brisbane	192.168.x.4
SQLAdmin5	Lisbon	192.168.x.5
SQLAdmin6	Bonn	192.168.x.6
SQLAdmin7	Lima	192.168.x.7
SQLAdmin8	Santiago	192.168.x.8
SQLAdmin9	Bangalore	192.168.x.9
SQLAdmin10	Singapore	192.168.x.10
SQLAdmin11	Casablanca	192.168.x.11
SQLAdmin12	Tunis	192.168.x.12
SQLAdmin13	Acapulco	192.168.x.13
SQLAdmin14	Miami	192.168.x.14
SQLAdmin15	Auckland	192.168.x.15
SQLAdmin16	Suva	192.168.x.16
SQLAdmin17	Stockholm	192.168.x.17
SQLAdmin18	Moscow	192.168.x.18
SQLAdmin19	Caracas	192.168.x.19
SQLAdmin20	Montevideo	192.168.x.20
SQLAdmin21	Manila	192.168.x.21
SQLAdmin22	Tokyo	192.168.x.22
SQLAdmin23	Khartoum	192.168.x.23
SQLAdmin24	Nairobi	192.168.x.24

Estimated time to complete this lab: 30 minutes

Exercise 1
Generating a View by Using a SQL Query Analyzer Template

In this exercise, you will use a SQL Query Analyzer template to create a
view and assign values to the parameters in the view.
C:\Moc\2071\Labfiles\L09\Answers contains completed scripts for
this exercise.

▶ **To create a Transact-SQL statement from a SQL Query Analyzer
template**

In this procedure, you will create a Transact-SQL statement by using a SQL
Query Analyzer template. Answer_Template1.sql is a completed script for this
step.

1. Log on to the **NWTraders** classroom domain by using the information in
   the following table.

Option	Value
User name	**SQLAdmin*x*** (where *x* corresponds to your computer name as designated in the nwtraders.msft classroom domain)
Password	**Password**

2. Open SQL Query Analyzer and, if requested, log in to the (local) server
   with Microsoft Windows® Authentication.

   You have permission to log in to and administer SQL Server because you
   are logged as **SQLAdmin*x***, which is a member of the Windows 2000 local
   group, Administrators. All members of this group are automatically mapped
   to the SQL Server **sysadmin** role.

3. In the **DB** list, click **library**.

4. On the toolbar, click **Insert Template**.

5. In the **Insert Template** dialog box, double-click **Create View**, and then
   open Create View Basic Template.tql.

6. Review the contents of the file in the edit pane.

   How does the generated script differ from standard Transact-SQL?

   _____

   _____

▶ **To replace template parameters**

In this procedure, you will replace template parameters. Answer_Template2.sql is a completed script for this step.

1. On the **Edit** menu, click **Replace Template Parameters**.

2. In the **Replace Template Parameters** dialog box, in the **Value** column, type **AustenTitlesView** to change the **view_name** parameter.

3. In the **Replace Template Parameters** dialog box, in the **Value** column, type the following statement to change the **select_statement** parameter:

```
SELECT * FROM title WHERE author = 'Jane Austen'
```

4. On the **Replace Template Parameters** dialog box, click **Replace All** to replace each of the occurring parameters with the newly assigned values.

▶ **To validate the syntax and create the view**

In this procedure, you will validate and execute Transact-SQL statements to create the view. Answer_View1.sql is a completed script for this step.

1. On the **Query** menu, click **Parse**.

   This verifies that the syntax of the newly constructed Transact-SQL script is valid.

2. In the edit pane, create the view by executing the script.

3. On the toolbar, click **New Query** to open a new Query window.

   This opens a new connection to SQL Server.

4. Write a query that uses an asterisk in the SELECT statement to retrieve all of the data in the **AustenTitlesView** view.

5. Execute the query to verify that it returns the desired results.

   What columns does querying the view return?

   _____

   _____

   What are the advantages of using SQL Query Analyzer templates for generating Transact-SQL scripts?

   _____

   _____

Exercise 2
Altering a View by Using the Object Browser in SQL Query Analyzer

In this exercise, you will use the Object Browser in SQL Query Analyzer to script and edit Transact-SQL statements that alter the view that you created in exercise 1. C:\Moc\2071\Labfiles\L09\Answers contains completed scripts for this exercise.

▶ To display the Object Browser

- On the **Tools** menu, select **Object Browser**, and then click **Show/Hide**.

  This displays the Object Browser pane.

▶ To locate the dbo.AustenTitlesView object

In this procedure, you will locate the **dbo.AustenTitlesView** object.

1. In the Object Browser pane, expand **library**.

2. Expand **Views**, and then expand the **dbo.AustenTitlesView** object.

▶ To generate a script to alter the view

In this procedure, you will generate a script that alters a view. Answer_View2.sql is a completed script for this step.

1. Right-click **dbo.AustenTitlesView**.

2. Select **Script Object to New Window as**.

3. Click **Alter**.

   This creates a series of Transact-SQL statements that alter the **dbo.AustenTitlesView** object, which was created in a new edit pane.

   What other types of scripts can you create that relate to this view object?

   _____

   _____

▶ To copy a column list from the Object Browser

In this procedure, you will copy a column list from the Object Browser. Answer_View3.sql is a completed script for this step.

1. On the **Query** menu, click **Parse**.

   This verifies that the syntax of the newly constructed Transact-SQL script is valid.

2. Expand **dbo.AustenTitlesView**, and then expand **Columns**.

3. Drag the **Columns** folder from the Object Browser pane to the edit pane, and then place the folder in the SELECT statement of the view definition after the asterisk.

4. Delete the asterisk in the SELECT statement.

▶ **To copy an object name from the Object Browser**

In this procedure, you will copy an object name from the Object Browser.
Answer_View4.sql is a completed script for this step.

1. In the edit pane, delete the **AustenTitlesView** view name that immediately
   follows the ALTER VIEW statement.

2. Drag the **dbo.AustenTitlesView** object from the Object Browser pane to the
   edit pane, and then place the object after the ALTER VIEW statement.

▶ **To validate the syntax and alter the view**

In this procedure, you will validate the syntax and alter the view.
Answer_View5.sql is a completed script for this step.

1. On the **Query** menu, click **Parse**.

   This verifies that the syntax of the newly constructed Transact-SQL script is
   valid.

2. Execute the script in the edit pane to alter the view.

3. On the toolbar, click **New Query** to open a new Query window.

   This opens a new connection to SQL Server.

4. Write a SELECT statement to retrieve all of the data in the
   dbo.AustenTitlesView view.

5. Execute the query to verify that it returns the desired results.

   Why should you enumerate all columns when constructing Transact-SQL
   statements?

   _____

   _____

Review

- **Displaying the Text of a Programming Object**
- **Introduction to Views**
- **Advantages of Views**
- **Creating Views**
- **Introduction to Stored Procedures**
- **Introduction to Triggers**
- **Introduction to User-defined Functions**

1. What are the benefits of views?

2. What are the benefits of stored procedures?

3. Why would you use a view instead of a stored procedure to encapsulate a query?

4. You have developed a query that joins the **member**, **title**, and **loanhist** tables to list the fines that are assessed, paid, and waived for each member and the title of each overdue book and to calculate the number of days that each book is overdue. Other developers are interested in leveraging the work that you have done to build their own queries. How can you best accomplish this?

5. Describe the three types of user-defined functions.

6. How is a trigger different from a stored procedure?

Appendix A:
Library Database Case Study

Introduction

The Library Database Case Study provides an overview of the operations at the West Municipal Library, describes the daily library functions, and presents the database that was designed for the library.

Overview of Library Operations

Before a database for librarians and members was implemented, an interview was conducted with the librarians at the West Municipal Library to assess the library's business needs. The decisions that the database designer made during the design process are explained in the following sections. The following figure shows the overall schema of the database that was designed for the library.

**Library
Database Diagram**

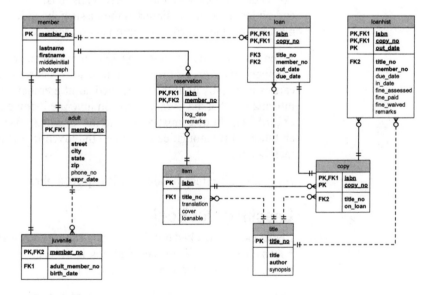

Daily Library Functions

Many daily library functions exist. The following are some of the most important.

Uniquely Identifying Books

Some books may have the same title; therefore, titles cannot be used as a means of identification. Librarians call books *items*. Items are identified by the International Standard Book Number (ISBN). Books with the same title can have different ISBN numbers if they are in different languages and have different bindings (hard cover or soft cover).

Reserving Books

If a member wants a book that is out on loan, the book is placed on reserve for them. When the book arrives, a librarian must notify the member who has been waiting the longest. Members can have as many as four books on reserve at one time.

Determining Book Availability

Librarians must be able to determine how many copies of a book are out on loan at any given time and which books are on reserve.

A synopsis that ranges from one sentence to several pages exists for each title in the library. Librarians want to be able to access the synopses when members request information about books.

Enrolling Members

To become a library member, individuals must provide their mailing addresses and phone numbers. A librarian then issues the individual a numbered, machine-readable card. This card is good for one year.

Juveniles (individuals under age 18) can be members of the library, but an adult member must sign for them when they join. Therefore, a juvenile member's card is good only until the associated adult member's card expires. The only information that the library keeps on juvenile members is their name and date of birth. The library must be able to detect when juvenile members turn 18 and then must automatically convert the juvenile memberships to adult memberships.

A month before membership cards expire, a librarian must notify the member.

Checking Out Books

Books can be checked out for 14 days. Members are allowed to have only four books checked out at a time. If a book is overdue, members have one week before the library sends a notice to them.

Members bring books to the front desk after they locate the ones that they want to check out. A librarian then runs the member's card through a machine that reads the card number magnetically. A screen displays information about the member's account, such as name, address, phone number, and the card's expiration date. Ideally, cards that have expired or are about to expire will be highlighted.

The screen also displays information about a member's outstanding loans, including title, checkout date, and due date. This information is useful because it is presented in a chronological sequence, with the most overdue loan appearing first and the most recent loan appearing last. Highlighting also indicates loans that are overdue or are about to become overdue.

If a member's account is in order, a librarian checks out the books. Librarians check out books by running a scanner down the book spines (the ISBN and the copy number are encoded on the spines). The ISBN, title, and author information then appear on the computer screen. If the books are not loanable, a warning message appears.

Checking In Books

When books are returned, librarians check them in by running a scanner down the book spines. The ISBN, title, and author information then appear on the computer screen, as well as the member number and name and the book's due date.

Occasionally, books are accidentally reshelved before librarians check them in. If a member tries to check out a book that the database lists as checked out, librarians need to be able to access the checkout information, including the member's name, check out date, and due date. If a member presents a book to check out that is still officially checked out to another member, a message appears that alerts librarians that the book is already checked out. Then librarians can update their records immediately by being forced to clear the previous loan before they continue with the checkout.

Generating Usage Reports

Occasionally, librarians must compile usage information, mostly for the Town Council or the Planning Commission. These groups usually want to know information, such as the volume of circulation, the popularity of various books, the reliability of return, and the average length of a borrowing term. Therefore, the librarians need to be able to prepare quick summaries of this information.

The types of questions that are frequently asked include the following:

- How many loans did the library do last year?
- What percentage of the membership borrowed at least one book?
- What was the greatest number of books borrowed by any one individual?
- What percentage of the books was loaned out at least once last year?
- What percentage of all loans eventually becomes overdue?
- What is the average length of a loan?
- What are the library's peak hours for loans?

Library Database Design

Based on the information that librarians presented, the project database designer decided to implement the entities from the preceding scenario in three groups of tables: tables that contain member information, tables that contain item (book) information, and tables that contain loan information.

Member Information

The first group of tables models the two types of individuals who check out books from the West Municipal Library. As the following figure indicates, the first group comprises three tables: **member**, **adult**, and **juvenile**.

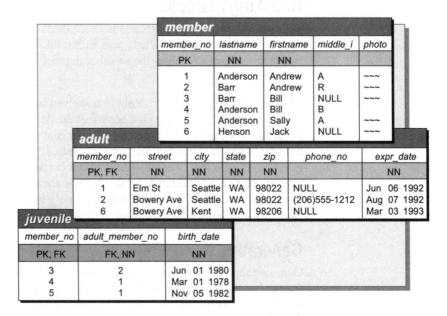

member

member_no	lastname	firstname	middle_i	photo
PK	NN	NN		
1	Anderson	Andrew	A	~~~
2	Barr	Andrew	R	~~~
3	Barr	Bill	NULL	~~~
4	Anderson	Bill	B	
5	Anderson	Sally	A	~~~
6	Henson	Jack	NULL	~~~

adult

member_no	street	city	state	zip	phone_no	expr_date
PK, FK	NN	NN	NN	NN		NN
1	Elm St	Seattle	WA	98022	NULL	Jun 06 1992
2	Bowery Ave	Seattle	WA	98022	(206)555-1212	Aug 07 1992
6	Bowery Ave	Kent	WA	98206	NULL	Mar 03 1993

juvenile

member_no	adult_member_no	birth_date
PK, FK	FK, NN	NN
3	2	Jun 01 1980
4	1	Mar 01 1978
5	1	Nov 05 1982

The **member** table is the master table, while **adult** and **juvenile** are subtables. All three tables use the **member_no** column as a primary key. Since the values in this column are different for each member and uniquely identify each row of information, the **member_no** column is a good choice for a primary key.

These entities could have been modeled in several different ways: as a single table or as **member** and **juvenile** tables. If a single table had been used for all members, many addresses would have been duplicated because juveniles in this model have the same address as their parents.

Librarians need to be able to track birth dates of juveniles only, so splitting the membership information into several tables eliminates the null column values that would have resulted for the birth dates of adults.

Dividing the tables in this fashion also models the scenario in a way that reflects the membership of the library: **member**-to-**adult** is a one-to-one relationship, while **adult**-to-**juvenile** is a one-to-many relationship.

Item Information

The **title**, **item**, and **copy** tables form a logical second group. The master table of this group is the **title** table.

For each listing in the **title** table, one or more entries exist in the **item** table because a book may be available in several languages, in paperback or hardback, and be loanable or not loanable. **Title**-to-**item** is a one-to-many relationship. Furthermore, for each listing in the **item** table, one or more copies of that item can exist. Therefore, **item**-to-**copy** is a one-to-many relationship.

title

title_no	title	author	synopsis
PK	NN	NN	
1	Gone With the Wind	Mitchell	~~~
2	Color Purple	Walker	~~~
3	Hotel	Hailey	
4	Winnie the Pooh	Milne	~~~

item

isbn	title_no	language	cover	loanable
PK	FK, NN			
1	1	English	softback	Y
2	2	French	NULL	N
3	3	French	hardback	Y
4	4	NULL	hardback	NULL
5	2	English	softback	Y

copy

isbn	copy_no	title_no	on_loan
PK, FK	PK	FK, NN	NN
1	1	1	Y
1	2	1	Y
2	1	2	N
3	1	3	Y
4	1	4	Y
4	2	4	Y

The **item** table has a **loanable** column. Rather than including information from this column in the **copy** table, the database designer assumes that all copies of a particular item are either loanable or not loanable.

Notice that the **copy** table has a primary key made up of two columns. This type of primary key is called a composite key. The combination of **isbn** and **copy_no** uniquely identifies each row in the table.

The **copy** table contains a duplicate **title_no** column. This group of tables has been denormalized to reduce the number of joins that are needed to retrieve information.

The **on_loan** column in the **copy** table is derived data—data that could be generated with a query each time that the information is needed. But the information is kept in the table to make it readily available and to reduce the number of calculations that must be performed. The **on_loan** column is populated by using information from the **loan** table (shown below). Because the **loan** table changes frequently, locks could prevent a user from obtaining this information. The **copy** table is more likely to be used in a read-only fashion, so it would not be necessary to prevent users from accessing information that is stored there.

Loan Information

The **reservation**, **loan**, and **loanhist** tables contain the library's loan information. The **reservation** table tracks current reservations for each book; the **loan** table tracks information on books that are currently on loan; and the **loanhist** table stores information on books that have been loaned and returned.

Note   In the following figure, FK1 implies a composite foreign key. FK defines a single column foreign key.

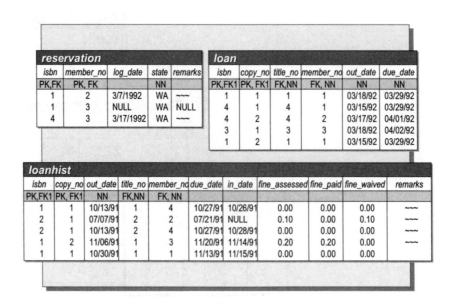

reservation

isbn	member_no	log_date	state	remarks
PK,FK	PK, FK		NN	
1	2	3/7/1992	WA	~~~
1	3	NULL	WA	NULL
4	3	3/17/1992	WA	~~~

loan

isbn	copy_no	title_no	member_no	out_date	due_date
PK,FK1	PK, FK1	FK,NN	FK, NN	NN	NN
1	1	1	1	03/18/92	03/29/92
4	1	4	1	03/15/92	03/29/92
4	2	4	2	03/17/92	04/01/92
3	1	3	3	03/18/92	04/02/92
1	2	1	1	03/15/92	03/29/92

loanhist

isbn	copy_no	out_date	title_no	member_no	due_date	in_date	fine_assessed	fine_paid	fine_waived	remarks
PK,FK1	PK, FK1	NN	FK,NN	FK, NN						
1	1	10/13/91	1	4	10/27/91	10/26/91	0.00	0.00	0.00	~~~
2	1	07/07/91	2	2	07/21/91	NULL	0.10	0.00	0.10	~~~
2	1	10/13/91	2	4	10/27/91	10/28/91	0.00	0.00	0.00	~~~
1	2	11/06/91	1	3	11/20/91	11/14/91	0.20	0.20	0.00	~~~
1	1	10/30/91	1	1	11/13/91	11/15/91	0.00	0.00	0.00	

It is possible to combine the **loan** and **loanhist** tables to reduce redundancy, but this may create other problems. The **loanhist** table is essentially a history of all loans and could become unwieldy. Over time, librarians may want to back up information from this table, so it makes sense to keep all of this information in its own table. In addition, this business model requires that several queries be made against the **loanhist** table. These queries would be easier to implement and faster to run if the history information were kept separately from the loan information.

The **loan** and **loanhist** tables also represent different functions of the application. When a member checks out a book, an entry is made to the **loan** table. When a member returns a book, an entry is made to the **loanhist** table, and the corresponding entry is deleted from the **loan** table. By maintaining separate tables for each function and denormalizing the tables, users can access the information more quickly. However, because the tables are denormalized, they require more maintenance. For example, when **item.title_no** is updated, the **title_no** column must be updated in the **loan**, **loanhist**, and **copy** tables as well. Because updates to the **title_no** column may be infrequent, denormalization may speed queries.

Appendix B: Database Schemas

Northwind Database Diagram

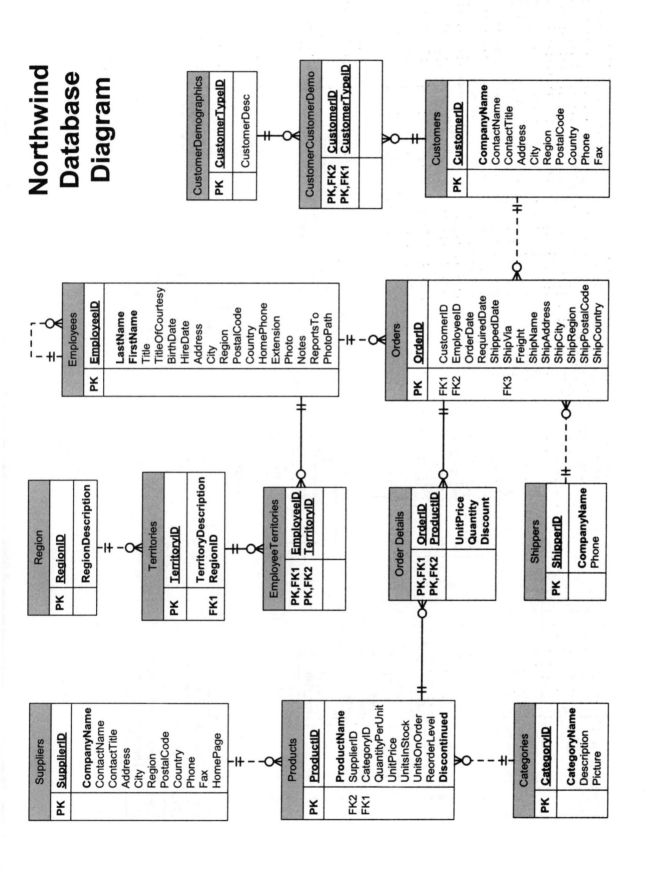

Library
Database Diagram

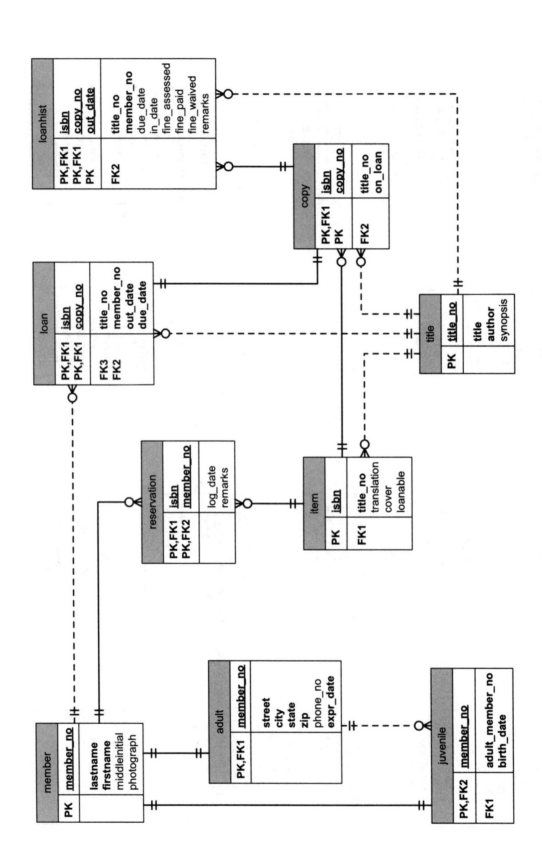

Pubs
Database
Diagram

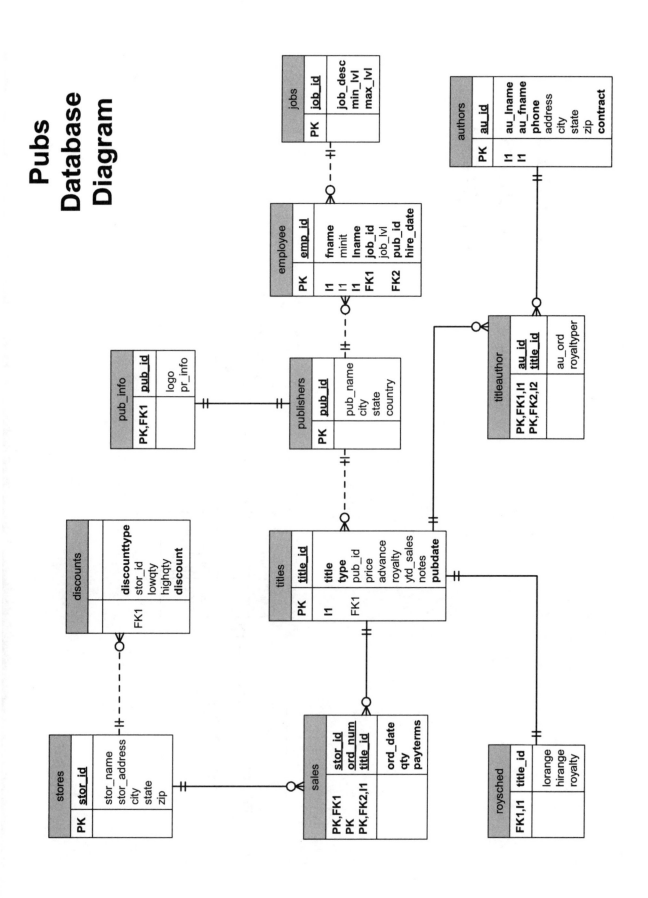

Joindb
Database
Diagram

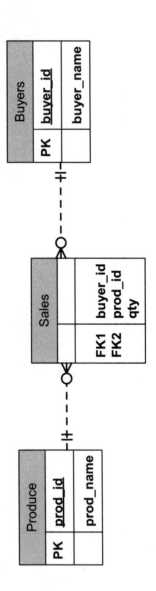

Buyers		
PK	buyer_id	
	buyer_name	

Sales		
FK1	buyer_id	
FK2	prod_id	
	qty	

Produce		
PK	prod_id	
	prod_name